To: Mrs. Borthwick
From: Clyde Earle
With every good wish
2005 Jan. 27

Acclaim for V. S. Naipaul's

BETWEEN FATHER AND SON

"By illuminating a heritage more emotionally profound than we suspected, these wonderful letters complicate and intensify our understanding of the sensibility behind Naipaul's novels and behind the armor of Seepersad Naipaul's brilliant son." —*Chicago Tribune*

"It is hard to think of a literary correspondence full of such rawness of emotion. . . . It is even harder to think of correspondents who have made such a large claim on each other's humanity."
—*The New York Review of Books*

"The arrangement of material is so skillful, and the narrative drive so strong, that on occasion it is easy to imagine that one is reading an epistolary novel. . . . These letters will bring readers to a better understanding of one of the English-speaking world's most enigmatic and self-effacing writers." —*The Boston Globe*

"Touching. . . . Heartbreaking. . . . There are marvelous exchanges of opinions and advice about the craft of fiction and the writer's life. . . . The final letters . . . seem like a vindication, an acknowledgment of a legacy, and further testimony to the power and endurance of this extraordinary father-son relationship." —Francine Prose, *Elle*

"Extraordinary. . . . Immensely rich in humanity." —*The Anniston Star*

"An invaluable record of [Naipaul's] relationship with his father. . . . The mood of *Between Father and Son* is one of remarkable fraternity, mutual aid and expansive admiration."

D0230426

"Remarkable. . . . Shows the humanity behind an extraordinary literary career. . . . As touching as any novel, as artfully written as any prose, perhaps the most human and compelling book to date with the name V. S. Naipaul."
—*Richmond Times-Dispatch*

"*Between Father and Son* chronicles the story of an extraordinarily sweet relationship. . . . Soon after his son arrives at Oxford . . . the father suggests, 'If you could write me letters about things and people—especially people—at Oxford, I could compile them in a book.' . . . It's not known what his son thought of this suggestion, but now we have that very book. It's almost enough to make one believe in a divine Providence."
—Joseph Epstein, *The New Criterion*

"Luminous . . . consistently articulate, interesting, moving."
—*The Times Literary Supplement*

"Fascinating. . . . Nothing is quite as revealing—or powerful—as the portrait evoked by this simple, unadorned collection of letters. . . . Together, the letters create a picture as wrenching as any novel, as vivid as any film."
—*Time Out New York*

V. S. Naipaul

BETWEEN FATHER AND SON

V. S. Naipaul was born in Trinidad in 1932. He went to England on a scholarship in 1950. After four years at Oxford he began to write, and since then he has followed no other profession. He is the author of more than twenty books of fiction and nonfiction and the recipient of numerous honors, including the Booker Prize in 1971 and a knighthood for services to literature in 1990. He lives in Wiltshire, England.

ALSO BY V. S. NAIPAUL

NONFICTION

Beyond Belief: Islamic Excursions Among the Converted Peoples
India: A Million Mutinies Now
A Turn in the South
Finding the Center
Among the Believers
The Return of Eva Perón (with *The Killings in Trinidad*)
India: A Wounded Civilization
The Overcrowded Barracoon
The Loss of El Dorado
An Area of Darkness
The Middle Passage

FICTION

A Way in the World
The Enigma of Arrival
A Bend in the River
Guerrillas
In a Free State
A Flag on the Island
The Mimic Men
Mr. Stone and the Knights Companion
A House for Mr. Biswas
*Miguel Street**
*The Suffrage of Elvira**
*The Mystic Masseur**

* Published in an omnibus edition entitled *Three Novels*

BETWEEN FATHER AND SON

BETWEEN
FATHER AND SON

~

Family Letters

V. S. NAIPAUL

EDITED BY GILLON AITKEN

Vintage Books
A Division of Random House, Inc.
New York

FIRST VINTAGE BOOKS EDITION, MARCH 2001

Copyright © 1999 by V. S. Naipaul

Introduction copyright © 1999 by Gillon Aitken

All rights reserved under International and Pan-American Copyright Conventions.
Published in the United States by Vintage Books, a division of Random House, Inc., New York.
Originally published in Great Britain as *Letters Between a Father and Son* by Little, Brown and Company,
London, in 1999 and subsequently in hardcover in the United States by Alfred A. Knopf,
a division of Random House, Inc., New York, in 2000.

Vintage is a registered trademark and Vintage International and colophon are trademarks of Random House, Inc.

A portion of this work was originally published in *The New Yorker*.

The Library of Congress has cataloged the Knopf edition as follows:

Naipaul, V. S. (Vidiadhar Surajprasad), [date]

Between father and son : family letters / edited by Gillon Aitken.—1st American ed.

p.   cm.

ISBN 0-375-40730-8

1. Naipaul, V. S. (Vidiadhar Surajprasad)—Correspondence.   2. Naipaul, V. S. (Vidiadhar
Surajprasad)—Family.   3. Authors, Trinidadian—20th century—Family relationships.
4. Authors, Trinidadian—20th century—Correspondence.   5. Fathers and sons—Trinidad.
I. Aitken, Gillon R.   II. Title.

PR9272.9.N32Z48   2000

823'.914—dc21 [B] 99-31089

CIP

Vintage ISBN: 0-375-70726-3

www.vintagebooks.com

Printed in the United States of America

10 9 8 7 6 5 4 3 2

CONTENTS

INTRODUCTION

The task of introducing this extraordinary and moving correspondence is a delicate one. In these letters between a father and a son, the older man worn down by the cares of a large family and the distress of unfulfilled ambitions, the younger on the threshold of a broad and brilliant literary career, lies some of the raw material of one of the finest and most enduring novels of the twentieth century: V. S. Naipaul's *A House for Mr Biswas*. Yet the letters also celebrate Seepersad Naipaul's achievement as a writer, not merely in the genesis and evolution of his single published novel, *The Adventures of Gurudeva;* but also, and perhaps more strikingly, in revealing the dedication of the true artist. For Seepersad Naipaul (Pa), the life of the mind—the writer's life—was everything: to record the ways of men and women, with a shrewd, comical and kindly eye, and to do that from within his own originality, was to live nobly. In his elder son, Vidia, he found a miraculous echo to this belief—miraculous, because there is no sense of a son's following in his father's footsteps, or of a father's urging that he might do so. There is a sense, rather, of the two men's being in step, neither embarrassed by any of the implications of the generation that divided them—and Vidia only seventeen when the present correspondence opens. The difference in their ages, and the fact of Seepersad's early death, have allowed Vidia to acknowledge the debt he owes to his father, and he has embraced the opportunity to do so in manifold ways in his work. In this correspondence, the reader will recognize the subtle, and unwitting, repayment of a father's debt to his son. Pa's deep concern for Vidia is a generous and never-failing tribute to the fine intelligence, and the responsive and sensitive spirit, of the younger man.

The heart of the correspondence covers little more than three years, broadly defined by Vidia's departure from Trinidad, for the first time, in 1950, to take up a Trinidad government scholarship at University College, Oxford, and by Seepersad's untimely death in 1953 and, subsequently, Vidia's going down from the university. By way of a postscript, the book concludes with a selection of letters which reflect his progress in the world during the three years which followed, culminating in the acceptance of his early fiction by a British publisher.

Momentous years . . . The government scholarships were few and far between. Representing a means of escape from the limitations of a narrow and backward island society, they were enormously prized and ardently competed for. 'Looking back,' Vidia wrote in December 1950, after his first term at Oxford, 'I realise the gigantic task I performed.' No less gigantic would have been the journey from an extended family upbringing in Trinidad to post-war England (the mother country), and an Oxford, home to the Morris Motor Works, drawing its undergraduates principally from the English public schools.

In *Finding the Centre* (1984)—readers of the present volume will note Seepersad's frequent injunction to his son to 'keep your centre'—in the essay entitled 'Prologue to an Autobiography', Vidia writes of his father and of the family's circumstances:

> He was a journalist for much of his working life. This was an unusual occupation for a Trinidad Indian of his generation. My father was born in 1906. At that time the Indians of Trinidad were a separate community, mainly rural and Hindi-speaking, attached to the sugar estates of central and southern Trinidad. Many of the Indians of 1906 had been born in India and had come out to Trinidad as indentured labourers on five-year contracts.
>
> In 1929 my father began contributing occasional articles on Indian topics to the *Trinidad Guardian*. In 1932, when I was born, he had become the *Guardian* staff correspondent in the little market town of Chaguanas. Chaguanas was in the heart of the sugar area and the Indian area of Trinidad. It was where my mother's family was established. Contract labour was far behind them; they were big landowners.
>
> Two years or so after I was born my father left the *Guardian*.

For some years he did odd jobs here and there, now attached to my mother's family, now going back to the protection of an uncle by marriage, a rich man, founder and part owner of the biggest bus company in the island. Poor himself, with close relations who were still agricultural labourers, my father dangled all his life in a half-dependence and half-esteem between these two powerful families.

In 1938 my father was taken on by the *Guardian* again, this time as a city reporter. And we—my father, my mother and their five children, our own little nucleus within my mother's extended family—moved to Port of Spain, to the house owned by my mother's mother. That was when I got to know my father.

In 1945, a sixth child, Shiva, Vidia's only brother, was born; and, in 1952, news reached Vidia in Oxford, initially in a letter, here reproduced, from his older sister, Kamla, of the impending birth of a seventh, Nalini, fifth daughter of the family. Vidia's mother, Droapatie Capildeo (Ma), was a seventh child, too—and in her case, the seventh of nine daughters. The voluminous Capildeo tribe—and notably Ma's two younger brothers Simbhoo (Capo S.) and Rudranath (Capo R.)—plays a vivid supporting role, often abrasively so, in the contents of the airmail letters that travelled from Port of Spain to Oxford. But the principal parts properly belong within the immediate family—in a personal sense, by Pa's preoccupation with the writing life; in a family sense, by Pa's deep feelings for the well-being of his absent older children, Kamla (in Benares) and Vidia at Oxford—and for the progress and development of his and Ma's variously adolescent daughters, Sati, Mira and Savi.

Kamla occupies a special position in this book. Two years older than Vidia, she was the first to leave home, becoming a student at Benares Hindu University, where life did not always run smoothly for her, and returning to the family, brought low by Pa's heart attack, in 1953. Brother and sister were particularly close. In the letters between them, which are well represented in this book, each invariably rebukes the other for not writing sooner, and Pa rebukes them both in the same manner. While the evenness of the relationship, certainly in their correspondence, between Pa and Vidia has been remarked upon, there is an enlightening carelessness in the absence of reserve between Vidia and his sister.

In terms of Vidia's letters, this is not an 'Oxford' book. While the life of the university is revealed, and Vidia's part in it, Oxford is of little moment to him. He works hard, suffers ill health and anxiety, poverty and depression; he makes friends and experiences happiness and a growing, if nervous, self-confidence. Two things really matter: the family, Pa and Kamla particularly, but Ma (with all her Capildeo relations) and his sisters, too—and the growing Shiva. And, of course, the ever-absorbing intention to be a good writer . . .

When Vidia left Trinidad for Oxford, Shiva was five. The brothers were not to meet until six years later. In his essay 'Brothers' in the posthumously published *An Unfinished Journey* (1986), Shiva remembers Vidia's letters home and the visit he made to Trinidad:

> Sometimes, the postman arrived with blue air-mail letters, the cause of much excitement in our household. Occasionally, I would listen with a kind of dazed astonishment to this notional being—*my* brother—reading a short story on the radio. When I was about eleven, this mysterious figure suddenly arrived among us. Why he should thus manifest himself, I had no idea. Still, it was an interlude of wonder; of intense excitement for me. I would go and stand in the doorway of his bedroom and gaze curiously upon him as he lay on the bed, smoking cigarettes out of a green tin. The tableau revived my father's fading image. He too, in the warm, quiet afternoons, would lie on that same bed, reading and smoking cigarettes.

This redolent image catches much of the spirit of this fine book, so expressively filled as it is with heart and drama; and it is a moving experience, when reading the letters, to watch the shifting balance, so delicately evolved, of a relationship between a good man and his good son; and of the natural yielding of the one to the other.

In preparing this book for publication, I have adopted a policy of non-intrusion, permitting the sequence of letters to tell its own story. Square brackets—[. . .]—rarely required, indicate a defeated comprehension of the holographic or typewritten word(s). I have, again rarely, revised punctuation to assist meaning; some small, but never significant, excisions have been made for the same reason, or to avoid the arrant duplication of news. Close family members are noted on their first appearance, but not thereafter; reference to the family trees will illuminate an understanding of relationships. Casual references to acquaintances and places are not clarified. The footnotes seek to define some aspects of Hindu ritual and practice, and focus to a degree on the names of books and authors—although not if these are 'canonical' or adequately described in the text of the letters themselves.

Particular thanks are due to The McFarlin Library at the University of Tulsa, Oklahoma, the repository of the Naipaul archive from which this correspondence has been drawn, and to Mr William Buford of *The New Yorker*, whose initiative and energy were critical to the process of unearthing it; and to Emma Parry for her shrewd assistance in the editorial undertaking. Above all, I am grateful to Kamla for permitting her letters to Vidia to be reproduced; and to Vidia himself, for his understandably disengaged approval of the project. It entertains me to reflect that this is a book he will never read.

Gillon Aitken
July, 1999

FAMILY TREES (Selective)

Seepersad Naipaul—V. S. Naipaul's father (1906–1953)

Persad (or Ramparsad—and fictionalized as 'Rapooche')	His elder brother
Hari	His younger brother
Phoowa	His father's sister
Sookhdeo	A rich relation by marriage, the husband of Seepersad's mother's sister

Droapatie Capildeo—V. S. Naipaul's mother (1913–1991)

The seventh of nine daughters, and the seventh of eleven children, notably:

1. Rajdaye
2. Ramdoolarie, divorced wife of Dinanath (the source for Seepersad's 'Gurudeva' in *The Adventures of Gurudeva*)
3. Dhan, the mother of Owad (later a lawyer)
4. Koonta, the mother of Boysie (later a doctor)
5. Ahilla, the mother of Deo and Phoolo
6. Calawattee, wife of Ramnarace
7. Droapatie
8. Simbhoo (Capo S.), elder brother, father of Deven, Suren and Sita (lawyer and politician; in England in 1950/51)
9. Tara, eighth daughter
10. Rudranath (Capo R.), younger brother (went to England on a scholarship in 1939, became Lecturer in Mathematics at London University)
11. Binmatie, ninth daughter

Seepersad Naipaul = Droapatie Capildeo

KAMLA	VIDIA	SATI	MIRA	SAVI	SHIVA	NALINI
(1930–)	(1932–)	(1934–1984)	(1936–)	(1938–)	(1945–1985)	(1952–)

I

September 21, 1949 – September 22, 1950

PORT OF SPAIN TO OXFORD

Trinidad
September 21, 1949

Dear Kamla,*

I wonder what is the matter with this typewriter. It looks all right now, though. I am enclosing some cuttings which, I am sure, will delight you. You will note that I went after all to the Old Boys' Association Dinner. I can count those hours as among the most painful I have ever spent. In the first place, I have no table manners; in the second, I had no food. Special arrangements, I was informed after the dinner, had been made for me, but these appeared to have been limited to serving me potatoes in various ways—now fried, now boiled. I had told the manager to bring me some corn soup instead of the turtle soup that the others were having. He ignored this and the waiter brought up to me a plateful of a green slime. This was the turtle soup. I was nauseated and annoyed and told the man to take it away. This, I was told, was a gross breach of etiquette. So I had bread and butter and ice-cold water for the first two eating rounds. The menu was in French. What you would call stewed chicken they called 'Poulet Sauté Renaissance'. Coffee was 'moka'. I had rather expected that to be some exotic Russian dish. Dessert included something called 'Pomme Surprise'. This literally means 'surprised apple', and the younger Hannays,† who was next to me, told me it was an apple pudding done in a surprise manner. The thing came. I ate it. It was fine. But I tasted no apple. 'That,' Hannays told me, 'is the surprise.'

I have just finished filling out the application forms for entrance to the University; I had some pictures of myself taken. I had always thought that,

---

* V(idiadhar) S(urajprasad) Naipaul's elder sister, then studying at Banares (also spelled Benares) Hindu University. The eldest of the seven children born to Seepersad and Droapatie (née Capildeo) Naipaul (see Family Trees)
† Fellow pupil, son of a distinguished black lawyer in Trinidad

though not attractive, I was not ugly. This picture undeceived me. I never knew my face was <u>fat</u>. The picture said so. I looked at the Asiatic on the paper and thought that an Indian from India could look no more Indian than I did. My face would give anyone the idea that I was a two-hundred-pounder. I had hoped to send up a striking intellectual pose to the University people, but look what they have got. And I even paid two dollars for a re-touched picture.

I am all right. I am actually reading once more. I decided to start preparing myself for next year by a thorough knowledge of the nineteenth-century novel. I read the Butler book;* I think it is not half as good as Maugham's *Of Human Bondage*. The construction is clumsy. Butler has stressed too much on passing religious conflicts; is too concerned with proving his theory of heredity. I then went on to Jane Austen. I had read so much in praise of her. I went to the library and got *Emma*. It has an introduction by Monica Dickens, which extolled the book as the finest Austen ever wrote. Frankly, the introduction proved better reading than the book itself. Jane Austen appears to be essentially a writer for women; if she had lived in our age she would undoubtedly have been a leading contributor to the women's papers. Her work really bored me. It is mere gossip. It could appeal to a female audience. The diction is fine, of course. But the work, besides being mere gossip, is slick and professional.

I think you would be interested to know how my $75 will be spent. I have taken over all your debts. $50 will go to the bank; $10 to Millington;† and $15 to Dass. I have about two dollars pocket money. I get this from Mamie‡ for teaching Sita.§ Sending that child to school to get an academic education is a waste of time and money. She is the most obtuse thing I have ever met. If you want to break a man's heart, give him a class of Sitas to teach. I wonder if you know that I have been teaching George.** He is dull but could pass if made to work hard. I am sure you will be glad to know that

---

* Samuel Butler's *The Way of All Flesh* (1903)
† Occasional Naipaul family servant
‡ Mamie (or Mamee): V. S. Naipaul's maternal aunt by marriage, wife of Simbhoo, the elder of his mother's two brothers (Capo S.)
§ V. S. Naipaul's cousin, Mamie's daughter
** V. S. Naipaul's cousin, son of his father's elder brother, Persad (or Ramparsad—and fictionalised by his father as 'Rapooche')

Jainarayan* is making splendid progress. Those people are a sorry lot. This devaluation business is going to make it even harder for them.

It is not for us at home to do extensive writing; that is your job. It is you who are seeing new countries, having new and exciting experiences which will probably remain in your memory as the most interesting part of your life. I must say, however, that your letters have improved enormously. I wonder why. Is it because you are writing spontaneously, without any conscious effort at literature? I think it is.

While you are in India, you should keep your eyes open. This has two meanings: the subsidiary one is to watch your personal effects carefully; the Indians are a thieving lot. Remember what happened to the trousers† of the West Indian cricket eleven. Keep your eyes open and let me know whether Beverly Nichols‡ is right. He went to India in 1945, and saw a wretched country, full of pompous mediocrity, with no future. He saw the filth; refused to mention the 'spiritualness' that impresses another kind of visitor. Of course the Indians did not like the book, but I think he was telling the truth. From Nehru's autobiography,§ I think the Premier of India is a first-class showman using his saintliness as a weapon of rule. But I am sure it has a certain basis in fact. Huxley may have degenerated of late into an invalid crippled by a malady that has received enormous approval by the intellectuals—mysticism—but what he said in his book** about India twenty years or so ago is true. He said that it was half-diets that produced ascetics and people who spend all their time in meditation. You will be right at the heart of the whole cranky thing. Please don't get contaminated; I will be glad when your three years will be finished; then you could breathe the invigorating air of atheism. (I don't like that word. It seems to suggest that the person is interested in religion; it doesn't suggest one who ignores it completely . . .)

I suppose that by now you have received the ten pounds. We got your diary. I could sense an underlying unhappiness and worry in it. I don't

---

* V. S. Naipaul's cousin, his maternal aunt's son
† The white flannel trousers of the West Indian cricket team visiting India at this time were famously stolen in Bombay
‡ Beverly Nichols' *Verdict on India* (1946) had occasioned much controversy
§ *Autobiography* (1936)
** Aldous Huxley's *Jesting Pilate* (1926)

think you were completely happy. I could imagine how glad you were when you saw Boysie* at Avonmouth. After all, who could be perfectly happy going to a strange land with only about seventy dollars to stay heaven knows how long? I doubt whether we could have stood the financial strain. I am very glad how things turned out.

I will write shortly. Goodbye and good luck.

With affection,
Vido†

[To Kamla]

Trinidad
October 10, 1949

My dear little fool,

You are the damnedest ass. Your letter amused me as I read the first few lines; then it became grotesque.

You are a silly stupid female, after all. I fancy you rather enjoyed writing that plea to a wayward brother. It made you a hero à la Hollywood. Listen, my dear 'very pretty' Miss Naipaul, you are free to indulge your fancy, and let it roam, but don't ever mix me up in it. I appreciate that the picture of an intelligent, sensitive ('he is the most sensitive of all your children') brother flinging himself at the dogs, as it were, eating out his heart, and drowning his sorrows in drink, at the departure of a dear sister is appealing and not without its melodramatic flavour.

You were the same over here. Do you remember your taunts at my getting a job? You enjoyed the picture you built up, the picture someone would form of me if he knew nothing of the family. A weak, bespectacled brother is frustrated by his lack of physical attraction. It grows on him, for he is intellectual, and he becomes a drunkard. He is easily led astray; when he falls for vices, he falls hard. The sister knew it all the time. She weeps as a fountain as she pens the bitter letter to her brother, inquiring if what she

---

* Boysie (or Boyzee): cousin, maternal aunt's son
† An intimate form of Vidia (itself a diminutive of Vidiadhar), the name by which V. S. Naipaul was and is familiarly known

hears is true, half hoping to hear that it is. You are a fool. He is easily led astray. Living in a family where generosity is bad business; where mediocrity and stupidity hold sway; where meat-eating is a virtue—he is ungenerous, he is stupid, he eats meat.

Am I easily led astray? Probably. By you. I could have, with profit, spent my money on myself. I always admire the human ability to forgo a pleasure, after that pleasure has been enjoyed.

If I smoked in Trinidad you well knew how I was at pains to hide the fact from you! Why didn't the ass tell me who was the slandering malicious 'friend' who had my welfare so much at heart?

You have insulted me, Kamla. This is going to be my last letter to you. I am easily led astray! Not you, who are fool enough to believe what one ass has said. This could have been entertaining, but you went all out to play the Hollywood role. At other times you kept us without letters for nearly three weeks. Now you dispatch three sermons. Vido is going to the bad. Stop him! He can't help himself, poor thing. Then the one to me: 'You want me to be happy. But how can I?' All this is very fine. Leave me out in future of all your daydreams. Try them on some English or Asiatic ass.

For three weeks past, I have been smoking. As much as with Springer and Co.* when you were here. That is bad, isn't it? I have been drinking excessively? Well, yes, water. It has been very hot. Listen, what have you people got against Owad?† I can tell you, Miss Hollywood, he is not a whit worse than any of your cousins. Of course, this will confirm, in your mind, the fact that I have gone to the dogs. But I don't give a damn what you think now. You have insulted me in the worst manner possible.

V. S. Naipaul

---

* Schoolfriends
† Cousin, Vidia's mother's sister Dhan's son

Miss Kamla Naipaul,
Women's Hostel,
Banaras Hindu University,
Banaras,
India

Trinidad
November 24, 1949

My darling,

I want you to promise me one thing. I want you to promise that you will write a book in diary form about your stay in India. Try to stay at least 6 months—study conditions; analyse the character. Don't be too bitter. Try to be humorous. Send your manuscript in instalments to me. I will work on them. I am getting introductions to quite a number of people— Pagett of Oxford included. Pa can put me on to Rodin, the star-writer of England's *Daily Express*. Your book will be a great success from the financial point of view. I can see it even now—*My Passage to India: A Record of Six Unhappy Months* by Kamla Naipaul.

Don't take everything in such a tragic way. I can't imagine how a girl like you so fond of laughter can't see the hilarious stupidity of the whole thing. If you go ahead taking everything to heart, your whole life will be just one lament.

But let us consider you—from the practical point. I have already paid back $150, and, by December, $200 shall be struck off. Not bad, eh? If you can't take it—tell your uncle* in London. Find out if his offer still holds good. I trust you are keeping in touch with Ruth.† If he says no, well, we'll see then. How much money have you in the bank?

Has the damned Gov't sent you your allowance?

My stay in Trinidad is drawing to a close—I only have nine months left. Then I shall go away never to come back, as I trust. I think I am at heart really a loafer. Intellectualism is merely fashionable sloth. That is why I think I am going to be either a big success or an unheard-of failure. But

---

* Vidia's mother's younger brother, Rudranath (Capo R.), at the time a Lecturer in Mathematics at London University
† Rudranath's wife, Vidia's aunt by marriage

I am prepared for anything. I want to satisfy myself that I have lived as I wanted to live. As yet I feel that the philosophy I will have to expand in my books is only superficial. I am longing to see something of life. You can't beat life for the variety of events and emotions. I am feeling something about everything—about this amusing and tragic world.

I have found it difficult to live up to my own maxim. 'We must be hard,' I say. 'We must ignore the pain-shrieks of the dying world,' yet I can't. There is so much suffering—so overpoweringly much. That is a cordial feature in life—suffering. It is as elemental as night. It also makes more keen the appreciation of happiness.

Please write to me only how sad you are.

There is one point I want you to help me stress. My thesis is that the world is dying—Asia today is only a primitive manifestation of a long-dead culture; Europe is battered into a primitivism by material circumstances; America is an abortion. Look at Indian music. It is being influenced by Western music to an amusing extent. Indian painting and sculpture have ceased to exist. That is the picture I want you to look for—a dead country still running with the momentum of its heyday.

Don't cry, my dear.

Your loving brother,
Vido

(I am sending the letter I got at the airport last night so that you could perhaps sense the adventure)

Hotel Wellington,
Seventh Avenue,
New York, NY
August 2nd
11.15

Miss Sati* Naipaul,
26 Nepaul Street,
Port of Spain,
Trinidad

New York is a marvellous place. Luxury and decadence. But what decadence! Newspapers 35 pages big selling for 5 cents.

But one fact hits the eye. The Americans are given overmuch, I think, to eating. They eat and eat. Eating-shops and hotels nudge each other in every street. I think it is pretty hard to get lost. The streets are numbered and so are the blocks.

So I wandered about this morning. I paid something like $3 to drive to and from the US steamship offices. Tourist class on an American ship is first class.

I looked hard for bookshops and at last I found one. It is really good. I could have invested $100 in books and felt no qualms about it. Books that I have long wanted to buy or read piled high. Courteous attendants who can tell you in 30 seconds flat if they have the type of book you want.

I bought a book, *South Wind* by Norman Douglas, for $1.28. James Joyce and Hemingway, Maugham and Huxley selling for the same price.

For the first time in my life people are calling me sir at every min. I am enjoying myself and—London me!—am not missing home.

I spent 3 hours each day on French language alone, 3 on Spanish etc. But then I wouldn't want you to work that hard. It all depends, as I say, on you.

---

* Sati (or Satti): Vidia's immediately younger sister, the third child of the family

Write me and tell me how you feel about studying for HC.* And don't worry about helping Ma for another two years or so. We will manage for the time being without your help. But a good HC will do you more good than one year's salary.

My best wishes for the examination.

Love,
Vido

62 Westbere Road,
London, NW2

Banares
p.m., 9/15/50

My dear Kamla,

Writing two copies of a letter is pretty tiring. To write home and then to write to you about the same thing is a heavy task.

That, however, is no excuse for my not writing you. It was sheer laziness. I thought the people at home had packed me up. For 3 weeks I got no word from them; in the meantime I had letters from people in France and Germany and several from friends here. The first communication I had was an official one—from the Colonial office.

I think you will be glad to know that I am absolutely happy. The only thing I need to make me feel the happiest man on earth is a girl, but what can I do? Nobody could ever like me; and I am despairing of myself.

To recapitulate what I have written in about half a dozen letters.

1. The Gov't was offering me a passage on September 19. This was ridiculous. I would have got here the day before my term opened. So I saved and with Shakhan's help decided to fly to New York and then take a ship to England. The government said: 'We are only offering you $464. Your trip costs $538, excluding the cost of your stay in New York. You will have to pay the difference.' I was so desperate that I said yes. But how I was relieved when they finally decided to pay everything.

---

* Higher Certificate

2. I was scared. I had never been on my own before. The idea of passing a night in a strange city and boarding a boat was terrifying. The boat was leaving N.Y. at 4 p.m. on Aug. 2; the plane was leaving T'dad at 9.30 a.m. Aug. 1. By 7 on the morning of Aug. 1, I was packed and ready to go. I didn't feel like shedding a tear. I had to be at the airport at 8.30. At No 17,* I learned that the plane was delayed. I was mad. I refused to believe. But it was so. So I kicked my heels in anguish at Woodbrook until 11, then took my luggage into dear old PA 1192† and we got to Diane at about 12. The waiting room was swarming with people who had come, not to see me off, but to see the airport. But the plane did come on time and at about 12.50, V. S. Naipaul was cut off from all family ties. I was scared, not unhappy, scared because I feared New York. Yet my fear passed away.

I began to enjoy myself.

[Note at foot of first page]: I met Ruth. She gave me a very unpleasant afternoon. I think she is a stupid, self-pitying shrew. A most detestable woman.

(Letter 2)

Now read on, darling.

We got to San Fran, Porto Rico at about 4.30 p.m. and left again at [. . .], this time for New York—8 hours' continuous flying away. Every moment of that day and that flight is imprinted on my mind. I can recall the faces of the stewards and stewardesses, the meals, the passengers.

At about 12 midnight we were over New York, acres of lights strung in asterisks mottled with red and green and blue. We grounded at 12.30; and I got a letter from the British consulate, instructing me to go to a certain hotel.

I took a taxi, felt like a lord at the hotel when a black porter took

---

* The Capildeo family house was located at 17 Luis Street in the district of Woodbrook, Port of Spain
† Registration number of the Naipaul family car, a Ford Prefect

my luggage in, calling me 'sir' every two or three words. It quite took my breath away. I was free and I was honoured. I was deeply happy. Freedom and desire achieved is sublime.

I got to the hotel at about two. I was about to go to a restaurant for a meal, when I remembered that I had a whole baked chicken with me—my darling mother looks after her children with all the poor little love she can dispose of—and I dumped the roti (wrapped in paper) in the waste basket and ate the chicken and a banana and drank ice-cold water. What the maid said on the following day when she emptied the basket, I don't know, nor do I particularly care to.

Next morning, I took a taxi to the steamship offices, taxied back to my hotel, had breakfast and went for a walk, bought a book; came back to my hotel, read the newspaper, took my luggage down to the port and boarded the boat. Simple. I was shocked that I had managed everything all right.

3. Voyage was very pleasant. I made several friends. A German woman (married and with husband aboard) whom I think I would have kissed, with ample co-operation from her, has invited me to Germany. I think I will go next year.

4. England has been proving very pleasant. Although my life with Boyzee is proving too narrow, I am enjoying it.

5. GIRLS—I met two. One I knew and saw for 3 days, took her to St Paul's and Regent's Park; but she has packed me up. She wants to be faithful to her boyfriend. Girl No. 2 was a Norwegian I met on a train to Oxford. We did some sightseeing together and I paid her the wildest compliments in French, vowed eternal love and wrote the torridest love letter (in French) I think I have ever written. She went back to Norway last Saturday. I think I will go to Norway this Christmas. She was very nice.

Your ever loving Vido

Trinidad p.m., September 15, 1950

V. S. Naipaul, Esq.,
62 Westbere Road,
London, NW2

Dear Vido,

It seems you have not yet received my letter. However, you do seem to be all right with cash, and I'm glad.

Your typewriter must be good to type so neatly; but I notice the C & O have a tendency to pile. But this may be due to faulty fast typing.

I hope the Penguin people accept your story. I am curious to see what it is like, but I half guess you would not like me to see it. I'm pretty sure it must be good, though. I can't imagine seeing you write a bad story. When writing a story it is a good thing to read good stories. Good reading and good writing go together. But you must have already discovered this.

Mr Swanzy* has paid me some fine encomiums on my short stories in his half-yearly review of *Poems and Prose in Caribbean Voices*. The review was also published in the last *Guardian Weekly*. On the other hand Mrs Lindo† (Jamaica) has taken me to task for sending in my published shorter story. She tells me that the BBC intended paying me seven guineas for it, but on discovering that the article had been previously published, the price was cut to £4 and 9/-, from which was deducted 9/- and something in the pound for income tax. So I was left with just $11, if you please. I have heard nothing, so far, about either 'Obeah' or 'The Engagement', though both have been sent up; and I have heard nothing about your poem. You had better write Mrs Lindo to let her know that you are now in England. Maybe she is mistaking you for me.

Have you written Kamla? She seems sad at your not writing her. Do write the girl and say nothing to hurt her feelings. We got a letter from her today, together with yours. She is ill with overwork.

Make contact with people like Thorold Dickinson‡ and other big shots

---

* Henry Swanzy, BBC World Service Producer, *Caribbean Voices*, a weekly literary programme
† Mrs Lindo, Jamaican Editor of *Caribbean Voices*
‡ Well-known film director of the period

in the film and writing business. You never know what good these people may lead you to.

So long as you use your freedom and feeling of independence sensibly it will be all to the good. Do not allow depression to have too much of a hold on you. If this mood visits you at times regard it as a passing phase and never give way to it.

Self-confidence is a very valuable asset and I am glad to know you feel confident; but don't underestimate people and problems. <u>Write often.</u>

Affectionately, Pa

[From Kamla]

Mon., Sept. 18, 1950

My dear Vido,

I received your two letters on Saturday afternoon but could not reply immediately because I had no air letters left. Anyway, I bought a few today. I have just returned from my music classes—sitar—and 15 minutes skating on my college corridor.

I do feel happy to know that you are happy. At last your dreams have been realised. It is now in your own hands to make or break the bright future that lies before you. Make the best use of your intelligence. Anyway, I know you'll make good. I am happy for you.

It is not that the people at home have packed you up. It is just that they are thoroughly disheartened. I may sound sentimental here but don't be angry. It's the truth. You should not write home in such an impersonal manner. You are fully aware that now Pa is left alone at home. You were his lifelong friend and now, as you said, family ties are cut. Do feel for them, Vido, and write them as they deserve. At least do that much. Pa wrote to me about a week ago saying that you had left home. He seemed somewhat unhappy. Said that he asked Sati to write you on behalf of the family. See what I mean. Be tactful with your English family,* will you?

You know, I feel terrible to have to be preaching Do's and Don't's to

---

* The Capildeo relations in England

you. But I guess I can't help it. I wonder if you take any heed of them? I could just imagine.

Pa sent me snaps of the people at home. You look lovely but that famous 'mooch' [. . .], I've deliberately hidden. Don't even try the experiment again. It is simply horrid. Mira and Savi* have grown like bamboos. I think you are in for a bunch of quite good-looking sisters . . . ahem.

Hey, you cannibal, since when degenerated? I should think that's a bad psychological sign, don't you?

You know, there is an Oxonian here—Colin Turnbull.† He said your college is quite nice but there is one disadvantage—trousers are very easily damaged in trying to scale the wall at night. So there, I've given you the hint. Colin will be returning to Oxford next year. He has promised to look you up. Be civil towards him.

You certainly seem to have gone torrid suddenly. A young Aeneas, eh? I don't mind it, but do be careful. You know what I mean. I would hate to have you placed in the same category as them West Indians. Don't ever let it happen. Go about yours nicely and gentlemanly. You are too young to have any particular girl. I say, don't you go and get yourself hitched to anybody. Boy, I hope you'd have some room in your heart and home for me when I get back. Save a little corner for me, will you? Girls mean money, Vido, and loans should not be indulged in.

I have decided to resign my job as secretary of the ISA—too much of a mental and physical strain. I am losing weight daily. It doesn't do my looks any good. The doctor has ordered me not to take milk. How do you like that? I have had a rash on my left leg, an abscess on my hip and all other signs of nervousness and overwork. Now, I am much better. I hope to make up during the winter. My Culture classes are being conducted in Hindi—I am learning nothing.

If you ever need anything, only ask me for it. Don't write home. Promise to ask for anything, won't you? I can even send cigarettes. Well, that is all for now. I'll write regularly.

Lots of love, Kamla

---

* Vidia's younger sisters, the fourth and fifth children (and third and fourth daughters) in the family
† Author, later, of *The Forest People* and other books about Africa—see Vidia's letter to Kamla of 11/8/51 and his letters home of 11/15/51 and 12/1/51

Be happy. But take good care of yourself. Be good. Ever loving Kamla. Have you written to Velma?* Pa has given me the latest rumour— Capildeo S. is coming to England for textile business!

Home, 9/22/50

Dear Son,

Your letter of September 17 we got yesterday. It has made me both happy and—to some extent sad. I thought that when Simbhoot† arrived he would be bringing you and Boysie cheer; that he would make the place a little more like home, with jokes and sightseeing and so on. I should not mind if letters do not come very frequently sometimes. You say Kamla has not written you; and Kamla says you have not written her. You write her and try to be kind in your letter. Kamla is only too anxious to hear from you as well as to write you. She probably did not know your address.

I have not failed with my developing outfit. The very first try was a success. I cannot enclose photos with this or else I would have shown you specimens. One photo of my developing I have sent to Kamla. It is Shivan‡ and Baido.§ A cute little snap. What I need now is a printer—you know, the equipment on which negatives are printed. Another humbug lies in the fact that I cannot get the right printing paper. Johnsons of Hendon Ltd, London, NW4, have plastic printing frames; more than this, they carry what they call a new Exactum Printer; also they stock gas-light printing paper of all grades. On this paper printing can be done with daylight. They are very cheap. See if you can send a few packets for me, for negatives, size 120. Also contact printing paper, grades vigorous, soft and normal. Tell the people the kind of camera I have, and they should give you the right stuffs for printing.

The *Guardian* paid me only $5 for the two Ramadhin** pictures; and five dollars for the story in the *Sunday Guardian*. Before these I think I got

---

* Girlfriend of Kamla
† Maternal uncle
‡ Shiva, Vidia's younger brother
§ Cousin, maternal aunt's daughter
** Sonny Ramadhin, fabled West Indian test cricketer

$3 for the uncle–aunt picture that came out in the sports page of *TG*. But my rice-growing story in the *Weekly* carried four pictures. They should bring me in at least $12, but of course you never know with these people.

I have not heard anything further on your poem. You know it has been sent up to London by Mrs Lindo. And I haven't heard more about 'Obeah' and 'The Engagement', which, like your poem, have been sent up; and acknowledged as having been received and retained for possible future broadcasting. Wait and see.

Your writings are all right. I have no doubt whatever that you will be a great writer; but do not spoil yourself: beware of undue dissipation of any kind. I do not mean you must be a puritan. A pity you spent some money badly re meeting Simbhoo; but such things will happen. It was gratifying to hear you could send us some money but everything is all right just now. Are you keeping a savings account? Yes, I think you do; I think you mentioned the fact in a previous letter. S.* used to also say some such things to Rudranath† when the latter had won his scholarship. I remember S's spirited objection and umbrage. You keep your centre. You <u>are</u> on the way to being an intellectual. He is only stating a fact. Acknowledge it mentally as such. Say, 'Thanks.'

I never had so much work as I am having nowadays. I hope I shall be able to keep up. I am no longer on the *Evening News*. They have shifted me to the *Guardian*. Since last Monday—General Election day—I have been working, at a stretch almost, from early morning to late night—nine and ten at nights. Don't see how I can find the time to do features for the *Weekly*. Even this letter I write at a snatch. I was asked to write a feature on faith-healing at about 12.30 yesterday; and I had to turn out the stuff first thing in the morning. The faith-healer's meeting that I was to describe actually never finished till midnight. This was last night. But I have turned in the story. What is strange is that I think it will be a good story—snappily written.

I like your decision to write weekly. I think I can easily manage writing once a fortnight providing the air-letter form is at hand! And providing that the letter, having been written, gets posted!

---

* Simbhoo
† Maternal uncle, Simbhoo's younger brother

I haven't bought the tyre. It will get bought when it comes to my not being able to go out—unless I had one. Like buying the battery. Let us know what is happening. Tell me about the fate of the poems you have sent in, and the stories. And don't worry about anybody or anything here.

No fear; we received all your letters. Only I find they took a long time in the coming. Once three letters, differently dated, came in a batch. Altogether we've got seven letters from you from the day you left home; plus a cable.

No harm in kissing a girl, so long you do not become too prone for that sort of thing. Love from everybody,

Naipaul

II

October 5, 1950 — January 1, 1951

FIRST TERM AT OXFORD

Home: 10/5/50
7.00 p.m.

My dear Vido,

It must be now about 11 p.m. in England. Your first day in the University must have long finished. I am both curious and anxious to know how Oxford reacted to you; or how you reacted to Oxford. Send me a detailed pen-picture of the day . . . Got your letter of Sept. 29; got one from Kamla, too. Both yours and hers came yesterday. So far so good . . . I think you are yielding yourself to needless worry about writing. I think you will have your hands filled with a lot of work at Oxford; and in any case you are hardly likely to find time to do any writing for money for a long time to come. So Andrew Pearse* tells me.

Don't be scared of being an artist. D. H. Lawrence was an artist through and through; and, for the time being at any rate, you should think as Lawrence. Remember what he used to say, 'Art for my sake. If I <u>want</u> to write, I write—and if I don't want to, I won't.' Long years ago, when I was about 14 or 16, I felt much as you are feeling now; eager to write, but writing in a kind of vacuity—utterly fictitious efforts—because what I wrote, or tried to write, had nothing to do with flesh and blood. I was simply writing stories that had no real counterpart with life. Now I know that if I am writing about Rapooche, I am for the moment Rapooche himself. I must therefore know Rapooche, be Rapooche. In a sense I am wholly myself; and yet I am wholly the character I am trying to portray. It's a matter of impersonation, I think, the kind of thing the actor does. This, I think, is the secret of getting to the inside of things. The mere fact that you are conscious of this lack shows that you're on the right track. Well, all this is

---

* Editor, the *Caribbean Quarterly,* attached to the newly founded University College of the West Indies

perhaps too much preaching; and I don't know whether I have succeeded in telling you what I wanted to say . . .

One cannot write well unless one can think well; only, in writing fiction one must be able to think as the character would think in given circumstances.

Like yourself, I made the mistake of sending a Ramadhin story—synchronising the dispatch with the last Test—to the *News Chronicle,* instead of sending it to the *Sunday Chronicle.* I had no idea they were two different papers, owned by different proprietors. I get some consolation from the fact that the sports editor, in returning the stuff, states that 'they are excellent material, but not for a daily newspaper as severely rationed for its newsprint as we are these days'. Why, ordinarily they might have returned the thing with just a stereotyped rejection note. Now that I re-read the story, I too find it 'excellent' material.

I am sorry Rodin was not too helpful. I shall write him. Really, I ought to have given you a letter of intro. It's the right way to go about these things, I suppose. He must be a big shot. Those who write features for such popular newspapers as the *Express* must be above the average. Sometimes it might be due to luck, too. For even I feel confident I could turn out a story or two worthy of the *Sunday Express.* Do not be too anxious. Your time is coming. But please make up your mind in advance that there might be lots and lots of rejections before you 'arrive'. Make up your mind for this, and know it is almost the necessary preliminary [. . .] Did you meet Mrs Capildeo R.?

Since you left home I have had a few first-rate stories in the *Sunday Guardian.* One on 'What the peasants think about the election' was particularly good. Even the British Council told me what a fine article it was, and that there is need for more such writings. Then another on a faith-healing service that I witnessed at Woodbrook. (My rice-growing story came out fine, too. Today I got a check for $20 for it. I had supplied my own pictures—four of them. I don't think I have been paid well enough. Fifteen dollars should be for the story alone; and the pictures should fetch at least $3 a piece. I intend to talk it over with Smith. But now I despair of writing many articles for the *Weekly.* No time, really. The work on the *Guardian* takes all out of me.

<u>Do</u> <u>send</u> <u>me</u> <u>a</u> <u>copy</u> <u>of</u> <u>R. K.</u> <u>Narayan's</u> <u>*Mr*</u> <u>*Sampath.*</u> The book is very favourably spoken of in *The Year's Work in Literature, 1949*—an annual

publication of the British Council. Narayan is spoken of as 'the most delightful of Indian novelists writing in English . . . in a way which no English writer of our time can rival'. It is published by Eyre and Spottiswoode, Ltd, 6 Great New St., London, EC4. The price is not given. I shall refund you the money. Also *The Authors' Handbook* (The Bodley Head). Re developer: send only a packet or two of 'Self-toning Daylight Paper'—vigorous, soft and normal grades. They won't cost much. I wish this sheet was longer. [Sentence deleted, with note saying, 'Parts deleted have been censored by me, Savi'] This is the time I should be writing the things I so long to write. This is the time for me to be myself. When shall I get the chance? I don't know. I come from work, dead tired. The *Guardian* is taking all out of me—writing tosh. What price salted fish and things of that sort. Actually that is my assignment for tomorrow! It hurts. Now keep your chin up, and far more important: keep yourself out of mischief.

Love from Ma and all, Pa

University College, Oxford
October 12, 1950

Dear Everybody,

What a delight to receive Pa's excellent letter from home. If I didn't know the man, I would have said: what a delightful father to have. He really writes extremely good letters.

It is now twelve noon. I have just returned from a tutorial, a weekly one-hour lesson with my tutor. I wrote an essay on *King Lear*, which he described as very pleasantly written and trenchantly argued.

For the first time I really find myself looking forward to letters from home. This morning, too, I had a letter from Johnnie Chenwing, the Chinese boy whom I taught at Tranquillity.* He is sending me ten pounds. I wonder why I impressed him in such a big way. At first meetings I usually do impress people, but I soon become my normal clowning self, and consequently go down in their esteem. But, I suppose, that is my character. Let

---

* Vidia's elementary school

it be. I am not sure whether it is to Kamla, or to you that I have described my first day at Oxford. But I think I have written to you already.

The people here accept me. I have quite a number of acquaintances, and to meet people, I have joined about half a dozen societies. I am interested in doing some drawing, because I feel the urge to draw and write poetry blazing within me. I have written quite a number of poems since I have left home, and I find material coming in floods to me. Thought and deep emotion is really all that one requires for poetry, besides of course a feel for words. When I was in London, I had one of my poems read by a writer whose novel was published last year. He liked it, especially the following lines:

> In a yellowing world
> Of yellowing leaves
> And yellowing men.

Beautiful words force themselves on you in this delightful climate. Listen to this. Read it aloud. I was trying to capture the sound of a racing train:

> . . . noisy trains
> clangorously clattering towards nothing.

I don't care what anyone says, that is a really excellent line. Again, describing Oxford:

> this elephant's cemetery where the cracked and the decrepit philosophies crack conglomerately in death.

Really fine, don't you think? You can see for yourself how vastly my poetry has improved. I have developed a greater feeling for words and can now truly appreciate Mulk Raj Anand's opening sentence of *The Liar*: 'Labhu, the old shikari of my village, was a born liar.' Few people really get that feeling for words. But enough of this.

I met Ruth; and I doubt whether I have come across a more stupid, arrogant, shrewish, self-pitying woman in all my limited experience. I went to see her for three hours. It was hell. I can hardly picture myself living with her and enjoying it. She seems to have a great hatred for the clan. I won't be surprised if Capo [Capildeo] R.'s churlish behaviour has not been due in part to her.

You've got to know that Oxford is a collection of more than twenty colleges. You hardly can get to know all the people you want. The 1948 people stick mostly to themselves and so on. If you want to meet people outside your group in your college, you've got to take part in many activities, you can go out every night. The Dean put the problem very well on Thursday night: everything is not to be found in books; on the other hand, it is folly to think that nothing can be found in books. The compromise is left to you. Yet it must be remembered that it is these distractions that are the essence of a university education. You've to win no scholarship. You don't want to beat every other fellow. If you do a reasonable amount of work then there is no reason why you cannot pass.

The toughest nut I have to crack here is Anglo-Saxon. It is an entirely new language, much more intricate than Latin. Satti can give you an idea how hard it is.

It is still not too late for your Ramadhin story. If I were you, I should send interesting bits of news to the *News Chronicle*. It may pay off. The papers are truly starved for news. But make it short and snappy. The news for instance of the cricket holiday in Jamaica and the civic reception, etc. made front page. You see what I mean. Send your Ramadhin stuff to any of the Sunday papers. It is not too late. Ramadhin is known to everyone in England, and very few know anything about his background.

The atmosphere of this college is more of a club than anything else. There is the Junior Common Room where the students meet and drink and smoke and talk, as though they were in any club. I have got to learn how to dance. Even Capo has advised me to try to learn. The lectures are dull and uninformative. I am going mainly to make social contact. It would surprise you to see the vast flock of people reading English. Most want to become writers. You are not obliged to attend lectures or write essays. You can do no work at all, if that is your inclination. But I have so much to read.

I am going out after this letter to see about the books Pa wants. Chen-wing has also asked for some books. I am going to send him some too. It is slowly becoming colder and colder. I shall soon start wearing my overcoat. Up to now I have been sticking to the unlined rubber raincoat. Please don't call a raincoat a cloak. England is teaching me to say thank you and please.

The beauty of Oxford grows on you.

I think I have exhausted myself now. I have rambled conversationally in the hope of making this letter more conversational.

Incidentally, I have a favour: could you send me a carton of cigarettes? Everyone here smokes and everyone offers you, and I have fallen back into the habit. But don't be horrified. But please send the cigarettes. They are so expensive here.

> Your loving son (and brother to the rest)
> Vidia

[Handwritten note]: Pardon the faults in typing. I have no time nor the desire to correct.

Home: 10/22/50

Dear Vido,

Something has gone wrong with my typewriter, so that the keys do not type to the end of the paper. Hence doubling this sheet like this.

Your letters are charming in their spontaneity. If you could write me letters about things and people—especially people—at Oxford, I could compile them in a book: *Letters Between A Father and Son,* or *My Oxford Letters.* What think you? Just here Kamla seems useless. You can do it, I'm sure. If you can bring the same quality of spontaneity in whatever you write, everything you write will have a sparkle. I believe this free flow in one's written thought is due largely to absence of anxiety. It is due to one not setting oneself too big, sometimes impossible, ideals. I know because it happens to me. Whenever I allow myself to become too anxious to please the person I am writing to or the person I am writing for, I generally lose balance and spoil everything. I begin concentrating not so much on what I want to say, but on what would most flatter the person I am writing to. The result is bound to be a stilted business. Don't care to please any person but yourself. Only see that you have succeeded in saying exactly what you wanted to say—without showing off; with utter, brave sincerity—and you will have achieved style because you will have been yourself. Much as many people will doubt it, this attitude of mind must be brought into play even when writing for the popular press. You must be yourself. You must be sincere. You must aim to say only what you have to say and to say it clearly. If in the chase for clarity you have to ignore a rule of grammar, ignore it. If for the sake of euphony you must use a long word, use it. My goodness! What do you think literature boils down to? To writing from the belly rather than from the cheek. Most people write from the cheek. If the semi-illiterate criminal wrote a long letter ordinarily to his sweetheart, it would be what most letters of such people generally are. If the criminal wrote this letter last thing before his execution it would be literature; it would be poetry. That's why Bunyan's *P. Progress* is great. That's why Gandhi's writing is great.

Yep! I am a contradiction; but I think I am in good company. Of Bacon it is said, 'His moral character was singularly mixed.' One might with equal truth say that character was singularly corrupt. Yet it is commonly accepted that the intellect of Bacon 'was one of the most powerful and searching ever possessed by man'. Or Macaulay was exaggerating again. And look at Goldsmith. 'He wrote like an angel, and talked like poor Poll.' Then there's Boswell, the man who was laughed at by the company he sought; the company he later adorned by writing the greatest biography ever written. It seems to me that it wasn't what these fellows were outwardly that mattered; it was the other self that they could summon. The mood they could put themselves in—that made them write how and what they wrote. Mohammed dictating the Koran in trance—don't think it was real trance—was not the Mohammed awake. Mood again. In a moment one can make oneself whatever one wants oneself to be. No wonder William James speaks of man's many selves. Maybe he's right. I think he is right. You may call to service your writing self; or you may call your politician self, or your conniving self, or your poet self, or your mystic self, or your saint self. So it seems to me. Conflict? Not if you have a well-integrated personality; not if you are properly psychologically weaned. But don't mix all this with the diseased state of mind modern psychologists call paranoiac reactions: those people who have their own fantastic logic—James Swami Dayanand Maharaj of Trinidad—former City Councillor, now a Rajah—parading Queen Street, with sash and sceptre (a small poniard), verily believing he is King of Somewhere!

You know, you should read some psychology. Don't be cynical about such readings. They form a part of one's education. A good book for you would be . . . oh, never mind.

Very sorry, but your Ma has just found out from Sarkar* that Customs Regulations make it extremely difficult to send away things like cigarettes. He says it can't be done. Still, I'll make more inquiries, for it seems to me the thing should not be so.

Well, I am sending you the Ramadhin stuff. See if you can place it anywhere. If it needs cutting down, cut it. Try the *Sunday Chronicle*, the *Sunday Express*, or *Reynold's News*. If you succeed in selling it, keep the money.

I could shoot a lot more talk, but I think I have said enough. Write lengthy letters about people—to me. If they become too long for an air form, send by sea mail.

Today was Hosey.† Everybody went to see the things, except me. But I did have a look from upstairs, and as the tajiahs‡ were passing the Rialto, I went across and took two snaps of hoseys and moon.§

I have collected a series of pictures on rice-growing in Trinidad— enlarged and everything. Some day I may use them. Locally they have already been used.

Don't forget to send me the Narayan novel—*Mr Sampath;* and the *Writers' and Artists' Yearbook* will be a very useful guide for me.

A talk I had here with an Englishman named Barker was very discouraging as regards finding markets for stories in England and in USA. He is night news editor on the *Guardian*, and has worked on newspapers in England and India. He was reporter, I think, on the *Daily Telegraph* (London). He has written some articles for American magazines and has also done some short stories.

What about your colds? Have you had any attacks? Let us know. Everything and everybody OK. Love from all, Pa

10/27/50

This I am now adding as a postscript; very sorry for the delay. This evening when I came in there was a letter from you. I have learned to recognise your

---

* A family friend
† Shia Festival of Mohurram
‡ Replicas of the tombs of Shia martyrs
§ Simulated moons featured in a ritual dance of the festival

letters by the colour of the paper. Sometimes in my letter you'll find me spouting a lot of talk; if you should find them absurd, forget them as so many banalities. In writing one must have something to say, but if one wrote only when one thought one would say the right things, one would seldom write.

I do hope you did succeed in meeting Radhakrishnan* again. To get the notice of such men a 'rebuff' or two is a cheap price for the privilege of an interview. And it is always the best to be quite frank about your position with such people. You could have said, in order to make conversation: 'My father has always looked upon you as one of the greatest minds of modern India. He has often said he never understood Hinduism so well as when he read your book, *The Heart of Hindustan.*' And you would have broken the ice, as they say. Contacts, Vido, contacts all the time. Let me go on. Suppose you had a fairly good chat with this great scholar, you could have described the experience of the incident to me in a letter—in a long letter, if that was necessary. I'd have delighted in the reading of such a letter; and I'd have kept it with other letters of yours. Write me weekly of the men you meet; tell me what you talked; how they talked; and you'll be amazed to know what a fine array of letters you have written in just a year's time. Let's go to work like that. It's an easy way and a good way; because the thoughts you embody will be free and light and spontaneous—precious qualities that go to the marrow-bone of good writing. Suppose you kept my letters, and I kept yours, we might find two books emerging instead of one. Who knows!

My letters then would not be just preachings, but descriptions of people and incidents in these parts . . . A Kamla, a Bhagwat,† a calypso night, a shango;‡ a chat with Baboolal,§ a chat with Rapooche. Do you see what I mean? You needn't send your letters by air if they are too long. Keep your centre. All's well at home.

---

* S. Radhakrishnan (1888–1975): Professor of Eastern Religions, Oxford; later, President of India (1962–67)
† A reading of the scriptures taking place over many nights
‡ An African religion
§ A peasant relation of Vidia's father

[From Kamla]

November 8, 1950

Dear Vido,

I am happy to know that you have taken to Oxford life. There is one thing, though, and that is, I don't think you should coop yourself up with books. You don't have to strive for any more scholarships and, believe me, the more you read, the more there is to read. Sacrifice neither schoolwork nor friends. Both, as you say, are very essential. There is the happy medium.

You know, about the cigarettes, I was told that the customs duty you would have to pay is enormous. It were better that you buy them there. However, don't think I am making excuses. If you want, I can send a few. See what the duty comes up to and then whether I should send more.

I received a letter from Ma, two days ago. She mentioned that you were better than Pa. You can imagine my surprise. I never queried.

Noble Sarkar has been inquiring after us and Ma has given the entire conversation. Talking about Ma, she has asked (very humbly) if both of us can help in paying Savi's fees. She said I should ask you. I have decided to send 5ors—$18—home monthly. That would be a great help, I know. I don't know whether you would be able to do anything. I am fully aware that your living would require about 3 times mine.

Anyway, write to me about this—don't mention it to anyone at home. If you think what I am sending is sufficient, then you should send nothing because I shall be coming to England, when you might need more money. Well, write and I shall decide, and don't write home scolding Ma.

During my vacation, I got a letter from Ramnarace Moussa.* Well, he wants this thing and that thing and a whole catalogue of books. I must buy them and when 'Ma is sending money', he shall enclose his. Do you mean to tell me that these people are not aware that I get no money from home? I wonder if I have come here to do business or to study. Really, I get so angry. He writes asking this favour, then goes on to bless me and in the two last pages of the form there is a further hint of these things he wants. This is the third letter. And I intend to answer it.

By the way, there is one thing I want of you. I don't know whether

---

* Maternal uncle by marriage, husband of Vidia's mother's sister Calawattee

you'd be able to get it. You know, Oxford prints specimen questions and answers in Eng. Lit. I don't know whether you'd be able to put your hand on a few of those, especially those of poetry. Really, Vido, I am studying for myself. Believe me, if you are original, you have failed. If you cram the book and transcribe it—1st class pass. What I would like to know is how the questions should be answered. A few days ago, we were given an exam—Coleridge as a poet—I was given 7/10 because I was 'original'. Another girl got a 7/10. My Eng. Prof. prefers hers and has asked the other students to 'learn her answer by heart'. She advised me to read it, which I did, and the honest to goodness truth, it was word for word with 'Comptons & Ricketts'—Lit. criticism.

Lots of love,
Kamla

[Two notes at side of pages]:

Please send a <u>Christmas card for Nanie.</u>* Do that much, will you?
Your rule for girls should be: 'Would Kamla think her a fool?' I have been following yours even before you asked. Don't worry!

Home: Nov. 17, 50

Dear Vido,

I think you defaulted a week in writing. You shouldn't. Always let it be a weekend chore to write home. To this schedule you should keep even if you miss a letter or two from our end. But you will find that more often than not there will be letter for letter; that is, when I (or we) receive a letter from you there will follow a reply to it. How long does it take to knock out a letter of this kind? Five minutes or so at most, and for my part I find it a pleasure. You say nothing on how you are making out with food. What do you eat, mostly? Speak on this in your next letter.

I think I have already told you how difficult it is to send cigarettes because of Customs Regulations. I know you will feel very disappointed, but so do we. Couldn't you get Boysie to get some for you in London? I

---

* Vidia's maternal grandmother

understand cigarettes are not quite as expensive in London as they are your way. And then again, the duty cost on sending cigarettes to you from here is likely to be so high that it would be cheaper to get the stuff in England. Anyway, they just don't allow you to send things like cigarettes from here. So far everybody we have asked has said it is just not allowed. Today your Ma was to find out the exact rule from the Control Board, but like herself, she tells me she didn't get the time to find out.

On the 11/10/50 your Ma sent you a 22lbs parcel containing: 6 tins grapefruit juice, two tins orange juice, 2lbs granulated sugar, 1 bott. Amchar* and a home-made cake.

Since last Monday—today is Thursday—I have been shifted to *Guardian Weekly*, to sub. And write stories and make up pages. The page-making is quite interesting work—almost as thrilling as writing an article; but up to now I am just learning. I seldom come home before 5.30 or later every evening. It is stiff work, but if I get to use my initiative in doing the make-ups without too much interference I am sure I won't mind the hard part of the hours at all. Fact is you get so absorbed in the work that time passes before you realise it is time to go home. More on this in a subsequent letter.

This week's human interest story: Chan Sadhu (Sanyasi) ran away with a young Brahmin boy of Tunapuna about a month ago. Only now, a few minutes ago, I got the news from your mother, who has just returned from Sookhdeo's.† She had gone to pay him $100.00 that was due him in interest. Nobody told us a word about his sly romance.

Second human interest item: Sookhdeo let off your mother with a hundred-dollar loan that she had taken from him when Kamla was going away. To that hundred he added $14 for you when giving a receipt for the interest payment. I suggest you write him a letter—not too fulsome—you quite appreciated the gift. He is human so will be pleased.

In your last letter—Nov. 6—you mention nothing about the Narayan book. Don't bother about the photographic things I asked you for, I don't have time enough for my camera now. But <u>do</u> send me the book.

Congrats on your *Isis*‡ success. Send me a copy of the *Weekly*. About

---

* Indian pickle
† Great-uncle by marriage, rich husband of Vidia's paternal grandmother's sister
‡ Oxford University literary magazine

the Carnival Queen story and Maugham piece in the *QRC* Chronicle:* You know, I had no copy of the *Chronicle,* so I asked Debysingh† to get me a copy. He said he'd send me one by Deven‡ if I sent Deven to him. Deven didn't meet him in the college today, but told me he'd go to him tomorrow. When he brings the *Chronicle* to me I shall send it to you without delay together with the Tranquillity School Mag. Which I have on my desk. You will see two x's in the body of your article. I think if you would delete the matter between the two x's; and also put some 'ands' in places of full stops, to make your sentences less telegraphic, it will be quite a good article. I could never get the courage to read the thing to the end. Some of the stuff you wrote in the *Hindu* were quite good, but I doubt if I could put my hand on a copy or two of that too-soon-dead paper.

Say, why not write an article or two for the *TG* or the *WG*§ here on life at Oxford. Make it chatty. If you wrote for the *Weekly* you'd get thrice the money that you'd get writing for the *Guardian.* Forget the *Evening News.* Sound Hitchens** on the idea, if you like; but I feel you could write right away. Four or five letter-size sheets in typescript should give you a good length, and you could get anything from ten to fifteen dollars for it—if it comes off in the *Weekly.* But if you could write with an eye to Trinidad so much the better.

Clippings or whole *Guardian*s being sent by surface mail.

All well at home, Pa

University College, Oxford
Nov. 22

My dear Kamla,

Thanks for your letter. I keep forgetting things. Only as I sit down to write to you do I remember what you asked me to get for you. I will try to remember tomorrow. Bear with me a while.

---

* Queen's Royal College, Port of Spain
† Teacher at QRC, an amateur writer
‡ Cousin, son of Vidia's mother's brother Simbhoo
§ *Trinidad Guardian, Trinidad Weekly Guardian*
** Editor, the *Trinidad Guardian*

I have no news, my dear, none whatever. I have been working very hard; but not as hard as I wanted. A feeling of emptiness is nearly always on me. I see myself struggling in a sort of tunnel blocked up at both ends. My past—Trinidad and the necessity of our parents—lies behind me and I am powerless to help anyone. My future—such as it is—is a full four years away. I have no doubt that then I shall be able to help. But how can I help you when you come to this country in 2 years' time? Perhaps, after I have settled here and made friends, I will find new openings. But I have nothing now. But don't despair. Once you are here and can get a job, that will be all. I would like to have you close to me when you get here; not that I want to pry into your life but that it would give me a feeling of deeper security. But all that is 24 months away.

My dear girl, my allowance is barely enough for myself. I smoke too much; but don't write home about that. I will do my best to send home £5 for Christmas, but I will only be sure after I have settled with the College Authorities. I am prepared to do some hack writing for anyone who would care to pay for it and next term I will write some articles for the *Guardian* and try to get some of my stories published over here. I speak of 'some'. Actually I have written only two; but I have been engaged on a novel. It is about 8 chapters gone—about 140 pages in any Penguin book; but it is only in a very rough form. I shall not touch it again until the end of next term. I am exhausted. I want new ideas to incubate a bit. I shall have it complete in a year's time. And think what will become of me if it is published! For I am sure of one thing—once it is published, it is bound to sell. It is a humorous novel.

Is there anything, my dear, I can get for you as a Christmas gift? Speak; for my allowance arrives in a week.

I got three letters this morning. I felt quite a big gun. 2 contained money; one was from home. Boyzee sent me a pound; the BBC sent me a guinea. They broadcast one of my poems on Sep. 24, did you know? But I, as you probably know, am no poet. I will, however, try to sell them those I have written. I have tried in 2 magazines, but they both promptly returned them—for a very good reason. They are very bad poems. I know it.

And now, about girls. I have conducted two highly unsuccessful love affairs this term. Only yesterday I rounded off one in a romantic way. The first girl—a Belgian and the most beautiful thing you ever saw—tolerated me for three weeks. Then she suddenly told me she couldn't come to tea. I was taken aback and deeply hurt. It appears that one of the stories I had shown her was, in her view, pornographic. Hell! I showed the same story to John Harrison* when he came to tea in my rooms last Saturday and he said there was nothing wrong with it. Anyway, she packed me up and sent me the most beautiful letter I have ever had from a woman. I shall quote:

My dear Vidia (she wrote),

I shall never forgive myself for hurting you and for this being the blackest day in my life—but do understand—it's not only that in society one must not accept your offence, which I myself forgive with all my heart; it is also and above all, as I tried to tell you, that I'm in love with another. I hate myself for the hours of pain I have caused you etc., etc. . . . .

How I wish that by some word I could add meaning to your life, etc.

Because you are intelligent, you rush this slow country's atmosphere and people—perhaps compromise, though hateful, is still best. You and another are the only worthwhile boys I have met so far in Oxford, but you shun your own anxiety, whereas I believe only anxious people worthwhile, and beautiful in their anguish.

Why don't you understand that your anguish proves your greatness, etc.?

Good! Not bad, eh? Imagine—your own brother, just turned 18 but lying to every girl that he is 22, drawing that letter from a girl after whom nearly everybody in the English class is rushing! I think the other chap was a better poet. The other woman who has been having 4-hour teas with me once a week is English and very stupid and I am relieved to be rid of her.

Goodbye now, my dearest Kamla, and keep well and don't write letters like the one above, because, you see, I *lied* to that girl.

Yours, Vido

---

* Art teacher at the British Council in the Caribbean

11/27/50

Dear Vido,

It would be a shame to waste such lovely space. Your last letter came a couple of days ago. I hope this will reach you before Christmas. Since you will be in London for the vacation, I wonder who will receive your parcel, that is addressed to the college and contains grapefruit juice, sugar, cake and so on. This was posted on November 10, so you should have some idea about the time it will arrive.

I hope, too, that you posted me the Narayan books before leaving for London. Ronald Millner, your New Zealand pen pal, has sent you a Christmas card; I hope you have sent him one too. If you haven't done so yet, you can still do it. The card is being sent you by ordinary mail.

We asked you to say how you are getting on with your food, but you have mentioned nothing. Of course we can't help you from this end if things aren't just right, but still, it is good to know.

It seems I may get a British Council Scholarship. Will let you know more next time—Pa.

In one short paragraph of D. H. Lawrence's *St Mawr* I have just come across these uncommon sentences: 'But his face was blank and stony, with a stony distant look of pride . . . She could see the cloud of hurt in his eyes . . .'

There are thousands of such sentences in this book which I got today. I have also got Hassan, a kind of Eastern tales of Old Baghdad; and Wells' *Short History of the World*. This book I already had, you will remember; but somehow lost it. A few weeks ago I bought Lawrence's *Letters*. Yet I no longer have much time to read; nor do I write articles for the *Weekly* that brought me an extra 25 or 40 D's in the month. It's a great loss, but as we say down here, what to do?!

Are you quite happy? You must tell me frankly. Barring illness, there is no earthly reason why you shouldn't be. Today after a chat with Noble Sarkar—he is a doctor now, and arrived yesterday—I thought, I'd sell the house, if need be, to make you take up some professional studies following your graduation. Try and win a scholarship—can you? I don't know what the odds are, if any.

You know, I wrote Capo R. and Boysie. Boysie wrote me, and his letter came today, but Capo R. hasn't replied. Well, let them keep mum.

The British Council rep. here is keen on giving me a B. C. Scholarship;

he's been complimenting me on my stories recently. But one stumbling block—to the scholarship, I mean—is my age. Already I'm in my 45th year, if you please. Stanley was so good as to hint to me what I should stress in my application; so also did Pearse. You see, the s/s is decided by a selection committee, with Hannays* in it. Everybody fears Hann as he's the Government's watchdog. But supposing I do get the s/s, I don't see how I can possibly take advantage of it. Who'll see home? That's the snag.

A Mr Steer, a graduate of Balliol College, Oxford—but went there from Birmingham Uni., I think to do a post-graduate course—is also keen to have me work with him. He is the Government's statistician; would pay salary of $160 (or more) to go up to $200. But again there's a snag. The job holds good for only five months. I have as good as turned it down. If I could only earn $200 monthly I'd have far less bother.

Pa

[Handwritten note]: The typewriter is fixed, as you can see.

University College, Oxford
December 1, 1950

My dear Kamla,

I sit before my typewriter and don't know what on earth to write. Frankly, I don't.

I am back in London for Christmas. I will return to Oxford on December 27 and work in the libraries until term opens in mid-January. I have brought all my clothes and half my books. And I am trying to work hard. I try not to go out, but all the work I do is for about four hours. Yet I am making some progress. I have collections and examinations by the tutors at the beginning of next term, and the big preliminary examination at the end of it. So I have to work hard.

Actually, the only thing that has me downright worried is the Anglo-Saxon. I hope I master it.

I asked for the specimen questions and answers at the Oxford University Press, but they had none. I am terribly sorry, and all I could tell

---

* Influential Trinidad lawyer, whose son was Vidia's contemporary at school (see page 3)

you is to float with the tide, but never deceive yourself. You know it's wrong. Well, you <u>know</u>. The other people just accept it as part of the Indian scene.

I have stopped writing, to prepare for my examinations. I have eight set books. Well, I have run through six, and have read one, and have not opened the other. For the past week and a half I have done fairly detailed studies of two. I have finished one of the two books of Virgil. The other I have done twice, but that was six months ago. So it won't be much to revise. So the Latin doesn't worry me.

You may be interested to know that about a week ago I had my first snow. It came down in little cotton-ball fluffs and after two hours, the earth was covered, but not the streets. I am looking forward to more. The newspapers have been forecasting it for the past two days, but none has fallen in my region of London.

I am not staying with Boyzee and Capo S. I am staying at Earl's Court. Not far from the Underground Station, about a minute's walk, to be exact. It makes the world of difference to have a room of one's own. Look, my dear girl, if you have to pay duty to *send* the cigarettes, then don't bother. If I have to pay, then send them by all means. Not Indian cigarettes, for heaven's sake.

Capo R. & S. have decided to buy a house in London. For £5,000! I met Capo R. a few days ago, by appointment. We had a meal at the Tottenham Court Rd Lyon's Corner House. He is taking up law. He wants to make money. He treated me very well, I think. But you never know with that man. He invited me down to Wallington, but I haven't been as yet. I detest that wife of his, whom you found so charming. What on earth was the matter with your judgement?

Boyzee's father's sister is dead—the last of the Deepan clan. I supposed that he will be writing you shortly about it. He is in the dining room of the boarding house at present, and I asked him what on earth I could fill up the page with. He told me. So I put it down.

Here's wishing you a Merry Christmas and all that. I can write no more. I have ransacked my brain and found nothing.

With love,
Vido

[Handwritten note]: Not posted

London
December 11, 1950

Dear Everybody,

I feel the urge to write a long letter home. For the past two days, I have been thinking more and more about home. I told Boyzee this, and he told me that the reason was probably that Christmas is not far off. I wonder. Christmas never meant much to me or to any one of our family. It was always so much of a glorious feeling of fun we felt existed somewhere, but we could never feel where it was. We were always on the outside of a vague feeling of joy. The same feeling is here with me in London. Yet there is so much more romance here. It gets dark at about half past three and all the lights go on. The shops are bright, the streets are well lit and the streets are full of people. I walk through the streets, yet am so much alone, so much on the outside of this great festive feeling.

But I was thinking of home. I could visualise every detail of everything I knew—the bit of the gate, for instance, that was broken off, the oleander tree and the withering roses. Sometimes the sound of a car starting in the road rouses me. The uncertain hesitant beat of the engine brings back No. 26 to me, smells and all. It makes me feel sad. Don't misunderstand. It makes me think about you people in a way I thought of you only rarely at home. It makes me feel ashamed of myself for not writing for the first four weeks in England, purely because I had no letter from home. I am really very sorry. Please forgive me.

And then for some inexplicable reason it makes me think of the early morning in the New York hotel. Eating large chunks of baked chicken— the most I had ever eaten at one sitting in my life. It was good, but oh, how dry, and there was nothing to wash it down with; even the oranges provided little moisture, and I had given away the bananas to a woman who had two children on the plane. Goodness, they were giving off a smell! Generosity wasn't all that prompted me.

Yes, I am thinking very much of home. I am thinking about all our problems. They hardly seem to exist here. One has to think hard before one realises that one's parents are in distress. A few nights ago, I felt that something had gone wrong in a big way. I wanted to send a telegram, but I changed my mind. Kamla tells me she is sending something like eighteen dollars a month. I will see what I can send when I return to Oxford in a fortnight. I will send at least ten dollars.

But do you know why I think of the chicken? You see, it made me feel how much you people felt and cared for me; and you can't realise how infinitely sad that feeling can make someone. One feels too weak to be caring about such a big responsibility—the responsibility of deserving affection.

As you can see, I am writing from London. I got here a week ago. I have left half my books and clothes at Oxford. The term opens in five weeks, but I want to spend the last three working with the libraries close at hand. I am working now, too, but find that I can't work with all that vigour that I had in 1948. Looking back, I realise the gigantic task I performed. I wonder how I stood up to it. But I re-read some of my essays that I wrote last term. They do read quite well. I try to stay in all day to force myself to work. I am progressing really. For the past week I studied *King Lear,* did some Virgil and read eighty pages of criticism on him, and did some Anglo-Saxon. I want to come top of my group. I have got to show these people that I can beat them at their own language.

I have stopped writing. I suddenly feel dry. I express myself in abominable clichés, and expressive words just don't come. So I have stopped. Actually I have added nothing for the past three weeks. That is good. It is better to let the mind lie fallow a bit.

The weather can actually make interesting news. Last week I had my first snow. It came down in little white fluffs; you felt that a gigantic hand had punched a gigantic cotton wool sack open, letting down flurries of cotton shreds. The camera doesn't lie in this respect. Snow is just as you see it in films and in photographs. It snowed for about two hours. The streets were not covered, but the tops of the naked branches of the trees were white with it—a white that showed more beautiful because the limbs of the trees were in comparison stark black. The earth was carpeted with white. It is very light stuff. A Cow and Gate* tin of it weighs less than a pound. But it stays long on the ground. If you went out your shoulders and your hair were sprinkled with the fluffs. The closest thing I have seen to it in Trinidad is the stuff that gathers in a refrigerator—not when it gets hard though.

The meals here are quite different from home. Usually you start with soup. Then you have the main course. A bit of meat or fish, potatoes (I have eaten potatoes every day of my stay in England, twice a day at Oxford) and either cabbage or cauliflower. Then comes a sweet. Apple and custard or some such stuff. Finally, coffee. You would be surprised how you get accustomed to the coffee habit, after lunch and after dinner. No rice, and I don't miss it. No roti, and I don't miss it. You have bread with your soup, or with the main course. My table manners, which just didn't exist when I was in Trinidad, have improved tremendously. Another thing. The family always has dinner together. In Trinidad this would be impossible, I know.

I met a bunch of West Indians the other day. Harrison gave me Chang's† address. I rang him up, and he invited me over. Selvon‡ was there, with his wife, and Gloria Escoffery. Gloria is a girl who, Harrison tells me, will be somebody one day. From the look of her, I doubt it. She passed around a manuscript of a short story she had written about the race problem. She didn't want me to see it. Then she began talking some rubbish about writing being an exploration.

'I write because I don't understand. I write to explore, to understand.'

Me: 'Surely you're starting from the wrong end. I always thought people understood before they wrote. And further. I always believed that writers wrote because they wanted to write and because there was the prospect of cash at the end of the task, if it were well done.'

All Gloria could say was a purely personal, 'Oxford ideals are getting you.'

She went on, however. She was still reading novels to understand life. What rubbish! Live life, I told her.

She was writing the short story to explain the colour problem. Selvon, who was very voluble and wise till I began to talk, said that the job was too big for a short story. So I said, 'My dear Gloria, why not write a little pamphlet on the colour question, and settle the whole affair?'

Selvon thought that writers had to instruct. I told him he exalted the

---

* British manufacturer of milk products
† Carlisle Chang, Trinidad Chinese artist
‡ Samuel Selvon, a Trinidad writer

members of the fiction-manufacturing class. Fiction, I told him, is the imitation of an action meant to entertain.

They held a post-mortem on me after I left. The next day Chang rang me up. Gloria, he said, had infinite faith in me. They all thought me a little queer, but that, I thought, was because I spoke a bit of sense, and told these culture-creators where they got off. The queerness, they discovered, was due to my reaction to England. How I enjoyed that evening!

Well, I have written over 1,200 words—enough to exhaust any man. Goodbye, and Merry Christmas.

With deep love from
Vido

[Xmas card]

Christmas Greetings My Son

[inside]

Because you are so dear a Son,
So thoughtful and so true,
It seems there is no Christmas wish
That's good enough for you,
So I'll just wish you—season's joy
And to it add this thought,
You'll never know what happiness
Your loving ways have brought.

With Every Good Wish
for
A Merry Christmas
and
A Bright and Prosperous
New Year

From Ma and Pa and the rest

Home: Wed., Jan. 1

Dear Vidia,

I am sorry I gave you the impression that we are desperately hard up. Nothing of the kind. Of course I no longer make the extras I used to make from freelancing and travelling. It is all desk work. But all this does not add up to our being in any great distress, and there is really no urgency for you to send us money. And as far as I am concerned, you should not work out during your vacation but relax and study a little—unless, of course, you very much want to do so for a change.

Gyp is dead. He was knocked down by a motor-van in our street at about 1 p.m. today and died some three hours later. He is now lying under the shade tree, a bag thrown over him. Tomorrow we shall bury him beyond the concrete patch. I shall miss him a lot.

Leaving Gyp dying, I left for the *TG* after lunch. As usual, I parked my car in Queen Street, opposite Rudd's Engineering. When I was ready to go home and came for the car at 5 p.m., good old PA 1192 was gone. I have reported the matter to the police. I may or may not get the car back whole. Just last week I had it thoroughly overhauled, so that it was humming like a new car, without a tick. Got a bill for $45.75, not including the cost of re-capping one tyre ($14) and vulcanising another. If I don't get back my car, or if I get it back burnt or in pieces, or with a good deal of its inside gone—I don't know what is the position as regards indemnity from the insurance company. I shall have to find out—probably from a solicitor.

Don't let these incidents worry you too much. It is all unfortunate, of course; but there are worse things than losing a dog and a motor car. Besides, I shall have to be compensated for the car by the insurance people. So you see there's nothing much to worry about.

I don't know exactly when your Mamie and the others will leave for England. They were to leave soon—in February or March—but now I hear Capo has written to say that they are not to leave until the Patna Street house is sold. The house is sold all right, or rather the money is not paid up. Anyway, I shall buy you the cigarettes. I asked Richards to take some cigarettes for you, but he said he would be carrying cigarettes for himself. We are not allowed to send away cigarettes. Jainarayan did send you two tins of Capstan, on a licence; but he was warned it was illegal to do so, and that if some cigarettes gift-parcels did get through during the pre-Christmas weeks, it was due to a mistake. By the way, you have not written Jainarayan to say whether you have got the cigarettes. Do drop him a letter. He's a very good fellow, and you know it. He is ever willing to do any little thing for us; visits home fairly often. The others hardly come. I have not seen Owad for months; seems he is peeved because I didn't allow him to drive my car.

And do drop Velma a short letter; then you may write her at no shorter interval than once every three months. Until your examinations are over you may write home once a month or once in six weeks. I know the time-consuming business letter-writing can be.

Do not mind Sati's roughness. She didn't mean a thing; just felt like having a friendly rough-talk, as at home. She was visibly hurt that both you and Kamla should misunderstand her. So when next you write say you knew it was just affection.

Your idea about writing for the *TG* is good, but write Hitchens first—enclosing a copy of the kind of stuff you do. But don't start until your exams are over. You can make some money if you write.

Thursday, 7.30 p.m.

PA 1192 seems to have vanished for good. No sparing of pains on the part of the police; patrol cars were out within a few minutes of my reporting the theft yesterday evening; but I have heard nothing about the car. A police-constable will come home to inform me as soon as the car is located. Saw Andrew Sinanan (Solicitor) this morning before reporting matter to insurance company. Signs are they'll indemnify without much bother, but must wait to know the fate of the vehicle.

Send the *Isis*.

Yours affectionately,

Pa

III

January 1, 1951 – April 11, 1951

LENT TERM, EASTER VACATION

University College, Oxford
January 1, 1951

Dear Everybody,

I am back at Oxford once more; not at the college, though, but in a room that is about ten minutes away.

I want to thank you for two things. First of all, I want to let you know how much I was moved by the Christmas card you sent me. Few cards have ever made me as happy and as sad at the same time. The card got to London Christmas Day. The day after Boxing Day, I came back to Oxford. The landlady and her daughter are both very kind.

The second thing I want to thank you for is the parcel. I never expected such a big parcel. One would think that I was going into the retailing business. It must have cost you a pile. All I need from now on will be two pounds of sugar every six months.

Kamla sent me charming pictures of herself. I gave Boyzee one of them. I have to buy her a present for her twenty-first birthday. I will buy it for her in a day or two.

I stepped on my spectacles yesterday and crushed the frame. Fortunately business goes on as usual in England on New Year's Day, and so this evening I have got my spectacles back.

The weather is pretty ghastly now. The sun hasn't come out for two days and it looks as though night is always threatening to fall in the following half an hour. It is snowing pretty regularly. I admit that when the snow is untrampled and everything is muffled up in a fleecy white, you have a beautiful sight. But when you have to walk in it on the pavements, it is a different matter. You skid, and the snow ceases to be white and beautiful, and becomes a sort of iced mud. Frankly I am wishing for the delightful weather of October—fairly dry, cool and at times cold.

You will have to bear with very short letters for the next two and a half months. I have my first examinations on, and I intend working as hard as anything. And you know what I mean by hard work.

Oxford is dull, nearly always, but now there are few students. In the colleges you find the solitary porter reading the *Reader's Digest*, and aching for company. Do you know, I am feeling tremendously homesick for London. London is a city for people who have grown up in cities. If you want noise without boisterousness, and crowds without crush, you should like it. Of course, its neon signs appear adolescent besides those of New York but about London there is a reserved, austere beauty. I don't see how I could live anywhere else but in London. Everything is at hand. Fleet Street, the big publishing houses, the museums, the picture galleries and wonderful cinemas and theatres. There is so much life in it. And you have only to witness London Transport at work to get a great thrill. At a station like Piccadilly Circus underground trains leave about twice a minute at certain times. Truly magnificent. Oxford's bus services, on the other hand, are, by universal mouth, unreliable.

Happy and truly New Year,
Vido

University College, Oxford
January 11, 1951

Dear Everybody,

I suppose that you have already received the letter I wrote home after Boxing Day, and so Sati will have to find something else to write about next time. Her English has improved considerably, I notice. Whether this was due to the unusual anger she steamed off at the time of writing, or a genuine intellectual step forward, I wouldn't know. Anyway, if getting mad is going to make your English better, stay mad all the time.

Or perhaps she wrote it under the influence of Christmas evening festivities. Anyway, I am very sorry if I didn't write. The fact is, I bought a number of Christmas cards to send home; but I didn't feel like sending them, and tore them up. Then I wrote an extremely long letter about two days before. Just last night I tore up a letter that I had written to Kamla—on an air-letter form, too. I get into certain moods and write things which, when read the following morning, read badly and are usually disgustingly maudlin.

I spent a fairly heavy Christmas. On the day before Christmas Eve, I went to Kilburn, and ate the heaviest meal I have ever eaten so far in this country. My two uncles and Boyzee were there. We ate so much that when we were finished, we literally could only move with great distress, and could do little more than look resignedly at each other. I spent Christmas Day at my boarding house. There was a little party given by the house-keeper. Terribly dull.

I am so glad to hear that the house is taking on a new look. It is high time. I have been talking to my tutor about what I should study in my fourth year, and he tells me it is too early to decide. So I will write to the Education Office and tell them that I am prepared to take the Diploma of Education. But reserve the right to change my mind later on.

Today, with Sati's letter, I got a card. From Golden.* The wretched girl had written to Mr Vido Naipaul, Oxford University, London, England. It is very flattering to be addressed Mr Naipaul, Oxford University, and have letters reach you. But think of the colossal ignorance.

I got back to college today. For the past two weeks I have been staying in lodgings in Oxford. I intend to go there every now and then to take a proper bath. The landlady has agreed.

Well, I have a pile of letters to write, and an exam the day after tomorrow. So cheerio, until next week.

Yours,
Vido

[Handwritten note]: I am writing a short article for the *Isis*—'Christmas in a[. . .]'.

---

* Vidia's mother's cousin to whom he was platonically attached at the age of fifteen or sixteen

University College, Oxford
January 11, 1951

My dear Kamla,

I am back in my own college rooms, and at my back the electric fire is on at full strength. Thanks for your letters.

You appear to be seeing quite a big hunk of India.

I have an examination the day after tomorrow, and in two months, I have my preliminary examinations, which I must pass, if I am to stay on at Oxford. So you will have to prepare yourself to receive fewer and shorter letters from me.

I had a letter from Satti. She gave me a thorough dressing down for writing only twice in a month.

You needn't bother too much about the cigarettes, if they are too much trouble. But here is something I want you to do for me. As you know, when I came back to Oxford two weeks ago, I stayed in lodgings. The landlady was very nice, and I told her that I would get her some tea. I would be glad if you could do the sending for me. The address is

> Mrs King,
> 12 Richmond Road,
> Oxford, England

Please try to, because I will be going to her home to have a bath, whenever I need one; as I have probably told you already, the bathroom is miles away from my room, and there is no privacy.

I have made no friends so far. Something, it seems, is wrong with me. I shall do my best, anyway.

I bought a number of Christmas cards—the college ones—but I tore them up. I didn't want to send them, and I don't know why.

I was reserving five pounds to buy you a present, but two things happened which have prevented me. In the first place, I smashed my spectacles, and, as I couldn't wait to get free ones, I had to pay to have them repaired. Then I discovered that walking in the snow requires good shoes; and I was forced to buy a pair of boots that cost me almost three pounds. So you will have to put up with me. I will be sending your gift at about the end of March. I hope you don't mind terribly.

I am afraid that I can't send home any money. The college has increased the cost of board by ten pounds a term and the scholarship money has remained the same. I am really just managing to live—very meagrely. And to have friends in this place, one must have money—to buy them drinks and tea.

Well, goodbye for now. I will be writing in about a fortnight's time.

Vido

Home: 1/19/51

Dear Vido,

The other evening I went to see an exhibition of children's paintings at the RVI.* And, for the first time, had the pleasure of meeting Mr Harrison. He seemed really glad to see me, and we sat talking for about half an hour. He appears to be quite impressed with you and says he is certain you will blossom into a greater writer. Within a day or two he will be going to Jamaica to put on the same show. The paintings are by English children in England. To me most of them appear too obviously childish, but of course I am no judge of these things. Last Monday—today is Thursday—I got a letter from you and another from Kamla. She wrote on the eve of her return to Benares from Calcutta, where she spent part of Christmas vacation. It is very good of you to think of sending her a present for her twenty-first. We will be sending her something, too—maybe cash, say $10.

It is almost three months now since I am sub. on the *Weekly*. Jenkins— you probably know the man—is editor, in place of Smith. A young Englishman, Bain by name, is also a sub. on the *Weekly*. Jenkins' job is to put the mag. in a new look. No doubt the man knows his stuff, but frankly, I think he is a good deal goofy. But he is a nice fellow to work with; doesn't give himself airs. I have asked Sati to post you a copy of the *Weekly*. Let me see you guess my pages.

I am curious to see a copy or two of the *Isis*. Could you post them right away?

Last Sunday the BBC read over 'The Engagement'. I forget the name

* Royal Victoria Institute

of the reader; but he was not an Indian. He read it very well indeed—much better than either Selvon or the other chap. They are still holding 'Obeah'. Heaven knows when I shall again begin writing a short story or two. I am too tired after work.

I think I have already told you why I have not been able to send you the poem you left here. The thing is still with Pearse, who tells me he wants to read it at leisure. Perhaps he will use it in his *Quarterly*.

You have by now of course received the Education Department's letter about your fourth-year study. Please write them and say what is what.

Today I left my car at McEnearney. The number of things they have to put right covered one and a half of their work forms. Repairs include re-capping a tyre—the front one that had developed, you will recollect, some flats; vulcanising another—if it can take it. The engine of the old jeep is purring as smoothly as ever. That's a really faithful car—almost human.

Mrs Capildeo has sold the house at Patna Street. I think they got $12,000 for it. Capo said he had bought it for $15,000. Your Mamee has made us a present of a pair of shears she had bought with the house. They are new brand; and she has asked us not to let the people at 17 know she has given them to us!

You really must send me a copy of the authors' handbook as soon as you can conveniently do so. Publishers: Allen Lane The Bodley Head. It is a book full of vital information.

I have read all the Narayan short stories. They are good stories, but not dynamic. I think it was Edgar Wallace who had once retorted to a highbrow: 'I don't write great stories; I only write good stories.'

Why didn't you spend Christmas Day with Capo S.? Really, it was just like you, wasn't it? Your Ma did a bit of grumbling at your living in lodgings or hotels when you could have avoided expenses by living the few weeks with Mamoo and Boysie.

When you get over your examinations you should write long descriptions of life at Oxford. I am sure they'd make good reading. I am sorry you tore up your long letter. Why, that thing must have been quite good. Such things very often are.

We spent last Sunday at Baboolal's. Brought 2 bagfuls of manure to put in for the roses, which bugs have almost wholly destroyed. The irony: we put manure to get new shoots. The shoots, as soon as they become visible, are bitten off by the bugs! Really, we put the manure to get the roses to satisfy the bugs.

Well, I think I have said enough. Write soon.

Yours affectionately,

Pa

[Note in child's handwriting]:

Dear Vido,

I am behaving a good boy. I send you 1,100 kisses. Shivadhar [Shiva]

University College, Oxford
January 24, 1950 [sic]

Dear Everybody,

Why on earth didn't you people tell that wretched Education Office woman off? If the Director of Colonial Scholars is getting anxious, why didn't he write straight to me from London? Don't let those Trinidad people play the fool. There is nothing to upset yourself about.

I gave no London address, purely because you could continue writing me at University College, as the people here have all letters forwarded. Send everything and all letters here. I will get them. So no more worry in the future.

This is the second week of my second term. I find the people friendlier. I have a little circle of my own friends now, and it makes Oxford so much more interesting.

I have received the newspapers sent me, and I am very grateful for them. I read the thing Harrison wrote about me. I wish I felt the same way about myself.

I have had my beginning of term 'collections', or examinations set by the tutors to see how much progress you have made. I had worked very badly last term, but the work I did in the vacation paid off handsomely. In the Literature paper I got an alpha beta. In the Anglo-Saxon there was no marking, but I did remarkably well, and in the Latin paper I got an alpha minus. Quite good, but the examinations are only six weeks off, and I still have bags of work to do.

I am sorry that you are having money troubles. I will do my best to send about forty dollars at the end of March or thereabouts. I think I will try to get a job of some sort in the three months' vacation.

The reason that people always write about the weather in this country is that it is forever changing. When I came up to Oxford at the beginning of the month it snowed every day for about three days; since the second week, it became very mild, but today has been much colder than yesterday. The weather provides interesting news. It seems to me that Oxford would not seem the same if there was bright sun. The skies are nearly always grey, and that is becoming. So when you say, fine day, it means something. In Trinidad you say, damn, another fine day. Here a day with sun and a blue sky is something you appreciate all the more, because you get it so rarely.

If Mrs Capo wouldn't mind, could you tell her to buy 400 American cigarettes—every person is allowed to bring in that much free of duty. I will pay her when she gets here. You really don't realise how essential they are to have friends. I don't offer people dinners or teas, because I can't afford to, but if I could offer cigarettes it would be better. So please tell her. And urge her not to forget.

I had a letter from Kamla, and from what she tells me, she is enjoying India, and from what she tells me, also, it appears that Satti has been having quite a time with her pen. I hardly get letters from anyone at home besides Pa, and Satti writes to put me and Kamla in our places for not writing.

Look here, I understand what letters mean. The porters probably get tired of my asking whether there is anything for me, and when does the next mail come in? I read my letters slowly, afraid to get to the end. But if I don't write, it means that I really cannot afford the time. Take this letter for instance. I began it at quarter past eight after dinner. It is now ten to nine. After nine, I can only do about two hours' effective work. And heaven knows who may drop in to see me, and I can't very well put people out of my room. So please understand.

I will buy a copy of the week's *Isis* and send it to you. I have a whole page this time. Really half, the other half is advertisement.

As I have told you, my time is limited. But after my exam at the end of this term, I shan't have another exam till June 1953. So I will have a lot of time. We have at Oxford all the big names coming up to speak on a variety of subjects. I could write a fortnightly Oxford letter that would contain news about West Indians in Oxford, and views of great men about the big world problems. I don't know whether in your capacity as sub-editor you could use a little nepotism; or would the ordinary *Guardian* care for it? Let me know. And how much do you think they would pay me?

Well, it is nine now. I must fall to work.

Cheerio!
Vido

University College, Oxford
January 27, 1951

Dear Kamla,

Thanks for your letter.

I am glad you understand about the birthday present, but I assure you I will make it up later on.

I did extremely well in the collections, or private examinations set by tutors to test you.

For some queer reason, I find myself unable to concentrate. This term, I have cut out all social activities, try to pen myself in to do some work, feel I am doing little, and keep on feeling, too, that there is little to be done. I wonder. I really hope I pass this examination. I think I will. I just wish it were over, so that I could catch up on my reading and carry on with my novel.

I am a feature reporter on the staff of the University magazine, *Isis*. It doesn't mean much, but if there is fair play, I should become at least assistant news editor by the end of the year. You would be surprised when I tell you that the majority of the students here are very stupid, and that the average intelligence is much lower than that of the sixth form of my years at QRC.

In my last letter, I remember saying that I find it difficult to make friends. Well, I find that as this term goes on, certain people are becoming more than friendly, they are positive bores. There is especially one Catholic who is doing his best to show me that he is that very fashionable modern type, the Catholic intellectual. But, goodness! He is as superstitious as any country Indian in Trinidad, believes in black magic, and that persons can be made ill by other people and so forth. And yet he had the absurdity to suggest that superstition was probably found in a cruder state in the West Indies!

At the beginning of this term the boat club people asked me if I would care to become a coxswain. I agreed, for it would be fun, I thought, to indulge in some form of outdoor activity. They tried me out a week, but I was pretty atrocious at coxing, so I have been dropped. And I am relieved. A coxswain is the smallest person in the boat. Yet he is in complete command, and is directly responsible for the lives of the crew, and the safety of the boat—slender shells, about 60 feet long and two wide, things which are so weak that a step on the wrong part would mean that the boat is destroyed. I don't mind terribly at being dropped. It merely means that I have discovered one more thing to be not good at.

I am waiting to see this term's expenses before I make a row with the Colonial Office. I have a feeling, however, that everything will be all right. I firmly believe that what I am to be has been cut out for me. That if I have to die tomorrow, I will die tomorrow. So I never worry. It is my only superstition, but I feel it deeply, and I am secure in it.

Do you know? I got some Trinidad papers, read them, and found them hilariously absurd. I never realised before that the *Guardian* was so badly written, that our Trinidad worthies were so absurd, that Trinidad is the most amusing island that ever dotted a sea.

The English are a queer people. Take it from me. The longer you live in England, the more queer they appear. There is something so orderly, and yet so adventurous about them, so ruttish, so courageous. Take the chaps in the college. The world is crashing about their heads, about all our heads. Is their reaction as emotional as mine? Not a bit. They ignore it for the most part, drink, smoke, and imbibe shocking quantities of tea and coffee, read the newspapers and seem to forget what they have read.

Please keep me alive with letters. Write at least once a week. I shall do my best to keep up from this end.

Cheerio!
Vido

University College, Oxford
February 12, 1951

Dear Everybody,

I was frankly quite upset at hearing about the car, but I am very glad that everything is now all right.

This is my first letter in two weeks, I have done no writing of letters for the past fortnight, and I now have a pile to write.

I bought a small gift for Kamla, nothing expensive—as a matter of fact it cost just about eleven dollars—but they say that on such occasions, the spirit and not the gift matters. l suppose she must have got it by now, but I have heard nothing so far.

Will you kindly tell Velma that I am just as embarrassed at not writing her, as she is probably angry with me. Tell her that I will write in a month's time. I probably will not to be able to write to Jainarayan till about that time, so could you tell him thanks very much for the cigarettes, he need send no more. I was very grateful for the promptness of his dispatch of the fags.

I had my first attack of asthma last week, and I slept almost continuously for two days. I am now fine once more, however, and alive as ever.

The days are lengthening once more. It is now almost five, yet it is still bright. I frankly am happy that winter is finished with, and that spring and summer are round the corner.

I will tell you something about this country. It is impossible to get rich. The income taxes are ridiculously high—about nine shillings in the pound after a certain stage, and it probably will go up with this heavy expenditure on re-armament. If you buy a car for £500, you pay about £120 extra for purchase tax. Everything has a purchase tax. For living, this country. For making money, somewhere else.

Sati knows of course that I was not killingly serious. But what did Meera* say?

I have sent along a copy of the *Isis*—one that has my name in it in small type. It is an absurd little magazine, as you will see. Because the under-

---

* Alternative spelling of Mira, Vidia's younger sister, the third daughter and fourth child of the family (see page 16)

graduates in this place are not all dazzlingly intellectual, as you probably think. There are asses in droves here. The reason why so many of them get ahead is that England offers just that scope for getting ahead. The boys in my sixth form, taken on average, are as good—probably better—than most of the people here. Gone are the days of aristocrats. Nearly everyone comes to Oxford on a state grant. The standard of the place naturally goes down. If you want to find superficial young men, and even more superficial young women, Oxford is the place.

I shall not write for some time again, so please prepare to do without letters, and understand the reason. My examinations are four weeks away.

But—although this may appear selfish—I will be very, very delighted to get at least one letter from one person a week.

Try, then.

Goodbye!
Vido

26 Nepaul Street
2.19.51

Dear Vidia,

The motor car is all right now; in fact, it is in a much better shape, the fenders and front bumper, which, you may recollect, were bent and dented, have been put right and painted. The front seat is now what is known as a bench seat, that is, it is a one-piece seat; and both the front and back seats and back-rests have been covered with green leatherette. Really, the car is prettier now than what it was. The insurance company paid every cent.

I find myself stumped for facts. Another six months or a year of inactivity as regards writing, and I may almost forget to write. Nowadays I am thinking mostly in terms of headlines and magazine-page make-up. The work is most interesting. Sometimes I think it is even more absorbing than writing. You could have no idea how much there is to it. Of course, you are not to take the *Guardian* for a model; still, it carries a fairly good make-up.

For the last week I have been reading *Newspaper Editing, Make-up and Headlines*—a ponderous textbook by Radder and Stempel. I never knew how little I knew about sub-editing—more so make-up—until I read this book. It is an American publication, but very good.

As soon as you are through with your examinations do send me a few copies—if you can manage it, half a dozen each of these papers, those underlined being preferable: *The Sunday Express*, <u>*The Daily Mail*</u>, <u>*Reynold's News*</u>, <u>*Sunday Chronicle*</u>, especially the popular sort. Distinguish them from the more highbrow and conservative sorts *(Liberty, Everybody)*. I want to study them for make-up.

Got a couple of letters from Kamla. She received quite a few lovely and expensive presents from friends in India on her 21st birthday. I doubt if she'd have done better in Trinidad. As regards her studies—I really can't say exactly what she is aiming at—I doubt if she herself is quite sure about this. She is supposed to be taking Indian Philosophy and the other things—culture and so forth—that go with it; and yet nobody is teaching her these things. BHU seems to be a slack kind of university.

By tomorrow your Mamee will know whether she can get passages on the *Golfito*, which is sailing from Trinidad on the 28th of this month. She is hoping to get the berths of two persons who are likely to cancel their passages. If this doesn't happen she will naturally have to wait. However, she has promised to take some cigarettes for you.

Dhan Mousie* has bought a new house, almost exactly like ours, but with one more room and two lavatories, on Dundonald Street. They moved in on Thursday. They had a Suruj Puran† this morning.

This letter must be rather fuzzy, but better so than none. When I mentioned magazines such as *Liberty* and *Everybody*, I meant to say these are not the sort that I want. They are more or less conservative in make-up and are highbrow.

I wish you the best of luck in your examination. Do not allow yourself to become a prey to anxiety, but take it cool; just aim to do the best <u>you</u> can, without show-off; that is, aim not to beat everybody, but just do the best you can.

Next time I shall write you a fuller and more satisfactory letter.

All is well at home.

Yours affectionately,
Pa

---

* Maternal aunt, Vidia's mother's elder sister Dhan
† Hindu ritual involving the reading of a scriptural text

[Handwritten]:

Dear Vido,

I am just filling up this space which Pa seems to have been unable to make use of. To be sure, you must be in the throes of very strenuous studies for your exams, and I, and in fact, everybody here, wish you a brilliant success. Rest assured that I am doing the best I can to get through my own exam which comes off Dec 4th.

> With love,
> Sati

Home: 2/24/51

Dear Vido,

I received a copy of the *Isis* two days ago; started dictating a letter to you—per Meera—and left off for want of an air form. Then we received another letter from you today midday.

The *Isis* is not bad. It is well printed and well edited and carries a youthful vivacity, but the by-line to the article 'Literary Schizophrenia' might have given the page a better appearance if it had been placed, say, midway into the middle column—and boxed. Your own piece is not bad at all.

Do you still want me to write to the man Rodin of the *Express*? When you are through with your examination try to place an article or two—or short stories—with Swanzy. Write as a West Indian for the West Indies. This may not appeal to you, but you are likely to get more money this way. And it seems to me you *do* need money.

Mrs Capildeo and children have booked passage by the *Golfito*. They leave on the 28th of this month—that is on Wednesday. We are sending you a 6lb parcel of sugar and a carton of Anchor Specials by them. I hope the specials do not get found out as 'cheap' or third-rate stuff. Let me know. The boat will arrive in ten days' time.

The School Cert. Exam. results came out yesterday. Rabi* came through with a first grade. (Let's see whether he'll write you.) Satti

---

* Maternal cousin

failed—for the second time; and Neel Ramdin achieved a third grade. I didn't see George's name, so I suppose he popped. In fact most of the private school students—500 boys and girls—failed; just 125 got through. Sitah Rajcoomar also fetched a third-grade pass.

The Ramnarines* have moved into another house. This time it's in Dundonald Street. The house is very much like ours; two-floor premises, with three bedrooms and two lavatories—what we call here 'the sewerage'.

I think I quite understand the position in which you are at Oxford. Everywhere you will meet shallow-minded people; but it is precisely because they are shallow that they make a lot of 'to-do'. I don't like to preach—least of all to you; I know you don't like preaching, but I can't help doing so at times. I suffered much in Jamaica because of the same superficialities; and yet they were each far more popular than I was. We must learn to look at people objectively. Perception is rare and intelligence is by no means widespread. Those who have it to any unusual degree often suffer terribly: they are the most lonesome creatures in the world. Look at Sinclair Lewis *(Babbitt)*. Yes, more often than not it is from such people that the world derives its true greatness. The intellectuals cannot but be different from the average. Sometimes in our very loneliness you will produce that which will be something new and which you otherwise could not produce. Spot your drones and microbes among your fellow-creatures, but do not let them put you out of your centre. AND DO NOT SAY YOU RESIGN YOURSELF TO OBSCURITY. Or if you do, say that in obscurity you will do your work. Let it be a shield to you from the noise and inanities of the rest; by no means a wet blanket.

If I get the time tomorrow morning—it is Saturday—I shall be sending you $10, and then every two months or so I shall send you some money. It should go some way towards helping you to throw a sherry party now and then. I know full well what this thing means and how necessary it is. Meanwhile be a man and cringe to none.

Pa

PTO

---

* Relations by marriage of Vidia's mother's sister Calawattee

Savi has made her name. She has come out with flying colours from an operation for the removal of her appendix. She was taken to the Col. Hos. eight days ago today and had the offending thing taken out the same night. She was quite brave about it.

Dr Mavis Rampersad, who works at the hospital, was most helpful. She it was who promptly visited Savi at home and later took her to hospital in her own car. Though she was off duty for the night she insisted on remaining with Savi, so that the girl should not lose courage. Everyday she visits Savi—three times or so; and brings the other doctors to see her too.

And Savi from the outset had a splendid recovery. Yesterday she told our Ma that she has become quite accustomed with being in the hospital. She'll be home within the next couple of days.

Pa

[Handwritten]:

Dear Vido,

Your Pa has given you all the good news already, so I have little to say. I hope you are taking good care of yourself, you must be careful especially against your asthma. Everybody home is well, including Savi, who though still in hospital is fine—Your loving Ma.

University College, Oxford
February 8

Dear Everybody,

First of all thanks for the two letters. They came within two days of each other, after a complete drought of correspondence for two weeks.

Now, look here. I don't want any money from you at home. You know you can't spare it, and I can get along well enough without it. Don't send any money, until I ask. I have not asked for the past seven months, and I sincerely hope I never have cause to ask. Thanks very much, anyway, for the offer.

I would like to know whether all journalists are disgruntled people who nevertheless cling to their jobs, cursing it in the meanwhile, or whether this is merely a hereditary sign. This morning, I was in a white-hot temper, because the assistant news editor tampered with all three of my stories. The man tampered with the first paragraphs. And from your advice given—on ever so often—I spend half my time thinking of a suitable opening. Take, this, for instance. I interviewed <u>Emeric</u> <u>Pressburger</u>, <u>the</u> <u>man</u> <u>who</u> <u>had</u> <u>made</u> <u>Black</u> <u>Narcissus</u>, <u>and</u> <u>a</u> <u>number</u> <u>of</u> <u>other</u> <u>very</u> <u>good</u> <u>films</u>, <u>and</u> asked <u>him</u> <u>what</u> <u>he</u> <u>thought</u> <u>about</u> <u>the</u> <u>latest</u> <u>film</u> <u>he</u> <u>had</u> <u>made</u>—<u>The Elusive Pim-</u> <u>pernel</u>. He said it was a lousy film. The President of the Club to which Pressburger was talking afterwards came round, asking me to kill that sentence. So, too, did the Chairman of the Oxford Univ. <u>Experimental</u> <u>Film</u> <u>Group</u>. I naturally refused. I find few things as irritating as having people tell me what to put in or what to leave out. Anyway, I began my report: ' "No, I am not happy over the E P. I think it is a lousy film," Mr E. Press- burger told the *Isis* last Wednesday.' And I headlined it 'The Lousy Pimpernel'. For the simple reason that what followed in the report was a dull thesis about the Film Industry. The fool changed the headline to 'Pressburger Speaks,' and rewrote my paragraph, 'E. Press. told the *Isis* last Wednesday, "I am not happy . . ." He was speaking about the film he had made, and continued, "I think it is a lousy film.' " Absurd change, isn't it?

I find I have a great liking for journalism. I feel it is such a great thrill. Everybody curses their papers, but they couldn't do better themselves—as even in Oxford, the *Isis* is held in contempt by people who can't write—and in any case they read them all the time.

Kamla tells me that home has been completely revolutionised. Miss Satti going out to dances as often as possible, and the girls wearing jeans. I am merely going to say I think it is just damned nonsense. I won't say any more, because Satti's feelings have to be considered. But put an end to this damned absurdity. Surely you can.

Incidentally, I had three stories in this week's *Isis*, covering almost a whole page. It is a great source of pleasure to attend people's talks and write 300 words that are as rounded and compact as a precis. At times I can criticise. Two weeks ago, I criticised George Schwartz in the *Isis*. He is a writer for the *Sunday Times*. And when Palme Dutt, the half-Indian boss of the British Communist Party, came to Oxford, I gave him so much hell that the Communists rang up the editor and cursed him. <u>I</u> <u>think</u> <u>a</u> <u>man</u> <u>is</u> <u>doing</u> <u>his</u> <u>reporting</u> <u>well</u> <u>only</u> <u>when</u> <u>people</u> <u>start</u> <u>to</u> <u>hate</u> <u>him.</u>

I don't promise to send as many as six copies of the *Sunday Express,* because it would mean waiting six weeks for them. What I will do is to send copies of the *Daily Mirror* and *Sunday Pictorial*—they are about the size of the *Weekly*.

I haven't even begun to learn to dance. And even if I could dance I doubt whether I could get a girl to take to the dances—they are all so damned big here!

A girl student, two inches taller than myself, *Isis* Reporter Philippa Gerry (you can see her name in the copy of the paper you have) has invited me to spend a weekend at her home in Devonshire. She is hoping her mother will agree. I have talked it over with Philippa, and she assures me that at no stage will I be pulled into a corner by either parent and quizzed about my intentions. So don't worry! But—I tell you everything, you see.

Vido

University College, Oxford
February 28, 1951

My dear Kamla,

What on earth are you trying to do with your handwriting? And not even giving me sufficient warning of it in your letter!

People have told me that my accent is almost perfect in French. The reason perhaps is that I speak English in such a foul manner. But now, as my English pronunciation is improving by the humiliating process of error and snigger, I find that French is becoming increasingly difficult to pronounce. It is largely a matter, I think, of using and not using the back of the throat. I hardly use the back of the throat. I open my lips wide apart and say 'gud' (good). The English would pronounce the word as 'guude'. Try it yourself. Say good your usual way, and you will find your mouth opening pretty wide. Try to keep the lips only slightly parted, and hear the difference.

This week, I had three stories in the *Isis,* that almost covered a whole page. Yet, though I am the best man on the news staff, and, as usual, the hardest-working, I doubt whether promotion is just around the corner.

A girl, a friend of mine, has invited me to her home in Devonshire. I told this to a boy at college, and he warned me against going. For, he tells me, at some stage of my stay, I will be pulled into a corner by either parent and quizzed about my intentions. As for the girl, I don't even pretend to understand her. Probably you, as a woman, could tell me exactly what I should believe.

She is on the *Isis* staff. She is a pretty foul reporter, and has little in. I let her know that I think her writing is pretty foul. She accepts it. Last term, I met her at a society meeting, and invited her to have coffee with me. On the way to the restaurant, I asked her to tea. She accepted all this, but under the impression that I was editor of the *Isis*. She was disappointed when I told her that I was a minor figure on the paper, and that if I were to die the following day, the *Isis* would probably carry on, without even an obituary. Anyway, she came to tea, and I read her the first two chapters of my novel. She invited me to her rooms for the next week. I went, taking along another chapter. Well, so it continued until the end of term, when she suddenly began behaving badly. She didn't want me to come to tea with her; would I mind terribly if she left my room right away? She would write me a note. I said I was sick of getting notes from women. She said, 'Very well, then, you are so damned sensitive, come to my room next week.' The same night I wrote her a bitter letter, criticising her politely. When I went to tea next time, we neither of us made any mention of the letter. It was the last week of term. We wished each other goodbye and Merry Xmases, all very politely.

At *Isis* conferences this term, I completely ignored her for the first four weeks. Then, she began to change again. She began sitting next to me, and putting her face next to mine to read a paper that I might be examining. One Saturday, in the fourth week of term, I decided I would go and pay her a visit. I went. There was a man preparing to go down the fire escape. My heart sank. There were two other girls, and the floor was littered with tea things. Introductions (she had pretended she had forgotten my name) were made, and the bloke went down the fire escape rope, while I stood silently, embarrassed, and trying to hide my embarrassment by smirking in a cynical manner. Then the man emerged as it were at the door and took the other two girls with him. I remained for an hour. She wanted me to stay a little longer. She began to give hints that she would care to see me again. The following Tuesday I went to her once more, and took her a tin of grapefruit juice. This she accepted and then shamefacedly asked if she, with a friend, could come to tea with me. I said yes. Shortly afterwards I got a letter from her, saying that her friend was booked up and couldn't come. So she came alone. Punctual as anything, and stayed until seven.

What should I think of her?

Vido

March 4, 1951

Dear Vido,

Savi came out of hospital on February 28, the day Mrs Capildeo and children left for England by the *Golfito*. Savi is thinner but looking much better than she did before the illness. We have sent you the carton of cigarettes and some sugar by your Mamee.

QRC had a very poor 1950, so far as winning scholarships was concerned. CIC* got all four, and Jean Brathwaite from the Bishop's High School carried away the Girl's scholarship. The CIC winners are: McKenzie—Languages; Bharath—Modern Studies; Cross—Science; Schacter—Maths. Cross and Schacter have tied for the Gold Medal.

Rajandaye Ramkissoon (girl's schol.) failed to get the schol., coming second. MacDonald of QRC (Languages) and Spicer taking Mod. Stud. each made second place.

This week news is scarce. Of course we have been having heavy rains—almost non-stop for two months, with recurring 'dry season' floods. But since a week now the rains have stopped and it seems the dry season has come at last. Your mother, who is somewhat of a geographer, says the heavy, prolonged winter in the USA was responsible for the late rains in the West Indies; and indeed, the papers did say something of the kind.

Trinidad cricketers are now in Barbados playing trial matches with the Bimshires.† The first match resulted in a draw, Jagbir being responsible for saving Trinidad from a defeat; not that he made runs, but occupied the pitch. On the results of these matches (BG‡ and Jamaica are in it, too) a

---

* College of Immaculate Conception, Port of Spain, the Roman Catholic rival of Queen's Royal College
† Slang word meaning Barbadians
‡ British Guyana

West Indies team will be picked to tour Australia. By then, it is supposed, Ramadhin and Worrell* will be back from India. You probably know that Ramadhin headed the bowling average in the Commonwealth team.

It may interest you to know that the rains caused a collapse of the Petit Valley bridge—that is the Capildeo bridge; not the cheaply improvised one, but the old Maillard concrete bridge that had been hanging for years much as a loose tooth. As a matter of fact the rains caused damages to crops and bridges and telephonic communications all over the island. Blanchisseuse for once was in fact marooned and the inhabitants there had to be carried food and other things by Government sea vessels.

Reverting to QRC—they got five House Schols.—Rabi wasn't one. Romily has been transferred as Acting Head of Nelson Street Boys' RC. I suppose he is happy over the change.

Shivan says that you didn't remember him with a card for his birthday. Kamla did.

[Handwritten]:

3/5/51

Got a letter from Kamla this morning. She says, 'For the past two months I have a growing longing to get back home or to England with Vido . . . I think that I am more homesick now than when I left home. I am becoming increasingly cynical and pessimistic. All this might only lead me to the pit of frustration. And after that I can't say what will happen. Right now I feel that it's no use living in the world.'

She says she is teaching herself ancient Indian history and culture, and keeps running to this professor and that for help. One whole year has gone and she hasn't had one history lecture.

Really, it all sounds quite depressing. I wonder if she could get transferred to a more responsible university, and whether this would help. You'd better write to give her some courage and advice. Affectionately yours,

Pa

---

* Frank Worrell, fabled West Indian test cricketer

Home: 7.30 p.m.
3/9/51

Dear Vido,

I hope I don't spoil this letter. I feel unusually tired this evening. I have been preparing to write you since a couple of days or more, but kept putting it off till I was in the mood. It seems if I waited on that you wouldn't get a letter another fortnight. So here it is.

For the first time since Kamla went away I have been quite worried about her. I really can't say what that girl is aiming for. Here is a university—believe it or not—that sets you subjects that it does not teach! If this is exaggeration it is only half so. I have suggested to her that if this awkward situation continues she should ask for a transfer to another university where there are better facilities for studying Indian history, culture and what not. Maybe she's sent you the letter, for I have asked her to do so, so that she may know what *you* have to say.

I don't think the sub-editor on the *Isis* did your story any great harm. I think his intro was a slight improvement on yours; but only slightly. With some more practice the first para of a story will jump and hit you automatically. So don't let this worry you. What I suspect happens is that you spend too much thought on an intro. Whenever you have a story to hit off just think how the London *Express,* or the *Mirror,* or *Reynold's* would have hit it off; for I notice that the style of the *Isis* is but that of the popular papers—weeklies and dailies.

Now, I would have respected the wish of the Chairman of the Experimental Film Company. You might have quizzed him on some other angle, and maybe you might have had a piece just as new, or almost as new. And that same man would have been useful to you next time—as an interviewee—not only for the *Isis,* but for the *Trinidad Guardian* and other newspapers. As it is, I have little doubt you have no sooner contacted one news source than you have lost him.

Except where Pressburger is a man who <u>never</u> <u>speaks,</u> 'Pressburger Speaks' is no headline or caption. It belongs to the old genres of the time when newspapers carried labels rather than headlines. A caption must say something; it must be concrete rather than abstract. 'Pope Pius and Divorce' says nothing. 'Pope Pius Sanctions Divorce' says everything. Nevertheless you will do well to let the subs have their way. I suppose they are genuinely keen on improving. Don't be too sensitive on this—at least not yet.

Off hand I'd have started thus: Mr Emeric Pressburger, who made 'The Narcissus', used a stark adjective for his latest picture—'The Elusive Pimpernel'. Asked by an *Isis* reporter what he thought of this new film of his, the producer (?) promptly said: 'Oh, I think it's lousy. I am not happy . . .' etc., etc.

And as to a writer being hated or liked—I think it's the other way to what you think: a man is doing his work well when people begin <u>liking</u> him. I have never forgotten what Gault MacGowan* told me years ago: 'Write sympathetically'; and this, I suppose, in no way prevents us from writing truthfully, even brightly.

Please don't send me the *Express* and the *Daily Mirror*. The *Express* I get right at the *TG*, and the *Mirror* is to be had for a few cents in almost any of the book-stores. I oughtn't to have asked you to send these. But send me the *Evening News*, the *Evening Standard*, the *Daily Mail*. <u>Also most of the copies of the *Isis* that contain your stories.</u> These will necessarily be back numbers; and I expect them first thing after you are through with your exams. OK?

By the way, I have been paid great eulogy by Swanzy on my story 'The Engagement' in his half yearly review. The broadcast was on February 18, but I didn't listen in. But a copy of the review was sent, as usual, to the *Guardian* and Jenkins showed me my piece. They are not publishing it. It seems—again believe it or not—mine was the only quite real and satisfactory story.

I am beginning to believe I *could* have been a writer.

One must have friends—says your Ma from behind the partition—but do try not to land yourself into a mess. She is referring to Philippa Gerry . . . As for me . . . I know it'd be no use my telling you anything by way of caution.

We are all quite well. My indigestion hardly visits me nowadays.

Accept the best from all of us.

Pa

---

* Editor, the *Trinidad Guardian* (1929–1934), first employer and encourager of Vidia's father's writing

University College, Oxford
March 28, 1951

Dear Pa,

I should have written long before this; but I was having exams; though they finished a good two weeks ago, I have been far too lazy to write. I didn't do at all badly in the examinations, and my tutor thinks that I should get a distinction. About three weeks before the exam, he told me, over coffee and cigarettes at a restaurant (this is to show you how delightfully informal tuition can be at Oxford), that I was worrying too much and working too hard. As a matter of fact, I shut myself off from every activity last term, except the *Isis*. There is no need to worry. I am convinced I have passed. I think the work done did me good, and I can actually feel myself growing intellectually. I am not so unsure of myself as I was when I first came here.

And now I must tell you about an *Isis* end-of-term party I attended. This party is given by the editor and proprietors of the *Isis*. It was at this party that I came upon the type of woman I have read about—the type that doesn't care a bit for writing but is extremely fond of writers. Being editor of the *Isis* has its compensations, I observed. I found, to my surprise, that people whom I never knew had heard of me as 'the bloke who writes half *Isis*'—referring to the news pages, of course. The editor was intrigued by my initials, and wanted to know why I always kept at V S, and never divulged the first name even. For you know that, in Trinidad, men call each other by their surnames, only women use the Christian names of their friends. Well, here you are supposed to call the people you know by their first names, but I still find it difficult. The news editor said that I was the best reporter he had that term. But no promotion as yet.

I have sent a story to Swanzy; and, brother, if it is accepted, I intend to churn the stuff out as fast as I can write. I can use the cash. A Frenchman, who read parts of my novel, told me I was gifted. He lives in the same boarding house in London as I do, and is on the French Service of the BBC. He wants me to finish the novel as early as possible, and pass it on to him. He knows people like John Lehmann* and others. He also wants me to

---

* Poet and publisher, Editor of *New Writing*

rewrite the Carnival Queen sketch—and the first part of it really does need rewriting—for the French programme; it will be translated into French. I don't know how long he is going to stay at the BBC, for the Govt has just decided to cut down on French Services and concentrate on countries behind the Iron Curtain. I have been turning over in my mind for some time now the idea of getting your stories published. I know no one yet; but I suppose by the end of the year, I shall be brought into contact with a number of people. Meanwhile, I think, the best plan is merely to send the short stories to a publisher, saying that most have been broadcast on the BBC. I will do my best, but we will have to decide in advance who will do the typing. Or at any rate how much! I suppose I can be trusted to act as your agent. Now, I want to tell you something. I have always admired you as a writer. And I am convinced that, were you born in England, you would have been famous and rich and pounced upon by the intellectuals. But you are not frightfully old. Shaw achieved success at about forty-four, you should try to keep on writing.

Your sister-in-law brought the fags for me; handed them over after drawing a picture of herself as being forced to lie to the Customs people, telling them that she smoked. And I damned well know that everyone coming to England is allowed 400 fags. Why do they go to such pains to let you know that you are in their debt? I intend to stay away from them. They can do nothing for me, except try to keep me down. Capo said, 'I see your mother is encouraging you to smoke.' I said, 'Yes, yes.' As soon as he saw that I was completely undisturbed by his sarcasm, and was replying with sarcasm to his sarcasm, he completely changed, and asked me about my exams!

The coarseness of those children struck me violently. I had just got back from Oxford. Their language jarred on me. I heard Sita saying in that wretched coarse Trinidad accent, 'I ain' wan' none nuh.' It sounds so frightfully illiterate.

And now thanks for the fags. The Frenchman thinks they are better than Camels. There's advertisement for you!

And now ease your mind: I am not going to Devon. I am spending a week with a college friend in Blackpool (this has its drawbacks, for the family is Catholic); I am spending a week in Cumberland. This vac I have been looked up by two friends—two more than during the last vac. One was an English chap who grew up in India. He treated me well last Tuesday. I was broke: we had coffee and lunch at the Regent Palace just off Piccadilly Circus—followed by tea at the Tate Gallery.

Here's a tip: the Penguins are issuing great books in their series now. Shall I buy them for you, or do you want to buy them in T'dad?

Vido

[Handwritten note]:

About the make-up of the *Weekly:* the Englishman handles features as though they were news. Yours is competent and will doubtless become better and better.

Observe how the English papers use photos . . . Every picture in a perfect rectangle *[2 illustrations].*

University College, Oxford
April 3, 1951

Dear Kamla,

I got your letter and your snapshots a few days ago. Of course I am owing you some letters, but I was too lazy to write.

I hate the way you refer to your birthday cake as a 'poor' one. I hardly think it was. I have never had a birthday cake in my life, nor even a birthday party, for you can never call those sweet drink and cake refreshments party fare.

I have some news for you. I wrote, and I think you will remember, early in 1949 something about a Beauty Contest. Remember? Well, since February 27, 1949, I have rewritten that thing at least half a dozen times. The last time I rewrote it was a few days ago, at the instigation of a Frenchman who worked at the BBC and lives in the same boarding house as I. He is going to have it translated into French for the French Service of the BBC. I have also sent a story to the Caribbean programme of the BBC, and by the looks of things, they have accepted it. If they really have, it means that for two weeks' work, I shall have raked in more than fifteen guineas. Not bad! And I am only eighteen! My novel is not complete as yet, but I have been working on it like a dog for the past fortnight, with little result. Of course, the ideas have come, but I have battered myself into a state of perpetual drowsiness, and need to rest for a few days before writing. One needs an absolutely clear brain to think of situations and people. But it is going on all right, and I want to have it finished by the end of June. The Frenchman has promised to sell it for me. He thinks I have a talent, and that I will be a success. Naturally, I don't think the novel is a great one, but I am writing it in the hope that I shall be able to get about a hundred pounds or so, and perhaps step into a delightful job after Oxford. But there comes trouble. If a writer has to write well, he has to live, and no man living within an office and being sure of four meals a day can write good stuff. Ordinarily writing comes from experience, and I have little experience: you know the way I live.

I hope you have come out of your despair. Please do. It is breaking my heart to know that you are unhappy.

You needn't worry about the girl. She is playing hard to get, she is trying to impress me with the number of people who are after her, and I am duly impressed, and withdrawing. I have come to the conclusion that having girl friends is necessary, but I am too passionate—you know what you always say about me, and I give each new girl far too much attention. I think therefore that I shall ignore girls altogether, until I have achieved success.

A college friend of mine has invited me to his home in Blackpool. The only knotty part is that he is a devout Catholic. I hope I do nothing wrong.

Oh, by the way, Arlette has become a nun. I have been seeing her sister Molly*—who is engaged to a Maltese bloke—at this boarding house. There are also two other Trinidadian girls here, very Indian, and very San Fernandian, and very stupid.

Please stop worrying, my dear, about yourself and, least of all, about me. And, as for home, you know how it runs. It is built on a solid foundation. You must realise that without us, the family has lost its heart.

The responsibility is mighty, I know, but it is not depressing.

Your pictures were charming, and the Frenchman said you looked as a Grecian goddess! And he has been married three times. So there!

---

* Arlette and Molly, friends of Kamla

I am glad that I have a sister as charming as you, and I am looking forward to the day when I can show you off in Oxford.

Cheerio, my darling.

[Handwritten]: The woman in Oxford got your sugar. She melted in gratitude and is sending you a letter.

Home: 4/4/51
9.45 p.m.

Dear Vido,

I have just finished chatting with Carr—the Belmont man.* He came to see me about a novel he is writing, wants me to read the chapters that he has completed, so I could tell him what I think of the effort.

We were very relieved to get your letter of the 28.3. It's something to know that the unusually long silence was not due to illness. As has so often happened, we got a letter from Kamla on the same day that we got yours. She seems to have got over her depression, and has decided to study on her own . . . I had no doubt whatever that you'd get through your examination. I suspect your greatest setback is your own anxiety; the goods you can supply, even with a modicum of study. I believe the 'open sesame' is the practice of indifference—indifference as to results after you have done your best, quietly, coolly . . .

The *Isis* is but a small thing. A year or two and you will be writing for more celebrated publications. You don't have to worry about us— so long as I keep going. Give yourself all the chance . . . Cut the Carnival Queen dispassionately. I believe at least a third of the stuff could be deleted. I recollect I had actually marked out the portion that seemed to me unnecessary . . . If the story to Swanzy has a West Indian theme, there's a good chance of its being accepted; but the payment nowadays is slightly less, say about ten guineas where it used to be twelve or thirteen. Still, few magazines will pay you better at this early stage . . . That Frenchman was probably just being polite: how on earth can

---

* Amateur writer in Trinidad

Anchor Specials, or any Trinidad cigarettes, possibly be better than Camels?

Jainarayan was home today. He said: 'You know, Mousa, the cigarettes came back. Vido didn't take them. The parcel had a note—"definitely refused". I believe the tax on it was more than the cost of the cigarettes.' A few days ago there was an item in the woman's page of the *Guardian* that you and some ten other West Indians had accepted an invitation from the Press Officer of the British Council to tour England to see some of the chief industries and things. On top of this comes the news that you'd be spending a week with a friend in Blackpool. Whatever it is I hope it turns out happy.

I suppose it will be quite some time before the new Penguins arrive here; so you may send me one—at most two. Yesterday I bought a copy of Deeping's *I Live Again*.* It is not quite the vintage, but it's a good story—a bit too rapid and professional. You come to know good books as good connoisseurs know good wines, I think.

Thanks for the magazines and papers. You needn't have sent the *Express*. I get it here.

[Handwritten]: Now there's a letter to write to Kamla, and it's late.

Affectionately,
Pa

University College, Oxford
April 11, 1951

Dear Everybody,

I am writing this from Blackpool. Blackpool is the big northern seaside resort of England. It is a big machine made to extort money from the people on holiday, full of fortune-tellers, gypsies, all named Lee, and all claiming to be the only Gypsy Lee on the front—eating places and amusement shops. Of course, the season has not yet started, but you can walk along the

---

* Warwick Deeping, popular British novelist of the 1920s and 1930s

front and see the machine being oiled for the season that begins, I am told, in June.

I am staying with the family of a college friend, a boy who stays on my staircase in college. It is a Scottish family, and very Catholic too, but I have never spent a more congenial four days in England. They do their best for me to feel at home, and I do feel very easy. One thing I have learnt here is the art of adapting myself to any new conditions. I have slept in so many different beds and rooms since I have left home that moving has neither horror nor romance for me.

A Frenchman told me that we must feel sorry for the British. He says that they are influenced by their women, their seaside resorts and their food. Their women can't cook, can't dress and are invariably plain; their seaside resorts are damp, wet places, packed with thousands of people being sucked of their money. Take Blackpool. The beach is pleasant, as pleasant as Trinidad's east coast, minus the coconut trees, but the water and wind are hellishly cold, and the water is always the colour of mud. Their food, he says, is fish and chips (fried potato).

This morning I did some forking in the garden back of the house. I worked for about an hour and I felt fine. I have never had the opportunity to do any work since I have come to England, and I think that I shall really apply for a temporary job on a farm in the coming vacation, not only for the money, but the air and exercise. Oxford is a comparatively small town. You start at the centre, and you find yourself walking along fields in ten minutes. When I got back to London from Oxford, the mad rush seemed to get me. I thought the people looked as though they were running, and it took me some time to feel that they were walking. The air of London is definitely unhealthy. In Oxford, I cannot sleep later than nine thirty. In London, I can sleep every day till noon, regardless of the hour I went to bed.

This Saturday I am going to Borrowdale, where the famous Bowder Stone is. Borrowdale is in the Lake District, and is further north. Don't think I am spending money. I am staying here free, and, as I am going to Borrowdale on a British Council Vacation Trip, the Colonial Office gives me return fare to Borrowdale from London, and pays me 7/6 each night I spend. As I came to Blackpool by coach, and this cost 18/-, and intend returning to Oxford, with my friend, hitchhiking, I shall come out very well, especially as the return rail fare is more than four pounds!

I had forgotten to tell you, but I had a letter from Rabi quite some time ago. Poor boy! I feel cruel. He had nothing to say to me, and went to a great deal of trouble to fill up his letter form. It was kind of him, anyway.

I hope Pa does write, even five hundred words a day. He should begin a novel. He should realise that the society of the West Indies is a very interesting one—one of phoney sophistication. In the Sookhdeo bunch, he surely can see a novel. Describe the society just as it is—do not explain or excuse or laugh. I regret I did not go about more than I did. But if I had, well, perhaps I wouldn't have been here.

Tell Shivan and Savi and Mira and Satti that I think of them; tell Savi that I feel very badly for not writing her, and for not sending either Shivan or her anything for their birthdays. But I can't help it.

I think Pa's birthday has passed. My best regards, anyway. And to Ma I send my love.

IV

April 14, 1951 – September 13, 1951

SUMMER TERM, LONG VACATION

My darling sister,

I got your letter a week ago. It came to me at Blackpool, where I have been staying with the family of a friend. I left only today, and am writing this from Borrowdale, where Ma's pen-friend used to live or perhaps still does.

My dear, I shall send all the books you ask for. No need to pay (until, perhaps, I go down on both knees, and plead, 'Please, sir, may I have some more?').

I performed (that's the way I usually do things) no blunders. The family is the most Catholic I have ever lived with. They believe, and they believe with all their conviction. Surely there is nothing wrong with that. It has built up a wall around them; but it has made them secure and they are not aware that what they believe is perhaps, or is, superficial and artificial. It has not made masters out of them. They are kind and generous. But this is, I suppose, because of the chastening knocks Catholicism is always getting at some time or the other. Power goes to anybody's head.

I have just realised that this is the first letter you have seen in my own handwriting for quite some time now. Is there any mighty change in it?

I am at peace with the world. It is a humiliating peace, but I am trying to learn to accept it. I cannot tell you why, for it may break your heart. For you, I know, have always looked upon me as a sort of intellectual giant. Haven't you? But what happens when a man discovers that he has been lying to himself all the time? He has lied so much he has grown to believe himself. Everything I say or have said makes me ashamed of myself. I find myself posing even when I am sincere. Must people always go through this stage? I was seriously thinking this morning how people could ever put up with me. I wish I could see myself as people see me. Perhaps it would be the last straw. Or perhaps I am not as bad as I think myself to be?

The boys who like me, like me because mine is a 'cynical flamboyance', because I pose as an 'enfant terrible'. Yet I sincerely am never aware of POSING. I suppose the reason is that in the WI [West Indies] we lived so completely within ourselves, we grew to despise the people around us. But the people ought to have been despised! A friend told me the other day that people don't like me because I made them feel that I knew they were fools. What do you think of me? And don't tell me of your cousins. They are all asses, as you well know.

I have come, regretfully, to the end. With all my love, my dear Kamla, from Vido

[From Kamla]

April 20, 1951

Dear Vido,

Well, yes. Your writing has become only a bit more illegible. Anyway, nothing to worry about. As a matter of fact, it gives me great consolation to know that not only my writing is illegible.

I am doing my annual exams. And what do you think has happened? My right arm has swollen. On the 18th, while doing my English Optional I, my hand suddenly went limp. I couldn't form the letters. You should see the writing. Simply horrid. God (No. I no longer believe in God. I can't even pray now.) alone knows how I finished my paper. Yesterday, I went to the doctor for fear any tropical disease has decided to become intimate with me. The doctor said the nerve (that funny nerve at the elbow) has gone a bit numb, maybe by leaning too much on it. So far the swelling is still there. I had my Eng. II this morning, with the result that it has come up a bit more, and is quite painful. However, I am carrying on with my exams. There is geography on Monday.

The last part of your letter is funny. Now don't tell me you have started all over again. For goodness sake live (and let live). Whoever likes you, or doesn't like you, is his affair, not yours. But one thing promise me, never take on to drink. I know what the result would be. So hang on to your senses. I will think you to be what I always know you to be. And believe me you are just what you are. So forget it.

I have got some hostel news for you. Somebody has entered into my room and stolen my wallet money and all. Now I don't mind the money in the wallet. But there was Pa's photograph and yours in it. I wish they would return them and keep the rest. Such is my luck. That money I had been carefully keeping to get myself some cotton saris for college. I went for my tea and when I came back it was gone. Why worry?

There is one boring American here. He has a beard, wears Indian clothes and talks in a slow drawling tone that wearies you. He is always trying to get you to go to this council and that. Really, a perfect farce he is. We call him 'walking Jesus'.

All my love, Kamla

Home: 4/25/51

Dear Vido,

I missed writing you last week; and it is almost a week now since we got your last letter telling about your Blackpool visit. Often enough when I am behindhand with these letters, it is due to—guess what?—yes, that's right—no air-letter form!

It should be the easiest thing to get; the Post Office is nearby; Sati, Mira and Savi pass there many times every day; but these people are undependable—even for such trifles as getting air-letter forms. Of course I am to be included among them, for, as you well know, I too pass and re-pass the Post Office many times every day.

You say I should write at least 500 words every day. Well, I have started to do so, but cannot say much just now. Let me first see how well the resolve works out. Even now I have not settled the question whether I should work on an autobiographical novel, or whether I should exhume Gurudeva.* I have confidence that I <u>can</u> turn out a novel; I have been making a detailed study of the structure of *Riceyman Steps,* and I believe I can easily do with Gurudeva what Bennett has done with Mr Earlforward and Mrs Arb. When, however, it comes to my attempting an autobiographical novel, I

---

* The eponymous hero of Seepersad Naipaul's only published work of fiction (see Bibliography)

find it quite easy matter to handle in parts and quite hazy and difficult in other places. What is difficult is the selection of the incidents.

You should work away on your novel by all means. It takes years to arrive, however good one may be; and an early start, I need hardly remind you, is a great advantage. Read Conrad for intensity of expression, but for the most part be yourself.

About my short stories: I can count on at least 11 that are in hand. But the mere physical effort to type these is tedious and repellent . . . I am often tired after work, and must be in a good mood to get back to work after work. It takes all the juice out of a fellow. So don't expect much from me. Another thing: almost every day I have had something to put right—the fencing east and south of the house, the garage, the garden—if I may call it by that name. I want to make the little place a bower. And I have already done a good bit in this direction.

Shivan is going to St Agnes' School (EC).* He is in third stage, but hardly does much work. He tells me children are requested, for a certain period, to 'go to sleep'—with heads bowed on desks—every day. I asked Shivan the other day: 'How long do the children sleep?'

Shivan: 'Till school over.' So there you are!

I have been with the *TG* sixteen months now, but they haven't given me a raise. A thing that is making me bitter—I suppose that's how a Communist comes into being—is that a third-rate English boy who, I assure you, does not one whit more or better work than I do is getting a far bigger salary than I am getting. Here in the colonies the white man is supposed to be a superior species—eating better food, living in better houses. I don't mind telling you I have somehow come to detest most of them. It's not my fault entirely. There's a man here named Barker (news editor) who talks as though he is the ace of journalists—he has some kind of a degree, a BA, I think, from some third-rate university. But actually the man is a bluff. If you have read Priestley's *Angel Pavement* you must have met Mr Goldie. This man is like Goldie.

Kathleen McColgan has returned to England. She tells me she has an uncle at Oxford—not in the university—and that on visiting him

---

* Church of England

she'd look you up. She is a good woman, in that she is not like Barker and company.

Kamla has written to ask us to send her 'immediately' a *Stembridge Geography—Southern Continent*. Your Ma tells me to ask you to send it to her because it would take a very long time if she sent one by surface mail from here.

Have you heard from the BBC in connection with your short story? Let me know.

A chap here named Allahar has been sending stories for the *Gdn Wkly*, getting them published, too; now it is certain that he has been sending in other people's words from English papers.

Everything and everybody OK.

Yours affectionately,
Pa

Next time I think I'll let your Ma have a shot at writing you.

University College, Oxford
May 1, 1951

Dear Pa,

Believe me when I tell you how happy I am that you are writing. You shouldn't let the choice bother you. It merely means that you have two novels to write. And you should not let age worry you either. You have probably heard me speak of Joyce Cary. He started to write after he had retired from the Colonial Service. He is now, I am sure, past fifty. I saw him last Sunday.

I think you will be glad to know that Swanzy will probably use my story in June or July. He wrote about a fortnight ago, telling me this, but asking me to rewrite the last page, which he thought was 'too literary'.

I did pretty well in my examinations—beta plus being my lowest mark—and my tutors are rather disappointed that I didn't get a distinction. But then only three men in the whole university got a distinction. I did the best in my college, anyway.

Please do not let the *Guardian* get you down. I know how much that sort of thing hurts, but please don't worry about it too much. As was to be expected, I got no promotion on the *Isis,* and as a matter of fact I think they are trying to ease me out. The whole of Oxford is run on lines so frightfully cliquish. You have got to belong to the circle of the boys if you are to get along. I came back late to the university this term and discovered that all the term's reporting had been already portioned out—and I wasn't included. I was later asked to pick up any extra news that may be unswept by the staff! This probably sounds familiar to you. But there are good points. I have been given my first feature to do. It is a pretty big thing, two pages with pictures, and it is going to deal with the impact of the expansion of Morris Motors (just outside Oxford) on the university. I hope I do something well. Only the big boys do get these kinds of jobs. So I suppose I shouldn't worry. I have been told, in writing and in word of mouth, that I shouldn't feel that I am not wanted on the *Isis,* that my work is liked, etc.—you know the usual waffle. But you never can tell with these people.

We had about a week ago four brilliant days at a stretch, but it is now cold and raining. What weather! But I like it. It is so full of change.

Boyzee, you will be glad to hear, has at last got into medical school, at Newcastle, which is a good hundred miles north. I am happy for him.

A boy called Abdullah is getting cigarettes from home—200 at a time—in gift parcels. Couldn't I be helped out the same way? I shall pay for anything. And please don't say don't bother to pay, for I understand the position.

At last I have found my own clearly defined circle of friends. It is pleasant to find that sort of thing. They are none of them terribly brilliant, but there is one boy, English who grew up in India, who is an artist and who failed his exams and is going to leave Oxford this term. This long summer vacation—16 weeks—is going to kill me with boredom, if I don't find a job. I hope I get one.

About the typing of your stories: don't people in Trinidad do people's typing? In England the rate is 1/3–1/6 per 1,000 words. The average-sized novel is roughly 70,000. So you can work out the cost of typing.

I should have written to Savi. But what news can I tell her, or anybody else for that matter? All I have to say I say. These letters are for general reading—and I hope no one wants carbon copies!

My love to everyone, to Ma and Shivan and Meera and Satti.

I have bought Kamla's books, and shall send them today or tomorrow.

Vido

Home: 5/9/51

Dear Vido,

The acacia is in bloom; not many festoons yet—just about half a dozen full-blown ones—but soon there'll be lots more. The tree is tall and lush, not at all like the ragged things you saw on Wrightson Road. Under the tree I have planted a bougainvillaea, the rich scarlet. I want to see it climb up and up, then hang in curtains of scarlet. I got the idea while passing St James Barracks. There, along the driveway, as you know, the purple bougainvillaea hangs from way up one of the old samans,* and it looks lovely. Kamla wanted me to plant a bougainvillaea against the car shed. This I have done and the stake has already sent out a shoot.

This flower-growing is like a tonic for me, a fine recreation that helps me to forget for a time the daily routine at the *TG*, though this is not saying that the work there is so painfully monotonous. That is the saving grace in the job. Within certain limitations called *Guardian* policy, or *Guardian* rules—you can exercise your ingenuity, and artistic instinct, if any—pageplanning, headline-writing, picture-placing, suggesting drawings, and so on. To set to work on a virgin sheet of newsprint and then to see it come back to you a magazine or newspaper page gives great thrills. Occasionally it can also give a bit of a headache.

I do seven pages in the *G Weekly* and two in the *Sunday Guardian*—pages 18 and 19, the business pages. Here the limitations are far greater: you cannot select just any type-head your fancy suggests. No; it's Bod. Ital. and nothing else. (In the Bodoni group alone there are Bod. Black; Bod. Modern; Bod. Ultra Modern; Bod. Extra Bold; Bod. Heavy, in addition to the couple of others already named.) One day I put Bod. Blk for streamer head and decks. I half knew the audacity would be questioned. Next day, Sunday, I saw the page back in its old Bodoni. So I stick to rules—when it comes to the *TG*.

You know, silly as it may sound, I find myself doing three (and very nearly four) stories at the same time. I mean I am doing three stories, not waiting to finish one before beginning another. You see, I've been reading Galsworthy *(The Assembled Tales—Caravan)* and Kipling's *Plain Tales*

---

* Rain-trees

from the Hills, and I've been getting ideas, and if I don't scribble down these ideas right away, I might lose them. And I have gone on doing this thing, now on this story, now on that, now on the other. One of the three I finished two days ago; the other two are more than half finished. I haven't put any on the typewriter yet. When I do then the work begins. But these first systematic jottings are good, I find. In that they give the story a unity and balance, and your ideas are preserved in more or less complete story form, even though you set to polishing up a long time after.

I don't want to give you the impression that I am writing like blazes; but I am writing, slowly and piecemeal, so to speak; and this is better than not writing at all. I feel exceedingly good at your encouraging words, because I know you are not flattering me and I have confidence in your opinion; still, I shouldn't like you to bank too much on me, for if I don't come up you'll be disillusioned; and this would be painful for both of us. Look, it isn't that I lack confidence. I <u>know</u> I can write; but it is also true that I get tired more quickly. Suppose I had nothing to do for six months, I have no doubt I'd write out my first novel. And I have no doubt it would be good, even though I may not easily find a publisher.

Do you recollect what Cecil Hunte* has said on the importance of note-taking?—of jotting down your impressions of people and things (and I'd add of capturing a mood)? It would be a God-send to you if you adopted this as a habit. You will find these jottings most useful some time, somewhere. You will have your characters ready to hand. Let me illustrate by putting down my impressions of Jenkins, off the reel:

Everything about him suggested lard. He was white as lard, thick as lard, thickly turgid as lard is turgid. As though to complete the impression, he habitually wore white; his very hair was white. 'Twas as though at some crisis in his life he had early vowed to his god that in fealty to him he'd go in nothing but white. He was short, rotund, obese; the heaviness and lardiness of him stuck to his tongue; for when he spoke, the words fell with a thud, as though that tongue was weighted at the tip with lead. When you looked at him well, he made you think of an overgrown baby: fat, round-

---

* Author of numerous 'How to Write' books

faced, chubby. It is said that the equable, sometime depressing but never unkind climate of England has its parallel in the temperament of its people. Mr Jenkins' physical attributes and lineaments had their parallel in his temperament. He was slow—oh, how slow! Until you came to know him well, you thought he was simply goofy; when you knew him better . . .

You might go on and on like this. It may be of no use to me just now, but some day it will come in handy: I might want a fellow just like this man in a story. The beauty of the thing is that you could seldom put in your character the same freshness if you described Jenkins say ten years later.

It would be a pleasure to send you a carton of cigarettes every fortnight, or at any rate, every month. But please find out from Abdullah how he gets his cigarettes—that is, how does the person sending him the stuff go about the matter. Jainarayan was here yesterday and he says you just cannot send cigarettes away at all. Find out from Abdullah and let me know in your very next letter.

You should welcome the ease-off from the *Isis*. You can do at least one feature a fortnight, writing the thing leisurely and effectively; and that should bring you even greater recognition than would just news-writing. And the fellow may be sincere enough when he says your writing is liked. Anyhow, accept it as that.

Congrats on your coming through your exam. You have done very well. After all, you nearly hit a distinction and the best in your college.

Cultivate Swanzy. Write on WI themes; not only fiction, but go in for factual writing also. These must be something better than ordinary descriptive journalism. They must have literary value. I have sent in a short—you know, that 'Mohun' piece. If it's accepted I'll give you half the proceeds. They still have my 'Obeah' in hand and I have reminded Mrs Lindo about the fact.

Look, do you know something of the inside of Ramlilla* or of Hosey or Shiva-Ratri.† If you do, write on these things for *Caribbean Voices*. And

---

* Pageant play based on the Ramayana
† Night dedicated to the Hindu deity Shiva

you should send in your Carnival Queen. All you need do is to cut out a whole portion out of the body of the article; make some of the sentence less telegraphic by just interposing 'and' and the thing is done. If you like I can do it for you from here. I have a copy of the mag . . . Well, no more room. Keep well as all is well at home. I had to type this on this paper for want of an air form.

Tuesday—5/15

Received your letter telling us about the things in your eyes. Are they the same thing we call 'cattle-boil'? It must be very difficult for you to write with those things. They hurt and make you feel uncomfortable like hell. You should have told your editor that you were in no position to write. But for these boils I would entertain no misgivings about the article. There are few things I have written that I thought were quite good, and I have handed in some just because I had to; and it has happened more often than not that these things came out much better than I had expected. Some of them that I thought were very bad were indeed very good. Over here, shortly after you left home, I wrote a Sunday article on Elodie Bissessar at the suggestion of Pearse; and while I did the thing in a low 'make it anyhow' spirit it turned out a very good thing. So don't despair.

An assignment like writing an article on the Morris works can be a devil of a thing . . . if you tried to take in every detail in your picture. Do you remember when I had to do that BC factory story? If we had allowed ourselves to say everything at the same time we'd have found ourselves in a muddle, no doubt. But the thing to do is to begin anywhere and say something on one aspect—then go on to another aspect; and so on and on—step by step. You will not have dealt with the story exhaustively: nobody does that, you know; yet whatever you'd have written would have had a completeness.

Last Sunday your Ma and I had been going round with the Tewaris—mother and daughter, using the good old 1192. We were heading for Benali, but heavy rain caused us to turn back from Chaguanas, and we ended up at the Ramdins. There I happened to get in with the doctor man—Deo; when I say get in, I mean I got into his car. I soon realised that the man was out on a bacchanal; told me that he'd not be returning till 10 or 11 in the night and was going anywhere there was a dance or things like that. So I jumped off at Arima and took a taxi back to Tunapuna, where I had your Ma and the Tewaris waiting for me. Medicine does not happen to be even the last thing that this fellow is thinking about; supposing you were like him, I'd prefer you a labourer; I mean I'd rather see you a decent labourer than a successful 'professional' such as this man is. We had two beers and a couple of whiskies at that fellow's, Ram Dharry.

I am reading a life of that poor Keats. No other biography—save Gandhi's and Nehru's (the latter borrowed by Bhisham and never returned) have moved me more. You know, I am not given to poetry— not the modern poetry we are having; but reading this book makes me see what a genius Keats really was—for the things he wrote at his age he couldn't be anything less; and to read what the fellows on the *Quarterly Review* did to him—no wonder it is said that the man was hurried to his death by these petty criticisms—so much like what is happening in Trinidad today. But you see how Keats lives and how he will go on living so long as the English language lasts . . . I had intended, at the first, to transfer the contents of this letter to an air-mail form. But this is now impossible; so I might as well go on typing more for the one and six that they'd charge me for mailing this.

Poor Kamla wrote—letter dated the same day like yours, and received on the same day. She says that she got the highest marks for her English papers; but that she doesn't want to do too well 'in this exam because they may give me a scholarship'. I really don't quite know what the girl means. Satti, who is coming to be a wit in some way: 'Oh, she is getting Indian foolish.'

And Kamla asks me why don't I buy for her Ma an electric washer? Well, I'd like to buy her more than an electric washer. I'd like to buy her a fridge; and I very much want to buy a tyre for my old car, and a battery and an inner tube; and the electric washer can't be bought for much the same reason that these things can't be bought. Look, the cost of living has gone up considerably higher since you people left; the extra thirty or forty that I used to make I no longer make; and my pay remains the same. I won't tell Kamla these things, for fear that old adage will hold good: 'Ignorance is bliss where 'tis folly to be wise.'

But <u>don't</u> let all this stop you finding out from Abdullah what to do to send cigarettes from here.

Well, it's time to get ready to go to work. Next week I'll be getting Thursday and Friday—both days being public holidays.

Keep well,

Your affectionate, Pa

[Handwritten]: I asked Sati to fill in this space—she declined; meaning she'd write a whole letter or won't write at all. Independent, isn't she?

University College, Oxford
May 9, 1951

Dear Everybody,

What weather! Really, it is the most unpredictable thing I have ever come across. Two weeks ago, it was hot and sunny, as any Trinidad day. Yet for the past week: grey, drizzly and cold.

I have just completed the Morris article. It is not as good as I thought it would have been. And now that I am in disfavour with the editors, it would have done me some good. But there are a number of reasons why it didn't turn out as well as I expected. In the first place, there are too many things for me to do. Then I didn't arrange my facts neatly enough before writing, and so I was hopelessly muddled. Then my eyes have been not too co-operative for the past week. Anyway, I shall send the next issue—a Festival of Britain issue—and you will be able to judge for yourself. Please let me know what you think of it.

I spoke of my eyes. Nothing serious is wrong with them. I have merely had two cysts removed from the right one and will shortly have another removed from the left. A really simple, 5-minute operation.

My, what a wonderful place the Morris Works is! I was taken around with a guide to myself as a member of the Press, and treated to the most wonderful lunch I have ever had in England so far. I spoke to the man who handles the editing of the five big Nuffield publications. He worked for a short time on Reuter and the *Daily Mail*. It appears that people are scheming and unscrupulous everywhere. He says he is glad to get away from the *Mail*.

I went canoeing the other day with some friends. Of course we didn't know the first thing about canoeing and it was only after we had capsized the canoe, ourselves and all, into the river, we realised that we were paddling it the wrong way. It was a funny experience really.

I really should send some pictures of Oxford home. The shops are littered with them: they therefore seem very vulgar. But I shall get down to doing it shortly. I myself have amassed quite a number of books since I have been in England. But I feel ashamed to say how many are paperbacked things, and how many Penguins there are!

Give my regards to everyone and what about sending me some photographs?

Vido

May 26, 1951

Dear Everybody,

My big story has come out at last—in this week's *Isis*. And my name is in biggish capital letters. Probably the first and only big article I shall ever do for the paper. It is really impossible to get ahead in that paper.

I shall send along a copy of the story as soon as my tutor returns the magazine. We have become rather friendly, my tutor and I. It is a very good thing.

This past week has been a very busy one for me. Last Sunday I gave my first big tea party. It cost me about twenty-five shillings. There were ten people in my tiny sitting room. And the room soon became very smoke-filled. We heard the door bang and used to wonder who went out or perhaps we would wait for a strange voice to learn if anyone new had come in. But it was quite a success. Boyzee fortunately came down for the first time that Sunday to see me. He came without warning and so the time I had set aside for preparation had to be spent showing him around Oxford. However, it was very nice to have him, and the boys enjoyed his company, and I suspect that he had tears in his eyes when he was leaving—he had enjoyed himself so well, and was perhaps sorry that he had never had the chance to live as I am doing, without any supervision and questioning by uncles. The party was my first big do, and I was so nervous that I didn't eat a thing. I was so busy seeing about the other people and forgetting so many things. The gas ring was occupied; the water refused to boil; and the tea I gave out was as thin as weak soft drinks and the colour of light brown paper. However, shortly after the badly disorganised tea, I passed round the beer—I had bought twelve bottles—and everybody was in quite good humour, after the fun they had all had over the rotten tea. It was a very successful party and was still going strong at a quarter to seven, when I had to throw them out to show Boyzee some more of Oxford. They insisted on taking him down to the college cellar for a glass of beer—the only hospitality an undergraduate knows—and so we went to the cellar for a glass of beer. Then I walked with him along the river, and back to the railway station.

I have decided to do some extra work for my final examinations. I am doing the novelists of the nineteenth century, and I have piles of novels to read. It is a good thing, however, as I shall be forced to fill up this massive gap in my reading. I have to read Dickens, George Eliot, Thackeray, Meredith, Pater, Henry James, Kipling, Thomas Hardy. The Assistant Curator at the Ashmolean, Harrison's friend, has given me one book of Hardy's and is prepared to lend me more. We have become rather friendly. He is very pleasant and the more so because he manages to talk all the time. He is extremely well read, and has no silly ideas about stupid novelists. I had him to tea in my rooms yesterday.

So I have settled down at last. I am not letting the *Isis* worry me, or anything else. As you can tell, from the mass of reading I have on, there is precious little time for writing. But I wonder if that isn't a good thing. Reading novels makes you think, and I have been doing a lot of thinking, which is all that matters. I read *The Old Wives' Tale*. By comparison with a Dickens' novel, it seems almost a booklet. It is extremely well written. I don't care much for the philosophy. The sad thing about life to the Bennett who wrote *The Old Wives' Tale* is that people have to grow old.

I do hope you are keeping up your writing. For heaven's sake do. You are old enough. You have no time to wonder what you have to write about. Your experience is wide and if you write merely one page a day, you will shortly find that you have a novel on your hand. About your short stories, I think it is high time we tried to find a publisher. About the typing: it costs thirty-six cents a thousand words. So if you have 70,000 words—the length of the average book—it will cost you under thirty dollars. We can try to split the cost, or use the money from your BBC short story. You will have to write an explanatory note stating that most of these stories are set in the West Indies. Personally, I thought Gurudeva a bit too short. I thought—as a matter of fact, as I look it over now—you could leave it out, seeing it is a sort of a half-caste story, neither story nor novelette nor novel, nor long short story. So send me a copy of the book, and copies of your short stories. KEEP COPIES FOR YOURSELF. I shall do my best for them. I promise nothing. But there can be no harm in trying.

Keep well, don't worry, and keep on writing.

Give Ma and Meera and Savi and Satti and Shivan my love. Thanks, Ma, for your letter.

The weather is beautiful. It is so warm that I am wearing a mere shirt—no vest. And I feel fine.

With all my love,
Vido

Old Gopal Bang,
PO Lanka,
Banares
May 29, 1951

My dear Vido,

It's now 11.10 at night. It is only since two days that I have begun studying in earnest. My eyes put me off a bit. Now, I am wearing a pair of dark-rimmed, maroon-tinged spectacles. I look goggle-eyed and silly. They are meant for regular wearing. But my vanity permits me to wear them only while studying or at the cinema. The result of my eye examination was that with my right eye, I could have read the first three lines, and with the left, only the first letters! Does this mean that they are very bad?

Guess what? I have come first in Cult. This means that I came first in all my subjects. But whether I have come first in my class I can't say. I shall know when college re-opens.

Instead of sending me photographs of Oxford why not send me a single copy of the *Isis*? I guess I am judging everything by BHU when I say that I don't want photographs of Oxford for fear of being disappointed. These huge massive brick buildings here, most impressive from the outside, are really full of nothing inside, mentally, physically and otherwise.

Do you know that Ma's birthday is in June—a card would do.

Keep well and lots of love, Kamla

Home: 6.9.51

Dear Vido,

Thanks for the *Isis* pages which I received yesterday. Your article was quite good, and if you were not hard-pressed and indisposed I'm sure you'd have done even better.

Kamla wrote today to say that she wants to get married but gives no more detail. We shall be sending you a parcel—sugar, grapefruit, pineapple. You haven't said anything about how Abdullah gets cigarettes sent him from Trinidad. <u>Please</u> <u>find</u> <u>out</u> <u>and</u> <u>write.</u>

Affectionately yours,
Pa

It's an awful house that we don't send you anything and it's a shame, too, that you don't ask for anything.

Pa

Dear Vido,

This is my letter and not Pa's. I just spared him those few lines.

Home is the same old thing. The usual fighting and quarrelling. Of course, all that is carried out between Meera, Savi and myself. Meera and Savi both team up against me. I suppose they do it just for fun.

I don't know if you realize it, but I am taking my School Certificate exam in December. I am trying my best to study hard. [. . .] helps me with my maths. That is really my worst subject. I am taking French lessons from [. . .].

In a letter I received a few weeks ago from Sita, she told me that you had become fatter, fairer and your voice more gruff. Is that true? Last week I wore your short white pants (home of course) and Pa took out a picture of me with it. I'll be sending you the snap of it. It is really a group—Ma, Meera, Shiva and myself. I hope you don't mind me taking it out in the pants. You know how funny you are.

At present our garden is looking splendid. There are nine pink rosebuds, and a lovely yellow dahlia. The oleander and the cassia are both flowering. We are getting more plants daily but unfortunately we have no room to plant them. I went days ago and bought eight verandah orchids for us.

In the King's birthday honours John Goddard (cricketer) got the OBE. At least I think it's that.

Well, that's all for now,

Sati

University College, Oxford
June 10, 1951

Dear Everybody,

This is the last Sunday of this term. When I go down, some time next week, I shan't be coming back till mid-October. I am going to France for a month and am getting a job for some time on an agricultural camp before I go.

I shall do my best with the Ramadhin story, altho' I think it is not quite the right time. But I shall try nevertheless. I suppose that you have received my *Isis* story by now.

I have got one picture of myself and have bought some of the college, but I am waiting for some more of myself before I send them along.

I showed my tutor a story I have written—written in early April—and he likes it very much. As regards writing, I have rested completely this term and it has done me some good, this rest.

Now the days are long. Lights go on about half-past nine at night and it is still quite light by ten. There is something sad about these long days—because you know that the length of the days keeps changing every day and that in two weeks' time the days will begin to grow shorter again until, in winter, it is quite dark at three in the afternoon. But this is the summer month, and in the early weeks of this term I have seen the trees grow green almost under my gaze. For one week a stripped tree—and I am thinking about the one I see across the street through my window—clothes itself in green.

The colours are the colours of paint from tubes—gay and as unbeliev-able as a coloured postcard.

I have done much reading this term. I read *War and Peace,* a novel in three volumes by Tolstoy, *David Copperfield,* E. M. Forster's *Where Angels Fear to Tread* and the big Bennett novel.*

I have just received a letter from Kamla. It contains news of the suicide of a girl I never knew, but whose fame had spread even to me—the Mud-dem girl. So she killed herself for love! One reason is as good as any other. The world is none the poorer, I think, for her death.

Please convey to Miss Millington my really deep grief at the death of her daughter. I don't know why, but people just seem to get news of bad luck. Tell her how sorry I am. It is difficult to feel someone else's sorrow as one does one's own, but I am truly upset. Give her my regards and affection.

I have learnt that Shiva is being hustled about from school to school. Isn't it a bit too early to give him wide and varied experience? But I suppose they won't take him at the Kindergarten. I don't think much harm will come to him anyway. I have been told that he is now of a reserved and contemplative nature; that in his mind he reviews the problems of the world, and dispassionately considers the meaning of life and death. Kamla is somewhat perturbed by this. She fears that he is becoming intellectual. And he is only six! Tell him I love him very much.

I suppose Ma's birthday has passed. I unfortunately cannot remem-ber the day. The only birthdays that are clear in my mind are Kamla's and mine. I merely know the months in which the others occur. I can

---

* *The Old Wives' Tale* (1908)

send no present to Ma. It grieves me, but I can't. All I can send is my love.

Well, I must fly now. I have a tutorial in a few minutes' time.

All my love to all—
Vido

Home: 6/19/51

Dear Vido,

I don't know whether you'll get this letter before you 'go down'. Still, I'm sending it. There is really not much to say, except that I shall soon be getting back to feature-writing—at my own request. Maybe the change will take place at the end of the month.

What about sending the Ramadhin story to *Caribbean Voices*, in your name? Or do you think they'll find it out—as being more or less the same version as what appeared in the *Sunday Gdn*? I shall be listening in for your sketch this Sunday June 24. Is it the story that you say you showed your tutor and which he liked very much?

Where is the agricultural camp on which you will be working before you leave for France? And do you mean that you will not be back at Oxford till mid-October? Because if this is so, I suppose it would be no good our writing you until you are back from France. Clear this up for us if you get this letter in time.

How I wish I could send you some money, but you know I just can't do so. I have sent a 3,000-word story to the BBC but I don't know whether Swanzy will use it. He has another story to hand. End of July, I'll be needing money to pay motor-car insurance; and they have raised the notes by 25%. This means I'll have to pay almost $100. Battery is giving way after 18 months' use and I need a tyre and tube. So you see how things stand and why I'm not able to send you some cash now and then.

We all seem to have a hard battle, but with resolution and courage we'll make it. I wonder if you know how glad I am that you are away and on your own and not depending on the Capildeos for anything. Oh. Those brothers! The less said the better; after all they are only conforming with the majority of mankind.

But I'm very proud of you and of Kamla also, and who knows that the hard times you are passing now will give place to better things, in good time.

Strange that while I had to look up the dictionary to know the meaning of cyst (upon getting your letter) my own eye should be developing the same complaint, so that I had to be on 2 weeks' sick leave. I went to work today. Make sure whether or not your cyst was due to the need of change of glasses consequent from eye strain.

All's well. Affectionately, Pa

Home: 7/23/51

Dear Vido,

I didn't know you would have been receiving letters addressed to you at Oxford. I was in a bit of a mix-up as to your whereabouts; and not getting any letter from you all these long weeks, made me all the more uncertain.

We are all very well, but I suppose you must be quite tired. I wish you could tell me what the work was like on the agricultural camp.

I am sending you today a money order for $10. It will help you see a patch or two of France. It's such a flea-bite, but I'd feel brutal if I didn't send anything at all.

We will be posting you a parcel with sugar, grapefruit, etc. There'll be some cigarettes inside the sugar. See that you get them. The parcel will arrive at about the middle of October, so you should be at Oxford to receive it.

I didn't hear your story very clearly. The fellow was speaking in a mumble. It had something to do about some people moving into a new house, the prose seemed rich. How much did you get for it?

My 'Obeah' was broadcast on July 14. Selvon read it—and read it very well, too. I haven't received the cheque yet. But I have had bad luck with 'The Mohun' story. They've sent it back! And I thought it was such a story!—especially as Mrs Lindo said it had interested her so much that she wished it was longer.

Really, I'm in no mood to write another and this 'reject' has dampened me quite a bit.

Your Nanie and the Sabadors are having big quarrels. The old lady keeps driving them everyday, but they can't get a house to rent or buy. Deo and Phoolo* sleep at us. The others remain at 17.

Gold Teeth Nanie† died last Sunday night at the Col. Hos. and was buried the following day. Your own Nanie wanted to bury her from the Col. Hos. But Tara Slo.‡ persuaded her that people 'would laugh'. After all, she left her house and land to Tara, Miss D'mouth, K. and Miss Dhan; plus jewels.

Write us some long letters about your visit to France. I wish I had a hundred dollars to send you. And you mustn't keep such a long time from writing. One begins to suppose that something dreadful must be happening to you. Kamla has had some trouble with her eyes, but is otherwise all right.

Love from all of us, Pa

University College, Oxford
July 30, 1951

Dear Pa,

Please ignore the other letter. I should have realised that there was a good enough reason for writing. You ought not to have sent that two pounds for me. Please don't feel badly about not sending me money. The discipline, you know, of not having anyone but yourself to depend on is quite good, especially for a man like me. I discover in myself all types of aristocratic traits, without, you know too well, the means to keep them alive. Whenever I go into a new town, I go into the best hotel, just to feel comfortable, sit in the lounge, read all the newspapers, borrowed from clerks who are usually very obliging, and drink coffee. I like comfort. And, whereas in Trinidad, I was tremendously shy of going even into a Civil Service Office, now I go everywhere, firmly believing that I have as much right to be there as anybody else. That is the

---

* Cousins, daughters of Vidia's mother's elder sister Ahilla
† Family friend of the older generation
‡ Maternal aunt, Vidia's mother's younger sister

one good thing Oxford has done for me. It is an expensive university. People expect you to behave easily, and, believe me, you do. Actually the process of my emergence really begins with getting on that plane. For the first time in my life I was dead alone—and I enjoyed it. It continued rather spectacularly with putting up at the expensive hotel in New York, being served obsequiously by porters and hotel waiters, and I found myself strewing tips around as though I had been brought up in luxury, when in fact I did so purely because someone else was going to foot the bill.

By now you will observe what is wrong with my typewriter. I haven't the time to have it repaired.

YOU HAVE ENOUGH MATERIAL FOR A HUNDRED STORIES. FOR HEAVEN'S SAKE START WRITING THEM. YOU CAN WRITE AND YOU KNOW IT. STOP MAKING EXCUSES. ONCE YOU START WRITING YOU WILL FIND IDEAS FLOODING UPON YOU. DON'T LOOK FOR DRAMATIC STORIES OR FOR HUMOROUS STORIES. AS SOMEBODY ONCE SAID, EVEN A HAND IS DRAMATIC. EVERYTHING IS DRAMATIC. MATERIAL YOU HAVE IT EVERYWHERE. LOOK BACK ON YOUR LIFE FROM CHILDHOOD UPWARDS. REMEMBER A SINGLE MAN OR INCIDENT THAT IMPRESSED ITSELF UPON YOU. AND A STORY WILL GROW. ANOTHER POINT. WRITE A STORY AS STRAIGHT OFF AS POSSIBLE. IN ONE DAY OR TWO DAYS. YOU WILL BEGIN LAMELY BUT LATER YOU WILL CATCH YOUR SECOND WIND. I HATE LECTURING YOU THIS WAY BUT I WANT TO HEAR THAT YOU ARE WRITING. I WANT TO HEAR THAT YOU ARE WRITING VERY VERY MUCH. YOU HAVE BEEN IDLE SUFFICIENTLY LONG. SIT DOWN TONIGHT AND WRITE THAT STORY ABOUT THE DROWNED CALF AND THE EXPERIENCED DIVER. THAT IS AN EXCELLENT STORY. YOU KNOW FURTHERMORE THE TYPE OF PEOPLE YOU ARE WRITING ABOUT. IN THAT STORY YOU HAVE THE MAN, HIS WIFE AND THE HORRIBLE WELL AT PETIT VALLEY. THINK. YOU FEAR IT. IT MIGHT MAKE A MAN LIVE IN CONSTANT FEAR, A FEAR BORDERING UPON INSANITY. HE WANDERS AROUND THE WELL. REASON WE ARE HORRIBLY ATTRACTED BY WHAT WE FEAR. FEAR GROWS UPON HIM TO SUCH AN EXTENT THAT HE DECIDES TO FILL THE WELL. HE STEPS ON A ROTTING PLANK. FALLS AND DIES. THERE YOU HAVE TWO STORIES. THINK, THINK AND WRITE.

I can hardly speak to you about writing. I can only urge you. Write straight off, even without correcting your typescript. Finish the story as quickly as possible. Remember, if a story has to have a unity, this can be achieved as best as possible by writing it straight off. And, believe me, when you get in the habit of writing, straight off, you will find that you have hundreds of unwritten stories. Put the rough stories away. Take them up about a fortnight later. And then revise them. Write one short story a week. You can afford to do this. Write. Style and Form and Character will gradually take care of themselves. Please write. The essential thing about writing is writing.

Forgive the lecture. But I want to hear that you are writing. You see, if you write about forty stories, you can choose about sixteen for publication. I have promised that I will do my best. As for me, please continue to have faith in me, until I advise you otherwise. Don't let one rejection make you faint. Writing for radio is different. What reads well in print may make bad radio material. My story which is being broadcast in September has had its prosy parts knocked off. The conversation is being used. Don't worry.

And don't believe that I think I am a good writer yet. I know my limitations. You are the best writer in the West Indies, but one can only judge writers by their work.

Vido

Home: 8/5/51

Dear Vido,

I am VERY glad to know that you will be having another story read in *Caribbean Voices* in September. That is good going; and the fact that you have some others, more or less finished, makes the going all the more prophetic. John Buchan had his first novel published at 19 while still at Oxford. So you are in good company.

I <u>did</u> write you about your story. I said the reception was bad and I couldn't make out the whole story, but just made out the drift of it. And of course I was most anxious to hear it. I THINK you got a good price for it. I got just 10 guineas for 'Engagement'—and it was longer than yours, I THINK. 'Obeah', by the way, fetched me 12 guineas. Not bad.

As a matter of fact, <u>I have</u> written up 'The Diver', but I don't quite like it. It was too easily and quickly done, and I half fear that if I send it to the BBC it will come back. Same thing with 'My Uncle Dalloo'. But I like this story. It is a portrait of Lollo's husband, deceased.

What about the Ramadhin stuff? Suppose you sent it in your name to the BBC's WI programme?

The joke you sent in to the *Manchester Guardian* appeared in blocked form on page 1. It was quite good. A lot of Trinidad legislators are in England just now. If you could get hold of some of them you could send in a story for the *Guardian*.

Although I said I was sending you the postal order for £2, I managed to add one more. So you should get three £1 orders in the envelope.

Go on writing, for progress' sake, and don't mind me. I am all right. I just want to see you do the thing. And I know you can do it. My God! At your age I could hardly manage to write a good letter.

I am going in for orchid-collecting—in a small way. I am using the shade tree on which to hang them. What I have are mostly locals, and most of them have long Latin names—which is the second discouraging thing about the hobby—the first being the expensiveness of it all.

Love from all, Pa

[From Kamla]

August 17, 1951

My dear Vido,

I am remembering you today as my 19-year-old brother. Whether you would like to be remembered or not is too much for me to say. I have been away from you two years and surely you must have changed—mentally and physically. Anyway, just take this birthday greeting as coming from me and don't be angry.

I haven't heard from you for a while, with the exception of that master five lines you sent on.

Still, I was glad it came. It saved me the thought that you were lost. However, you not writing is a good sign, I should think, either you are happy or you have metamorphosed into the Englishman. If not, then what?

On Sunday I leave for Patna. I hope to be there only for a few days.

I shall be posting on the Independence Day paper to you. I couldn't read it but, with the casual glance through, it looked interesting.

Today, we were given another holiday, for Rakhi—when sisters tie bracelets of silk threads on their brothers' hands, feed them sweets and put a tika* on the foreheads. Then, their brothers give them a sum of money. Remunerative, isn't it?

Well, that's all for now. Be a good boy. All my love and Happy Birthday.

Kamla

[From Kamla]

Aug. 18, 1951

My dear Vido,

I should have written long before this, but I never had the slightest idea that you would return so quickly.

By the way, Pa, in his letter, said that he is sending you another small sum of money. I do not think you should return it.

I have a firm belief that you are overworking yourself with story-writing, college work and that silly agricultural farm. Oh, I did write to you, I had completely forgotten.

You are always very worried about something—money, for instance. You should take things easy and not kill yourself in swanning all over the place. I do not know how many things you are trying to do at a time. I am here and I can get loads of stories (of course, I'm an absolute dud at it, but still I can furnish facts to Pa), but I have realised that it's just impossible to do two things at one time. Think of your health first and everything last, and no more agricultural camps.

I envy you slightly. But I am extremely happy to know that you had a lovely quiet stay. You and your women. I am sure they must cost some money. Still, I don't mind but don't go beyond the limit.

---

* Red dot on forehead

I wrote a letter to Capo R. at his Wallington address. I doubt if it would ever get to him now that he has moved from there.

I wish I could be with you for Christmas, but I had better shut my mouth and my mind.

I say, your letter paper, you know what I mean. A few of the girls have gone quite goggle-eyed over it.

The Khurannas will be bringing something to you.

Keep well,

> All my love,
> Kamla

Home: 8.19.51

My dear Vido,

It was hard news for us that you've had an operation for the removal of your appendix. Your Mamie wrote us to say so. According to her, you would have left hospital last Wednesday. I hope you <u>have</u> left and that you are all right; that your asthma too is not troubling you too much. It is plain that you've been having some difficult time—first with your eyes, then a month of farm work, then your appendix. As soon as you can write, please tell us about yourself. To date, except for the letters from your Mamie we don't know what's the position.

The BBC broadcast a version of the last six months of poetry and prose contributions to *Caribbean Voices*. Your story was mentioned, and a little later, my own was mentioned too. Samuel Selvon's first novel got a word or two, and I'd be a liar if I didn't admit that far from feeling well about it, I felt peeved with myself. Wish I were in his shoes.

Can I write at least two stories a week for the *TG*, plus a novel? How I get along is like this: I quietly scribble down my story in bed in the evening; then type it in the office next morning. The next half-day I take it easy at home, or go out for the facts for another story.

The fact is I feel trapped.

Kamla's last letter said that she had fever for about a week. Her eyes are also not very good. We are sending her something by the Khurannas, who will be leaving for India via England on September 1.

Owad is leaving for England on the 13th October. If he really does so, we will be sending you a parcel by him. We have sent you five packs of Anchor Specials by Miss [. . .] of [. . .] Girls', who will be in the UK by about the middle of September. I begged her to take a carton, but she said she could take just five packs—half a carton—because she was also carrying cigarettes for someone else.

Do write us to give us all the news about yourself. With wishes for your speedy recovery—

Affectionately, Pa

Home: 8.20.51

My dear Vido,

Your letter sent from your Mamee's reached us yesterday. Also the pictures of yourself and your college. And what pictures! In those in which you look as though you were still under a shower bath you look thin; in the one in which you sit on a stone wall you look grand. We are relieved to know that you are coming out well after the operation. I am sending you £3 per money order, so that you could get some nourishment which you will certainly need. If funds permit, I'll send you some more money later. But the £3 I'm sending you at this same opportunity.

We are all well at home and just now I'm having a bout of worry because I have been sitting for a portrait (oil) to Johnson—*Guardian* artist—and I get a bit nervous whether I have done right. I'll be paying the man piecemeal, you know.

Yesterday I had my first sitting at White Hall, for two hours. There Johnson takes an art class; and while the students were sat drawing a hand (plaster cast) he went on doing me. When the sitting was over and I had a look at the thing, I got a pleasant surprise. It was me. And a fairly large canvas too. I'll have to do some more sitting—on Monday and Friday afternoons, from 5.30 p.m. to 7.30 p.m..

Don't let this annoy you; I am paying for the picture at my leisure and convenience.

I have developed a craze or mania for orchid collection—already I have some 8 or 9 varieties of them—mostly local ones, so far. But one which I got at the Botanic Garden is worth at least $20. I got a tiny plant for

2/- per a friend in the gardens. It's a very expensive hobby and I am going
to stop as soon as I have got just two or three more of the orchids that I
want.

Tell your Mamee that I shall be ever grateful to her and your Mamoo
for what they have done for you. Your Ma has written your Mamee.

Your Ma is sending you a 'box' parcel by surface mail.

1. Contains: 5lbs sugar in tin
2. 3 tins grapefruit juice
3. 2 tins orange juice & 2 Jamaica Soap (Dream)
4. 2 tins pineapple juice
   Look for 3 pcks of cigs. In sugar.
5. 1 Bott. Guava Jelly
   Also 2 copies *DG*.

> Yours affectionately,
> Pa

University College, Oxford
August 20, 1951

Dear Everybody,

As you probably know by now, I have spent some time in hospital.
A rather pleasant two weeks in fact, down with that shameful disease—
appendicitis. Sophistication seems to breed it! For the second time since I
have been in this country I have had my asthma—it came on with the
appendicitis and gave me a bit of trouble, for coughing with a cut in your
stomach is decidedly painful.

The doctor gave me an injection of adrenaline for the asthma attacks
and it worked wonderfully. Within five minutes I was able to breathe reasonably well.

But I really enjoyed the stay, especially as it was free. My holiday in
France, however, has had to be abandoned and I am naturally disappointed.

I am staying with Mamee—perhaps for a week—and then, if strength
permits, I shall travel about England, as far as money permits. The illness
has had another bad effect. You see, for the three weeks that preceded it, I
wrote every day and I had really found myself going. Yesterday I tried to

continue where I left off but it was no use. That, more than any thing else, distresses me.

I am glad that joke about the *Manchester Guardian* appeared; but the people haven't even sent me five shillings! They have sent nothing as a matter of fact.

I am really quite well now and there is no need to worry.

No more news I am afraid; I am not in the mood to write really. When I am I shall probably dispatch a longer letter.

I was 19 on holiday. And—oh! I feel so old.

Love to everyone—Vido

Have you received the photographs yet? Send me a cutting of the *M. Guardian* joke please.

University College, Oxford
August 29, 1951

Dear Kamla,

Thanks for your letters and for the birthday card.

Laziness, laziness—blame that for my not writing before. It may be of interest that I had my appendix taken out, but that is really no excuse. After all, I was able to walk three days after the operation. It meant, however, that I had to cancel my trip to Cannes. With the money refunded I intend to go to Paris for a fortnight. For a long time I was undecided; typewriter or Paris. But I need a holiday—after 3 weeks' farm-work, and 4 weeks' enforced rest.

At present I am staying with the Capos in their new house at Clapham. They have been rather kind to me, but I miss the freedom to which my lone-wolf year has accustomed me: a room of my own and at least one chair and a table. The children nauseate me.

News: Richard is married to an ugly, 30-year-old Englishwoman. You can guess the type. I ran into Richard and his mate at Oxford about 4 weeks ago, when they were on their honeymoon. Fool! Fool! And bigger fool she!

I am naturally upset about your eyes. I do hope you regain proper sight soon. I am in the best of health myself.

Afternoon

Have just returned from the city, where I bought my ticket for
Paris. I am travelling by plane, and will leave for Paris next Tuesday
(Sep. 4).

The typewriter on which this letter is being completed is not my own,
as you can guess. It is Capo S.'s.

I look out of the window before me and I see the side of a large red-
brick cinema on my right, and trees and red-brick houses, one like the
other, on my left. It is late summer, and the worst of the hot months is gone.
Now all England is preparing to subside into the mellowing tones of
autumn, and the countryside will seem scorched into a brown-red haze;
then lorries and motor cars will kick up whirlpools of dead yellow and
brown leaves. The English autumn is definitely the most beautiful thing I
have experienced, and I look forward to taking walks in Oxford during the
term that comes in seven weeks.

My position, as far as money is concerned, is not as desperate as it
was in the last two weeks of June, when I was literally penniless, and literally, too, didn't know where my next meal was going to come from. But
something always did turn up—a friend, usually. And the man at the
Ashmolean Museum at Oxford bought me regular teas, and even gave me
two pounds. But all that is past; there is no need to worry now. I am comfortable. Please don't blame yourself. I never expected the money at all. Pa
sent me three pounds a month ago. The money hurt me more than anything
else: I know how much they had to deprive themselves of to send $15. I
shall send them five pounds at the end of September, from the money that
I hope comes in for another one of my stories that is being broadcast next
month.

I am writing pretty steadily, and the old problem of what to write about
no longer bothers me.

I can let you know that all is not well in the state of Capos. Capo S. has
been here for a year now, and has not yet got a job. There is constant talk of
going back to Trinidad. I can sense a straining of the relations between the
brothers. The children are not very fond of their cousin: they parody
him, and Deven occasionally roughs him up. The house at Wallington has
been sold, and Ruth, by herself, is moving to Brighton. So there! Judge for
yourself.

About the cigarettes, I think I told you that I had to pay a whopping big duty on them. So kindly send me no more.

Goodbye and I hope your eyes get better soon.

Vido

[birthday card]

On your 19th Birthday!

[inside]   Happy Birthday Greetings, Son—
             May every hour be gay,
             Success crown all the hopes and plans
             You cherish on Life's way;
             The Best of Luck and Good health too
             Be yours today and all Life through!

To Vido—

From Ma
Pa
and Everybody home

18 rue de la Sorbonne, Paris 5
September

Dear Everybody,

I have been in Paris for a week and have only just come across a post office.

Paris is wonderful. But it is terribly expensive: a meal costs about 8 shillings. I am all alone, but I have always been meeting interesting people.

In Paris one feels freer than in London. The people here are more relaxed and I feel at home. My landlady, too, is wonderful. Of course, I am not terribly healthy. No pains or anything, but I get tired very quickly and have to stop and rest every so often.

Would you believe it? I am a mere 10,000 words from the end of my novel. I have sent part of it to the man at Oxford. He thinks it is good, and, what is more exciting, eminently readable. So there. By the end of this month, I am going to send it to publishers. Frankly I am in no doubt about its being accepted.

There are thousands of Negroes and Arabs in Paris, and they are treated excellently by everyone. And how incongruous it is to see Indians looking for all the world like Parisians under a heavy tan, talking French! How strange it is to hear a little Indian boy muttering complaints to mama in French! And to hear Indo-Chinese speaking French!

Of course the first sentence I spoke on French soil was: *'Où sont les toilettes?'*—i.e. 'Where are the lavatories?' I was in a panic, for at school one is respectable, and no one ever does ask the French for lavatories. I order food at random—largely vegetables—and don't know what on earth I am going to get.

I will write some more before I leave Paris; but goodbye now!

Yours,

Vido

Paris,
September 13, 1951

My dear Kamla,

This is my last day in Paris. I have not been having a wonderful time, as all good postcard-writers say. I have been having a quiet, agreeable stay.

Originally I had planned to leave on Monday the 17th, but I have had to change my plans. As usual: a woman. This time she was Finnish. We met in Montmartre, the painters' district, and we spent three delicious days together. She even put off going to Finland for a day. But she left yesterday and I can't bear to stay on any longer in Paris without her. She is marvellous really. She has spent a year in America and, despite this, she is fascinating. She collects turtles and records of Arabian music! And when she said that she was going to call one of her turtles—we had bought two in a Paris shop—after me, what could I do?

I would give anything to be able to see her in Finland before term begins and to spend a month with her during the Xmas vacation. But—money! money!

I am not terribly healthy. I am very weak and constantly need to sit down. And I find it difficult to sleep.

What can I tell you of Paris? It is wonderfully full of monuments. But I sense an underlying unhappiness among the people. Paris is a jaded city, littered with monuments to dead and mocking glories. The glamour evaporates in a night and you realize that the grind is as hard as in England. The world has nothing new to offer. Only people can be exciting.

And frankly, as Maugham says, beauty is a bit of a bore.

I am afraid I am a terrible brother really. Sending you only very sketchy notes. Forgive me, will you?

I have only a few hours in which to get ready to go to the airport.

Love, from Vido

V

September 20, 1951 – January 8, 1952

MICHAELMAS TERM, CHRISTMAS VACATION

Dear Everybody,

I owe you a long letter and I sit down tonight with the intention of writing the longest letter I have ever sent home. So if this letter is long, and if you get no more for a fortnight or so, you will know that the reason is that I have exhausted myself.

Well, this letter is going to be divided into three parts—my thanks and my advice; Paris; and my slight achievements and disappointments. Don't be too alarmed by that last word!

Well, aren't we all quite mad! Imagine my dear old man having his portrait painted in oils and going into boyish ecstasy over the fact; imagine him, further, suddenly conceiving a passion for expensive gardening. Well, it is mad, perhaps, but I like it. I approve, if my approval helps at all, that is! What amateur and immature Customs-dodgers you are, my dear people. Your Campbell-soup box arrived just crated with sugar. The sugar-tin lid was off, and the tin itself seemed to have been the victim of a malicious attack. It was dented and battered; half the sugar was spilled in the box and was, when I got it, a neat pastel grey. And there were these incriminating cigarette packets sitting so obviously, so loudly begging to be seen, that I am surprised you have not been rounded up for questioning. I saw something about ½ bar soap (local) in the blue inventory stuck on the parcel; but no soap arrived. It doesn't matter, anyway. Thanks very much for the parcel. But listen now, please don't send any more parcels unless I ask for them. Sugar I don't need. I have given Mamie the 6lbs you sent me by her. Guava jelly is exotic: I pass that. Cigarettes involve too much trouble. So just don't send any parcels unless I ask for them. There was quite a batch of letters waiting for me when I got back to Oxford today (I did not have them forwarded to Paris) and among the letters was a note from Rostand, about the cigarettes. I shall drop her a line tonight, when I get through with the mammoth task I have set myself. So that's that, as far as acknowledgements of gifts and letters are concerned.

It is upsetting that dear little Shivan hasn't got into Tranquillity yet. Not that I think his education is going to suffer, but I am afraid that he is not allowed to sit the exhibition examination. Give him my love. I am afraid I have to give up Mira and Satti and Savi as dead losses. I sincerely hope I get rich enough to do something for them. What do those girls do all day? The news that Shivan is beating pans is distressing. The news that he used the kitchen floor as a lavatory is amusing and, on second thought only, shocking.

And now a word about the £6 I have received so far from you. Receiving the money is painful to me. It makes me quite unhappy. If I need money I shall write. Don't send me money you cannot afford. I can take care of myself for the time being. Now this is important: I want a copy of *Gurudeva*; and I want copies of all the other stories you have written. I shall pay you back the £6 by having those stories typed and sending them to publishers. I am not doing this all on my own drive. I had tea with Swanzy at the BBC in Oxford Street two days ago, and here, as far as I can recollect, is what he said of you, Pa: 'Your father is a damned good writer. His stories are as good as, perhaps better than, those stories by Indian writers that are published in this country. Why don't you try to get him a publisher at the same time you look for a publisher for your novel? He is a realistic writer, but he has a sense of humour. He describes Indian ceremonies with charm; though one does get tired of the details of these ceremonies and of Indian marriages (reason for the rejection of "Mohun"). I can't understand why he isn't better known in Trinidad.' So you see you had better send me your stories. And, oh, there was more: 'He is a natural writer; but I think he is the one writer in the West Indies whom I would urge to have DISCIPLINE. He tends to grow wistful about the older generation; but that, perhaps, is because he is of the older generation.' So send me your stories.

While I am on the subject of Swanzy, I had better say that I got eight guineas for 'The Mourners'.* Personally I think it is a good story. That was the story my tutor liked. Swanzy said that he owed me an apology for hav-

---

* Vidia's first published short story

ing the story read by a Jamaican girl. He promised to give me some reading parts some time. I don't mind getting the extra cash. And, now, about my magnum opus: *The Shadow'd Livery*.* Satti will probably remember the name. This morning, at half-past eleven, I wrote the end to what has turned out to be a 277-page thing in typescript (a little more than 70,000 words or 210 pages in an ordinary-sized book). The man at the Ashmolean Museum here, who has read the first 50,000 words, thinks it highly readable. So it appears that, with luck, Father and son will have first books out at almost the same time. I hope one of us does strike the jackpot!

You ask about my health. I am fine. To demonstrate how close the affinity between Pa and myself is, I must say here that I know what his indigestion pains are. In Paris—where they eat only 2 meals a day—I developed it for 2 days. But it was to be expected. 3 meals a day for 18 years, 4 meals a day for one year, and then, suddenly, 2 meals a day! Since I began taking my four meals a day I am fine, thank you.

I have some news for you; but keep it under your hat. The Capo brothers don't get along too well. There is no open hostility but both parties criticise each other to a neutral like myself; and there is talk—now almost the intention—to return to Trinidad before the end of the year. I feel sorry for Capo S. He has managed to get no work. The bright hopes promised by his brother just didn't exist; further the M. Sc.'s behaviour is repugnant to them. He treats the children, Mamie thinks, rather ill. He grows angry when his brother's friends come home; and, on occasion, is deliberately rude. They don't like it here, I can tell you. But they have treated me quite well. It was on Mamoo's typewriter that I pounded out the last 25,000 words of my novel. They gave me an egg a day for almost a fortnight—and eggs are rationed and expensive here.

Shall I save Paris for another letter? It is quite late now. Yes, I think I will. I am terribly sorry I didn't make this a whopping letter, but I want to have something to write about next time.

By the way, something got me quite annoyed. That *Manchester Guardian* thing. Lord, they just didn't print what I wrote. What asses the

---

* Vidia's first attempt at a full-length novel, with the title later given to a book about Trinidad by a fictional character (Foster Morris) in *A Way in the World* (1994)—see Bibliography

sub-editors can be sometimes. Isn't it surprising how much things can upset you? That upset me all afternoon.

Well, goodbye. Love to Ma and the rest.

> A loving son and brother,
> Vido.

Kindly remember me to Jainarayan. He probably curses me, but ask him not to.

Sep. 29, 1951

My dear Vido,

I ought to have written long before now, but I had been in a hell of a worry and fret because of the carrying-ons of your cousins Deo and Phoolo. I had never realised, until about three weeks ago, how shockingly 'advanced' these girls have become. You know, they live with us; and I found myself—and still do find myself—in a position of not knowing what to do: whether to tell them to go away or to let them go on with their lamentable perversity. These girls have become so ultra-modern that they make no distinction between Negroes, Mussulmans or any other people. Deo says, without the semblance of a blush, there's nothing bad or ugly in a Hindu girl marrying a Negro boy. Her actual words: 'What does it matter as long as you can be happy?' As to Muslims: 'Why, they are only human.' They have not merely expressed these things as mere opinion. They are nostril-deep in the thing. A week or so ago Phoolo brought in a young black-as-coal (I assure you I do not exaggerate) dougla.* She wanted to know what I thought of her marrying this man. Your Ma and everybody else was at home, around the table. I could not but be cold to the fellow. And after about five minutes of desultory this and that kind of a talk, left. The two sisters—Deo and Phoolo—walked with him to the gate. And this is what shocked me most—says Deo: 'He is a nice fellow. Much better than Parsad.' Now, this Parsad was another suitor that Phoolo had brought in one or two evenings before: a handsome young Hindu boy of about 23, a civil servant in the GPO.†

---

* Half Indian, half African
† General Post Office

When both your mother and I observed that the man—the Dougla that is—was dougla, Deo *insisted* he was all right, a pure Indian of Madrasi parentage. And this girl, Phoolo, aided and abetted by the elder, had been going around with this dougla, with the straight intention of marrying him, for many a long month. Now, she assures me that she has given him up.

But it is not with Phoolo that I have been having any trouble, but with Deo. The girl has gone head-over-heels, as they say, in love with a Mussulman named Isaac Mohammed, a drummer in the Indian orchestra that plays for Radio Trinidad. Twice or thrice a week this girl *must* meet this Mussulman—a seller of pallets on the road—and must be out with him till late at night. Her own brother tells me he has seen them go to the pictures. Phoolo tells me that the other day Deo took him into Stephens even to see him approve the measure and pattern of a skirt she was getting. I have come upon these two at nine at night promenading—with our own Mira leading the way.

And Deo insists she will not marry. At the first she denied knowing the fellow at all; now she blatantly tells me that she has known him for more than a year; but that more than talking with him there's nothing. I don't mind telling you I can hardly believe her. She goes to a desperate extent to meet this man. She'd say she was going to her mother's for a short time, when in fact she is gallivanting with this Mussulman boy, who hasn't even so much as a settled job to live on. And pretending she is just going to Dhan's, she takes Mira and Savi with her. Can I put up with this thing?

I have begged her over and over to give up going to Radio Trinidad's studio. She could hear the programme much better at home; but even while saying, sure she hates Mussulman and does not care a jot about going to the studio, the studio is where she is going to.

Deo never goes out in company. She goes out alone and at dusk. Deo goes to see a friend off by the Colombie. She goes aboard. The ship sails away 11 p.m., but Deo does not come home till 1 or 1.30 in the morning . . . comes, too, in a car, with a married man (Mangatal) boy-friend. She goes to the ship with us in *our* car. She remains on board ship all the time, without so much as a word to your Ma or to me that she will not be returning home with us.

I cannot help thinking that this girl has already gone astray . . . none of the family would take her, except Dhan; and I am afraid that if she does anything funny, I'd be blamed because the thing happened from my home.

She abhors marriage; she is openly contemptuous towards the Indian way of life. I know orthodox Hindu conditions are discouraging; but I think this girl's abhorrence springs not from any knowledge of things Indian, but rather from her stark ignorance of things Indian. The Hindu religion has left no impression to the good. Girls who are apathetic towards marriage are often enough people who enjoy the satisfaction of cohabitation without the responsibility of marriage. It may be clever, but it is also a cowardly attitude . . . You will wonder that I should allow myself to be so extremely agitated in this matter that after all does not touch my home.

But it does touch my home . . . what about the example these girls are setting?

Not a word of all this to Deo and Phoolo. In the first place I'm trying hard to get them out of the mess. Most of the members of the family hate them. I must show them sympathy and understanding . . . Give me your view on this matter. Write c/o the *Guardian* . . . Will send the stories soon.

All of us are all right.

Affectionately,

Pa

Home: 9.29.51

Dear Vido,

We received your very satisfactory letter a few days ago. I <u>warned</u> your mother that parcel of hers would be shattered by the time it reached you. I had some concerns that the cigarettes will be discovered by the Customs people. That too was Mrs Naipaul's handiwork. All right then, we won't be sending you any more parcels.

Did Swanzy really speak so highly of me? Then, why the Dickens he sent back my story? Anyway, the booklet and the stories will be following the letter surface mail. But mind, the copies of some of the stories are not quite the copies that I sent to the BBC. So you may have to patch up.

I have some slight recollection of reading *The Shadow'd Livery* somewhere, but I can't remember in what place. Nobody seems to know anything about it.

You wrote a very sweet letter indeed. Write plenty more like it. Short letters are not half as satisfying.

I am sorry for Capo S.—really I am. And I must be a darn good judge of human nature, for I had secretly correctly summed up the situation. Those children will be in trouble if their parents returned to Trinidad without them.

As soon as your novel is accepted, write me. I'll put it in the *Guardian*. And, in the meantime, do send me the short story. We couldn't hear so much as a sentence. Reception was extremely bad, and after about ten minutes they shut off.

Want to hear something about Shivan? His teacher, a girl, asked him what kind of work did his father do; and Shivan assured her that his father was a <u>DOCTOR</u>. And the good lady believed him and never knew me as anything else until she met your mother. I suppose 'Doctor' sounds big to Shivan much as it sounds big to most people.

I do two features every week, so that not much time is left me to write anything else—unless I took no time off for some sleep every day in ten. Of course I am well-known as a writer locally—but only locally, and for local fame I don't have any great craving.

All of us are very well at home. I like my portrait. Cost me $52. Want to get another for your Ma. Have my own in the middle, with you and Kamla flanking either side of the wall downstairs.

Love from all, Pa

Univ. College, Oxford
Sep. 30, 1951

Dear Kamla,

Well, I am back in Oxford; the term has not begun, and none of my friends are about. So I am really quite alone. I wonder if many people have been alone as I have been for the past year, and for most of my 'years of awareness' as a matter of fact. The point is I find people—especially these bright young sparks at Oxford—quite insipid and their conversation and company tedious. I am too old for this place. In Oxford all the boys play at being grown-up. It is most distressing. I really do hope you have not been as lonely as I.

It is with difficulty that I prepare myself for the term's work. As you probably know, I idled all last term. I wrote 2 essays instead of the customary 8. But I had many decent excuses—eye trouble, and asthma and things of that sort.

If my typewriter were good I would type off another story for the BBC. I have already had two broadcast and I do need the money from the third. On the twentieth of this month at about half-past eleven in the morning, I wrote 'The End' to my novel, about which I have been dropping hints for the last sixteen months. Well, *alors c'est fini*. And what a relief! The man at the Ashmolean Museum here has the novel now. He has already read ⅔ which I sent him before going to Paris. He is very pleased with it; thinks it readable, funny, and 'extremely well-written'. Frankly I am inclined to agree with him. Tomorrow I am having tea with him, and will hear his opinion of the novel as a whole. It appears that a good friend of his is a director of the publishing firm of Secker and Warburg— reputable people. And he has undertaken to do the 'peddling' of my opus. Wish me luck. I shall be so happy if this novel brings me some money for Ma and Pa.

I am afraid I have become a writer. The more I write, the more I want to write. And I don't enjoy writing. You see, characters begin to live in your mind. One character has been keeping me awake for a couple of nights. Let her grow; I shan't throw her out of my head just yet. While she is with me, I am not worried. It is the same sentiment you know that prompts you to eat the yolk of an egg after the white—or to keep the best part of a meal for the last bite—or to keep your highest card for the last hand. Does this make sense? It should.

As I grow older, I find myself doing things that remind me of Pa, more and more. The way I smoke; the way I sit; the way I stroke my unshaved chin; the way in which I sometimes sit bolt upright; the way in which I spend money romantically and foolishly. I am afraid Pa won't like this. For he will presently have no secrets from me. The more I learn about myself, the more I learn about him. Please don't lose your affection for Ma. She is worthy of all that we can give. We oughtn't to disappoint her. She is the type that suffers in silence, poor dear! I love her; but who has shaped my life, my views, my tastes? Pa.

And now there is something you must do. I want you to expect nothing great from me. Never think that someday you will see my name in lights. I don't think you will. And I don't want you to be hurt or disappointed. I had a frightening dream last night. I promised myself, crying, to write 1,000 words a day for, 'You see,' I told myself, 'you have only one more year of life. You have cancer. Write 1,000 words a day. For every 1,000 words you write, you will get £1,000.'

University College, Oxford
October 1, 1951

Dear Ma,

I had tea this afternoon with Ian Robertson, the man at the Ashmolean Museum here. He is very pleased with my novel, so pleased, in fact that tomorrow he is sending it off to the director of the publishing firm Secker & Warburg. Let's not expect too much anyway. But this publisher is a friend of his and he had already been told to expect my novel that is going, in a crudish, criss-crossed, pencilled and penned draft, to him.

Ran into John Harrison last Saturday, had lunch, and spent about four hours with him.

Manin and Mamie treated me excellently while I was ill. Mamie, of course, was ever kind to me. And even Manin, now a sad and disappointed man, has softened. Capo R. and I got along famously. Don't ask me why. But even Boyzee wanted to know how I manage to talk pleasantly and be talked to pleasantly! So there. No need to fear of any fiery tempers. I have besides a standing invitation to stay at their house in London whenever I want (for short periods, of course). As far as I know it is definite that Capo S. is going back to Trinidad—perhaps next Feb'y, unless something big turns up. Which I hope for, but which is, sadly, unlikely.

I hate to talk about the weather, but it is autumn now; the leaves are growing brown and falling, the mornings are chilly and foggy.

Love to everyone.

Vido

PTO

Shirts here cost anything from 30/- to 60/-. Naturally beyond me.

In about three months I shall be needing about 2 shirts. If you buy them and wash them, I shall have to pay no customs duty. Better yet, mark my name on them. This is just a warning. Don't buy any until I send the money.

Vido

Please don't send me money.

Room No. 40
Women's Hostel,
Benares Hindu University
Oct. 4, 1951

My dear Vido,

Now if I were only near you, do you know what I'd like to do—give you a good knock on the head. You and your dreams and your writing and what next? I don't know what should follow. You are living in this world and all you are doing to yourself is making your life miserable by trying to live out of it. What you do need is a good dose of 'me'. But it's impossible to do it from this far.

Another thing, I am expecting you to do real good, not only in writing but also in college. I will be disappointed with any other result.

Next. Will you please stop trying to do two things at one time—Are you a Napoleon?

You are quite all right, you are fit for this world, and every other thing (even to be dumped with the sea at times), so stop getting fancy ideas into your head.

Everything you say does make sense. But I am afraid I don't like you to be so profoundly sensible.

I wish you every success in your novel. And I mean it from the bottom of my heart. But I can't help but worry over your overworking yourself. It's really distressing to me.

Good grief! I have been preaching too much. But I jolly well mean all I have said.

Tomorrow college closes for the Puja vacation. I am staying right here.

The light in my room has attracted thousands of tiny insects, which keep flirting with you all the time. The result is that I am on my bed, far away from the light, writing this letter.

There are many things that I have to say but all I shall keep in my heart till I see you personally—say the next 18 months. Don't worry, time will fly. Do you wish to see what I look like sometimes—if I am the same Kamla? I often think of you but it's impossible to connect your present self with what you were at home.

Now be a sweet little boy, will you, and STOP DREAMING!

Lots of love,
Kamla

Now don't feel sad over my sending this cheque, because I should feel hurt.

[From Kamla]

Oct. 13, 1951

My dear Vido,

I wish you wouldn't talk so about yourself. It seems that we are in the same boat—terribly worried about home. Really, I have become so thin that people refuse to believe their eyes. But that really doesn't matter.

Don't let that novel of yours get you down-hearted. Take it easy in your college days. Maybe, something would turn up later. But you can't expect to do good at one shot.

I expect my letters of home must have reached you by now. Well, Ma and Pa are there and if they can't control Sati while we are away, it's really too bad for them. But one thing, if I find this affair going on at home, then, I surely won't stay. What's going to become of those three sisters, I really can't say. Gosh, how I wish they were all boys. Anyway, let's hope for the best, I might be going home in a year's time. At least, I will have to.

I think what you should do now is to stop worrying. You know you just can't expect to make money and study at the same time. But what I think you should really do is this—study, get through your exams and return home for a job (please don't get wild) or else try to get a job in the WI University. You know that what you like is a luxurious life and in England, it's impossible to have a luxurious life. It is time you learn to be practical in life.

I would so like to do all I can for you. But, you know how it is. All I can ask you, please dear, is to have patience for one year, after which I would be able to send you the extra £20. Just be very patient and economical for one more year. Don't think of marrying for money. You know it's no good. Make your own money and you'll enjoy it all the more.

All my love, Kamla

[Note]:

I haven't been anywhere for the burning summer or during the last vac. Do you know why? I said it was because I wanted to study. But I was lying. It was because I had no money. And I am sure that for a time I was the only human being on the campus. Let this give you some courage. Be brave and keep smiling. Something will turn up.

Oxford,
November 8, 1951

My dear Kamla,

I am most dreadfully sorry about the delay in replying, and, as usual, I can offer no excuse. It was downright laziness on my part and perhaps discourtesy. I must thank you very much for the £5 you sent me. It was very useful.

You know, I do wish I had about £200 more a year to live on. Life here would be then simply perfect. As it is, my walls are bare: I can't afford suitable pictures. I can't afford to have many friends—usually people who could be useful to me later on—because I can't buy them drinks. My holidays are the dullest things imaginable, because I can't travel either abroad or even in England. I can't buy a decent typewriter: my old one is just finished now, and I have at least one story that should have been sent to the BBC a long time ago, and for which I would have got another eight guineas. I can't afford shoes. I just have two old pairs that soak in water; no black pair. I have no decent mackintosh, and only a poor overcoat. All in all, it is pretty grim. Look, if you know of any rich girl who wants an intelligent husband, recommend me, will you?

Home affairs. Sad, isn't it? Just in case you haven't, you must hear now that Deo is chasing penniless men, Phoolo niggers, and Tara douglas. So there! And think of Satti and the rest. You know, you never can trust girls and I find great difficulty in trusting Satti. Even when I was teaching at QRC, embarrassing rumours reached me—from boys who didn't know she was my sister. I wish you would write her some stern letters. Women perhaps know how to talk to women. I am really worried.

More sad news. My novel has been rejected by one publisher. The evening of the rejection I was as low as on that evening of the scholarship result. Now it is in the hands of a second publisher and I am waiting, waiting.

About 4 weeks ago a bearded man came into my room. I didn't know him. He fumbled for my name, I helped him, and he announced that he had known you in India. His name is Colin Turnbull. He is getting to be quite a boy here—his picture in the *Radio Times,* talks on the BBC, a book commissioned by Harrap's. I am going to spend the next weekend with him. I hope he isn't homosexual. Nearly every other man one meets in this country is homosexual.

I had the Capo S. brood up here about three weeks ago. The children, as usual, were terribly bad-behaved, and it was most embarrassing showing them around. I have never seen kids of seven or eleven in this college before I brought my cousins. However, everything passed without incident; and after all, they were kind to me when I was ill.

I wonder what plans you have made for your livelihood after India. Do let me know something. I have none about my post-Oxford career, but I am not worried. Something always turns up for me. Who knows, my novel may be published next year!

Because I spent almost four months of the vacation working, being ill and writing a novel, I naturally had no time to do much college work. It has therefore piled up and I am trying to work hard this term.

So life continues as dully and insipidly as ever for me—here. And when I think that I wanted so badly to come to Oxford and England! My only consolation is that life would have been infinitely more insipid in Trinidad.

Love,
Vido

Home: 11/10/51

Dear Vido,

I was glad that you destroyed the letter you intended sending to Satti. It would have hurt her terribly and done her some harm. Satti is not a bad girl, you know. She is tall now and looks very dignified to and from school. She is very sensitive, and when not in a bad mood has a sense of humour, so much so that she is sometimes apt to become or to appear frivolous. If you asked her, 'Well, what are you reading?' she'd teasingly reply, 'Comic Strips, and True Romances.' In fact she <u>does</u> read comics, but True Romances and such stuff only when some other person such as Velma drops home a copy. For the rest, the girl is really working hard, studying late nights for her exam, which is only a few days away.

All of my children, so far, are good children. Some, like Savi, are at times shockingly rude, but none of them is innately so. Of course Satti is stubborn sometimes. The other day she wanted to go to inter-college football match. I said she should take Savi and Mira with her. She insisted on going alone, but in the end climbed down her stubbornness. I feel you'd do her a lot of good and put plenty of ambition and pride in her—pride about race and religion—if you'd write her and tell her things endearingly. She'd be very proud, I know. But condemn her, and you'd tie knots in her that would be difficult to loose. I would rather you wrote her a letter or two, even if you had to skip writing a general letter.

Phoolo and Deo left us quietly yesterday morning. Deo had been carrying away her things piecemeal for a week or more. All my begging and scolding that she give up the company of low people and that of her drummer boy-friend seem to have been in vain—throwing water on a duck's back. What you said about them is very true, indeed. I, too, am in a better frame of mind since they have gone.

Alladeen has given me two of his pictures: a pen and ink drawing of a Hindu priest poring over a book; and a large pastel work of a shango dancer. He put before me some half a dozen pictures and asked me to have my pick. He suggests that I allow him to do a portrait of me as soon as he gets the time to do so. But I think I'd let him paint your Ma's portrait instead.

I think you should write home at least once a fortnight as a rule. After all, what other link is there between you and home but letters? You should write more regularly, however short your letter.

What about your novel? Has the publisher replied yet? You must tell me all about it. I am quite well and so is everybody else. Three of my orchids have flowered, but I don't mind saying the Monday Throat was quite disappointing: an insignificant flower, almost colourless, without fragrance. But the Butterfly is a little beauty, I assure you. Butterflies do mistake it for a butterfly. And my Cedros Bee has been in bloom for two weeks and still looks pretty fresh. Alas! I have no Cattleya to speak of. They are much too expensive—at least $10 for one plant; and the best one costs $200, believe it or not.

I have what I am told is a very rare orchid; Silogene, it's called, but I'm not sure I've spelt the name correctly. Love from all of us.

Pa

University College, Oxford
November 15, 1951

Dear Everybody,

Pa has guessed the reason why my letters to home just stopped dead. The novel has been rejected. But I have got over my depression. The news about my novel just made me quite indifferent to everything. Today I feel mentally flabby, not having written anything since Sep. 23, not having read anything besides college books since term began.

I wonder if you will be impressed. But, at any rate, I can try. So far I have read all Chaucer and all Spenser—together with about 1,000 pages in double column of Bible-size print! This week I am reading *Paradise Lost*. So perhaps you can appreciate how much work there is to do.

Thanks for the photographs you sent. You all certainly did choose the poorest light? By the way, is Satti wearing rimless glasses? They would look grotesque on her face. Mira is, I am afraid, the most distinguished-looking of the 3 girls. Tell Satti I wrote her an extremely nasty letter, but tore it up. I criticised her handwriting and her studies—lack of, rather.

Tomorrow I am leaving for London. I am spending a weekend out of Oxford, with a man who knew Kamla in India. He has returned to this country as a sort of religious crank: he has grown a beard and is a vegetarian. He gives talks on the BBC and writes an occasional letter to *The Times*. He is full of praise for India, for Benares and for Kamla, and assures me that Indian university degrees are not altogether despised. As an old Oxford man, he should know.

Love to all, from
Vido

University College, Oxford
December 1, 1951

Dear Everybody,

I am so glad that the disquiet at home has disappeared.

If I have not written frequently home this term it was because I really had much work to do. I had to read all Spenser and all Milton—and that is really a lot of reading.

I spent a weekend, about a fortnight ago, with the family of a man who knew Kamla in India. I thoroughly enjoyed my weekend for the man had a car and, together with some other friends of his, we were able to go driving about—from Horsham in Sussex to Chichester, where there is a wonderful cathedral, to Portsmouth. We got to Portsmouth about eleven Sunday night and returned to Horsham at about 2 in the morning. Next morning we were in London. I visited the Capos, then my friend took me to his club in the West End; I left London for Oxford by the 1.30 coach. Very pleasant and very interesting.

My tutor, I am happy to say, is pleased with my work. It is true that I do not write many essays—I have written only 4 this term—but when I do write an essay it turns out to be a really excellent one. This is not boasting; for my tutor is truly impressed. He wants to see my novel; if he thinks it is good he will first of all get the college to give me a grant of £15 to get it properly typed, then he will try to get it published. Robertson at the Ashmolean remains impressed by the novel and seems to be in no doubt that I will get it published some time and that I will be a good writer one of these days.

Because of this, my Dean (whose father was the Headmaster of Eton) has grown much more friendly towards me and has promised to pay for the repair of my typewriter, and this will cost about 50 shillings. 'Indians,' he said, 'are very charming, very practical, some even geniuses. But you are so startlingly incompetent.' I took this all in good humour.

This term shall be over on the eighth of this month. I was hoping to go to Spain, but my money will not perhaps permit this. But no worry. I have a lot of work to do and I have to get back to my short stories. I think I shall spend the 8th–14th in London. There is a German in London whom I want to see; I have no doubt that if I play my cards correctly I may be invited to Germany to spend Christmas! Let's hope anyway.

And I shall tell you this about the Germans I have met: they respect Indians, and are attracted to them. I was sitting in a restaurant one day. A girl—blonde—sat opposite me and began smiling. I smiled back and was then instantly laughing, for I found the situation highly amusing. It turned out that she was German. We chatted for a while and then she left. There was, too, the charming woman on the ship, a sixty-year-old German woman whom I met in my lodgings abut 2 months ago—mad on Hinduism and mysticism, the German in the National Gallery in London, who insisted on being friendly and on taking me to a room where the German painters were represented sketchily.

It is getting cold now. A few days ago I bought a pair of gloves—24/- —but necessary.

It is strange—but during this term my circle of acquaintances has suddenly grown and I find all my afternoons occupied. I have also acquired the habit of having tea in restaurants and coffee at 11 p.m. in the Randolph, Oxford's most expensive Queen's Park hotel, where the coffee costs a shilling a time!

This morning, for instance, I had coffee with Robertson. Tonight I am going to see a play. Tomorrow there is a showing of the Film Society. Monday I have tea with someone. Tuesday a meeting of a literary society, with a buffet supper provided by the Dean. Wednesday some Europeans are coming to tea. Last night I went to an At Home of our new Master. All this does sound madly exciting on paper, and perhaps will appear so in retrospect, but it does not seem so to me at the moment.

By the way, let Pa know that I don't like his I'd's and we've's. Use the apostrophe as sparingly as possible.

Love, Vido

1/8/52

My dear Vido,

I have just read your letter in which you speak of having seen the Capos off. They will be landing Friday, this week. I wonder whether Capo S. will be as glum as he used to be with me.

I wish you had told me what size shirt you now wear. You ought to have done this more than a month ago; in which case you would have had the shirts by now. If I do not hear from you on this matter in a fortnight, I shall be buying you 3 shirts, size 14½—the size I wear. You do not have to send us any money. If you do I'm bound to feel rotten about it. We are not quite so badly off, I assure you.

I don't mind telling you, I have even wasted some money. I was fool enough to pay Johnson $15 to do me a small seascape in oil. He ought to have given me it at least a fortnight before Christmas; he told me he had finished the thing—of Maracas Bay—but that he had left it at his house 'today'. The truth is he had not done the picture at all. Up to now I have not got the Pict. Talking about pictures . . . I have framed and hung up your broad unfinished watercolour of the Aiknath shops, at Petit Valley. It looks good.

I have some more snapshots of the homefolk. I have given the negatives to get enlargements and will send you them as soon as I get the pictures; also to Kamla.

I am jammed up with work tonight. I have to finish a 2-instalment story on food production and The Marketing Board. Must do it tonight, for tomorrow morning I have to go for a story on match-making. Yet another story, partly finished, is on 'The Last of the Grass Cutters'—you know, those fellows who bring green grass to stables away from the Caromi Swamps. Naturally when I run through with these I want to rest, loll or sleep.

Kamla has not written us since November; not even a Xmas card. But Velma and Joy were luckier. They got Xmas cards from her.

Last Saturday I tried to do a watercolour painting of the pond in the hollow of Rook Garden. It does not look good. The pond looks more like a rock than like a pond!

I did better doing a seascape from a small photograph of one of the old 'Trinidadians'.

I am worried over Kamla. I can't understand why she is not writing home, yet writing to other people. Please tell her to write.

Sati might have been writing you tonight or tomorrow; but I have just spoiled one of those letter forms—and have used hers. My typewriter, too, is behaving badly, n & g sticking, the v not typing. Your Ma tried to oil the works while I was typing this letter for you. Result: the oil spread over the paper.

Be cheerful. When the time comes you <u>will</u> get a job. If you don't get one right away, you have home. Write some short stories for extra money. Collect them later. Home is bright and gay. Plush carpets and so on. Next week I might have the outside of the house painted. We never forget you for a day.

Pa

VI

January 16, 1952 – April 4, 1952

LENT TERM, EASTER VACATION

University College, Oxford
January 16, 1952

My dearest Kamla,

I returned to Oxford two days ago. The vacation that has just gone by has been the worst I have ever spent in this country. I was extremely depressed and felt intensely homesick. But now I am picking up once more, as the saying is.

Thanks very much for your card. And I realise that in a few days your birthday will be coming round. I shan't send a card, but I offer my best wishes.

Oh, by the way, I am on another Oxford magazine. It is the *Oxford Tory* and, as you can judge by the title, it is a political magazine. But I am not unduly worried by the politics of the paper. I am in charge of layout; and I have designed a cover. I shall send you a copy of the paper, when it comes off the press.

I promise that I shall write both to home and to you once a week. It has been such a long time since I heard from you, but I am to blame for that, I know. I should like some news about you—about your plans. When are you leaving India?

If you have felt as intolerably lonely as I have been feeling for the last five weeks, I realise what a cad I was not to have written. But I do apologise most sincerely and can only offer the excuse that I was so upset that I couldn't even read a newspaper with ease. But all that is over now—I hope. Oh, it is so difficult to grow up! The years seem to stretch endlessly before one and one cannot see the way ahead.

Pa tells me that you haven't written home for a long time. He appears to be hurt and I can understand. Please write him. Many times I fall asleep wishing that I would wake up and find myself back home, that I could nip across 'next door', to Rialto; or that I could ride to Point Cuman for a dip in the sea.

Having done no work whatsoever during the vacation I intend to work as hard as I can this term and I hope my health and my state of mind permit this.

I received some charming photographs from home recently and I understand that some were sent to you, too.

Ruth and Capo R. did invite me for Christmas and I did accept. It was a good thing I did, too, because I was indescribably unhappy. Ruth likes you very much, but I can understand why you felt that you would go mad if you had to live with them for much longer.

Capo R., Owad and myself went to Southampton to see Capo S. off. It was a tiring trip. We got there on Friday 29th at 10 am. We were told that the boat had been delayed till 9 p.m. At 9 p.m. we learnt that the boat wasn't coming till the following day! We did see them off in the end though, and I sent some gifts for the people home.

Please write home soon,

Love,
Vido

1/24/52

My dear Vido,

This letter should have been written earlier, but because I didn't write it the moment the Capos handed us your Xmas presents and your letter, it didn't get written till—now. The best time to write a letter to a fellow is immediately you get one from him.

Thanks for the lovely Xmas presents. Shivan was quite proud of his painting set and jigsaw puzzle. Your Ma's chocolate we all enjoyed; and the Abdullahs* lasted me some three days.

I am very sorry I can't send you the shirts as I had threatened. My car was involved in an accident and it is costing me $90 to put right. I have paid up $10 and owe the garage man the balance. So this leaves me quite 'broke'.

The Capos returned looking happy. I haven't gone to 17 for 8 days, so

---

* Turkish cigarettes

I can't say whether any change has taken place. He was quite nice to me, anyway.

Sati and the others have returned to school. I don't quite know whether Sati intends taking HC. If she does not get a first grade she'll of course do so. I doubt whether she has done better than second grade.

Mira failed her exam—for the second time. Savi passed—coming 20th. Deven is back at QRC on the Exhibition; and Sita is attending the Convent. Suren* is going to Eastern Boys' Gov't, where Romily is HT.† Shivan may get into Tranquillity in April, when Romily's uncle is expected to take up the principalship.

Kamla has stopped writing us. She should tell you why.

Your affectionate, Pa

(Your Ma writes the other side.)

My dear Vido,

Thanks for your Christmas gifts. I do hope you are in the best of health as Mamie say please take good care of yourself and don't be too careless.

Kamla has not written us a line since Nov. neither a Xmas card. I will be glad if you can find out the reason from her and let me know. She can never realise how much harm and grief she is causing. I cannot see the reasons for not writing us.

Well this is one thing I am begging you not to do don't marry a white girl please don't. Mamie told me that the girls are just crazy over the boys that go to England to study, they feel that they are very rich, and when you marry them your life is done with, I don't say you will do it. Your aim should be your study, nothing else. I suppose there are plenty Indian girls in England studying. If you marry one of them only when you are through with your education, I shall be very pleased.

Your loving, Ma

You should get yourself accustomed to slanders and mischief-mongers just ignore it.

---

* Cousin, younger son of Vidia's mother's brother Simbhoo
† Head Teacher

Jan. 31, 52

Dear Vido, A while ago, I typed off a letter to Kamla. We received a letter from her yesterday—after a two-month's silence. She said she was not writing because she was 'extremely, extremely, extremely hurt' by a letter from me. She admits that it was very baby-like of her, and suggests that I write her 'some nice letters' and it would be all right. She says she needs petting. Well, I sent her a very flattering but nevertheless sincere letter, which, I hope, will make her regain her centre. I don't think Kamla's health is as good as it was when she was here. It seems she is living under a tremendous nervous tension. She seems to dread her exams, which, by the way, begin on March 27. I know just what is happening: people expect her to be top, and she is anxious—over-anxious—to justify their expectations. Hence her state of anxiety. You too, I find, are subject to the same sort of thing. Get rid of it. Learn to do your best and to do it calmly and coolly.

I suggest you to write her some nice letters. She must be painfully lonely and homesick. Nostalgia can become an illness. Give her a lot of courage about her exams. I think this letter will reach you in time, and you have just to rush your letter right away.

Will you send me a copy of the magazine for which you have planned the cover?

I see Selvon has had a novel accepted by the Wingate Publishing House, and it has been recommended by the British Book Society as its 'Book of the Month'. Lucky fellow. The book, entitled *A Brighter Sun*, deals with a marriage of two teen-age Indian children in Trinidad. My own idea. And I doubt whether Selvon knows really much of the realities of the Indian way of life in these parts. I don't mind admitting that the thing depressed me. I feel—very foolishly of course—that I have been robbed of my theme.

Are you writing some short stories? You should, you know. This Selvon success is likely to make me do some work, too. I am so sure I could write anything as good as Selvon can—but more so on Indian themes. But, of course, Selvon has youth in his favour.

Capo S. has started work in Port-of-Spain. He had given up Caroni. Dangerous place. Do you know ex Leg. Co. member C.C. Abidh* was

---

* C. C. Abidh, former member of Trinidad's Legislative Council, had defeated Vidia's mother's brother Simbhoo in elections to the Council

shot dead one night, about nine o'clock, in his house at Charlieville? This happened about a week ago, and nobody knows who is the killer.

You promised to send a letter a week, but you are not doing so. If you at all start a letter you will dash it off quickly enough, just touching on the events of the day, or even of the hour. Your Mamee has been telling your Ma about 'how the English girls are having the West Indian boys dancing on their (the girls') fingers'. And your Ma is worrying a lot. She thinks you may go and get yourself married to a white girl, and she would like you to marry no one but an Indian. Your Mamee has told her there are 'lots of Indian girls from Trinidad studying in England'. If an investigation were made, it would show that by far the majority of inter-marriages end in failure.

Keep out of the mess.

Your affectionate
Pa

Dear Vido,

At last we have received a letter from Kamla after two months. She said in her letter that she was extremely hurt in one of your Pa's letters. The car got in an accident, the repairs has cost us $100 but the starter is to be fixed. What a beginning for a New Year. Well, I hope for the best.

Books are very expensive for this year. I am feeling the pinch. If education of children was as expensive as it has now become I don't think I could afford it. But on the whole everything has gone up. Try to secure your health and be a good son.

Your loving Ma

University College, Oxford
January 31, 1952

Dear Everybody,

I got your letter yesterday. I am happy to know that the things I sent reached home safely. It appears that Mamee has drawn a picture of unsullied Trinidad youth being lured to a fate worse than death by white sirens. Of course the picture is false. When you hear that So and So had a hell of a time in England with the girls, the girls are not to be blamed, but the boy pitied. Even in Trinidad one can have a hell of a time with the girls! And, believe me, in this country perhaps more than in any other, one is constantly aware of the differences in class. These differences are real, whatever anyone may say. If someone can find his level only with the cheapest women, well, what are we going to do?

The circles I move in, however, are different. Perhaps it is distressingly without the required feminine leaven, but you have nothing to be worried about. Money attracts the English girl just as it does the Indian girl. The fact that I am poor does rather effectively knock me out of any marriage mart. English girls are no looser than girls anywhere else, and despite what one hears about French women, they remain as difficult to get at (for poor me anyway) as any others.

The women I have known I have met quite by chance. Acquaintanceship is struck up almost unconsciously. These meetings hardly ever ripen into any enduring sort of friendship. And this, I must confess, I find rather distressing. I am afraid I was not cut out to be a monk. If I wanted to have a hell of a time, I could do so very easily, by pretending to myself that I am without intelligence, and that I am just as stupid as the boy from Tunapuna who gets a third grade, and is sent by parents 'to go and saw some more'. So, I think you have very little to worry about. I tell no one I am rich. I am not blessed with a striking appearance, and I am not a man of distinguished associations. A thorough nonentity, in other words.

Well, I have got through the press the first issue this term of the *Oxford Tory*. And in two days the second shall be out. Layout is interesting, and though we work with uninspired and unimaginative printers, I think we have brightened the magazine up considerably. The magazine gets me nowhere in Oxford, of course. But I have almost complete control of it and, as I haven't even Tory inclinations, you can imagine the thrill I get out of working on it. I am also learning a lot about layout—learning the hard way—and any experience of this sort is desirable.

About Kamla: I have had no letter from her for quite some time. I do not know whether she is ill. I believe—or rather suspect—that she is being childishly petulant. Let us hope she snaps out of this attitude of non-co-operation.

I am working slightly better this term than I did the last. And I feel sure that I will improve as the term gets on. During the past two months I have been prey to the gravest emotional upset I have ever experienced. And calm of mind—a thing which most of us have nearly all the time, without knowing how marvellous it is—is only slowly returning. I say this not to disturb you, but to explain the surliness of the few letters I wrote. The pains of growing up, I suppose.

The college, by the way, paid for the repair of my typewriter: 30/. I am being treated with extraordinary consideration by the college authorities, and I do hope that I do not let them down.

To write this letter, I stopped off reading, in a desultory way (for it is a dull book), Conrad's *Lord Jim*. I have to write an essay for the select college society on 'The Use of the First Person Singular in English Fiction'. It is an interesting subject, but it involves much reading, much dull reading.

I can feel that the writing in this letter has been rather woolly. I hate writing badly, at any time, but when the spring comes and the sun shines, and the girls emerge from their winter cocoons of dull heavy overcoats and bring life and gaiety to the streets with their bright cotton frocks—well, then, I may feel myself once more. So far it has only snowed for two days this year. Rather disappointing!

Love,
Vido

February 6, 1952

Dear Pa,

Here are two copies of the magazine which I control in all but name. I have had, as you can see from the title page, to do nearly everything. I re-write articles, and design the pages. Last term the paper was extremely dull, with one column stretching right across the page, large unreadable paragraphs and no sub-headings.

Perhaps you may find it strange that I am running the Tory paper in Oxford. I myself am surprised that I should be doing so, and I honestly cannot recall the trend of events that has made me control the paper. I suppose these things just happen. Up to the end of last term I had never heard of the magazine. This term I run it. I have designed what several people call the best advertising poster they have seen in Oxford for some time. And the paper is on the up and up. The first issue sold more than any other.

Don't worry about my politics. I don't bother about them at Oxford. Here I can see too clearly that people only play at politics, without any great sincerity. And I have a strong suspicion that this attitude is carried on in later life. Being a politician is just another career to the people here. In any case, the pictures that appear in the number for Feb. 5 were obtained by me from a Communist. He could hardly believe his ears when he learnt that they were to be printed in a Tory magazine.

I am also enclosing a copy of a programme of the college play. We had our first night last evening, and all the seats were sold. This is as gratifying to me as to any other member of the cast, for I did the publicity, and it is largely publicity that sells the seats for a first night. But trouble soon arrived. The king* died today. He is in some way connected with our college, and so the Dean and the Master decided to cancel the play altogether. I then had the job of de-publicising, i.e. taking down posters and letting the town know that the play was cancelled. After an hour of this work, I and my band of helpers were informed that we might put on the play tomorrow. So followed another round of re-publicising!

Oxford has a population of 100,000, most of whom are workmen who live on the Morris Car Works, a few miles east of Oxford. Yet I spent only £14 on publicity, and did a pretty good job, too.

Love,
Vido

University College, Oxford
February 9, 1952

Dear Kamla,

Thanks for your letter. I am glad that nothing very serious had happened to you. Although I must own that I suspected that your refusal to write was mere perversity.

You must forgive this old typewriter. It jumps at regular intervals. The back-spacer has to be used if I don't want to give the impression that I am writing in columns. There, I have forgotten to back-space again!

---

* King George VI (1895–1952)

I myself have been trying to do some hard work, and I am slowly getting into my stride once more. My depression has almost disappeared and this makes me quite content. I suppose you will be working harder than ever by the time you get this letter, and you have my best wishes.

Actually I have been terribly busy for the past three weeks, what with editing the *Tory*, and with publicising the college play. But tonight was the last night of the play, thank goodness, and I can call my time my own. I have to write a paper for a college society in eight days' time, and that, too, involves a lot of work.

The winter is going out reluctantly. We have only had two days of snow, and I find this a trifle disappointing. I am looking forward very much to the spring—to five weeks from now, as a matter of fact. I am doing my best to get out of this country for a little while. I think I shall go to Paris again. I find it a wonderful city for relaxation. The cut of the foreign travel allowance to £25 a year does rather curtail one's activities, but I know a French boy in college who has promised to let me have some francs, if I give him the equivalent in sterling.

I do not know what has happened to you—about your scholarship. In either case I think I shall be happy. It will be good fun (if we have the money) to have you in England. And I suppose you will enjoy another year in India. I do wish I could come to India to see you and the country. But this is a dream only, and I hardly expect much to come out of it.

Feb. 17

Sorry to have stopped. But I had to write a 5,000-word essay on 'Some Uses of the First Person Singular in English Narrative Fiction'. It is finished—in a rough way—and I shall spend most of today polishing it.

I don't know whether you find the same difficulty, but I find that there is very little to write about. I am well, I am working better and I have enough friends. I have done nothing wrong so far and intend to keep it that way.

The weather remains the only subject of discussion and it is pretty foul at the moment.

It may interest you to know that Gocking* and his family are in

---

* Teacher at Queen's Royal College

Oxford. I have visited them about three times. Gocking is here on a course of study. At his age, too! Don't you think that it is an absolute waste of money?

All my love, my dear Kamla,

from,
Vido

University College, Oxford
February 19, 1952

Dear Everybody,

It is now 8.10. In five minutes I have to read a paper to the college literary society, the Martlets, on 'The Use of the First Person Singular in English Narrative Fiction'. It is only this afternoon, before dinner, that I finished the essay. Although I wrote the bulk of it a few days ago, starting at ten one night, and working right through till three the following morning, I found that after long abstinence from writing I wrote only with great difficulty, and it was only after the first two thousand words that I got into my stride and began writing really well and intelligently.

Then I waited a few days, and this evening wrote the last 600 words. These are not good words. The criticism is unusually bad, and the attempts at humour are gross and vulgar. But it is too late now to change anything.

The Martlets is an old literary society in Oxford. In the old days before the war we had outside men coming to give lectures, men such as Lord David Cecil, and the famous critic C. S. Lewis. Now, every fortnight, the members of the society gather, usually in the Dean's rooms, drink port, settle down and listen to a paper read by an undergraduate.

A man usually writes only one paper while he is up at Oxford, but I got elected so damned early that I may have to write two papers, or even three. But this is my first. I am only slightly nervous, particularly as I know most of the people I am going to talk to.

This week has been quite a hectic week for me. First, getting the *Tory* out. Secondly doing a poster for the Oxford Experimental Theatre Group, and designing others for the same group. By the way, I have become infinitely more knowledgeable on the subject of typography. So much so that the printers who do the *Tory* have said that they regretted that I did the layout. They can put nothing over on me. It is the best compliment, I suppose.

And now I really must stop, and go to this meeting. I shall complete this when I return, and let you know how the whole thing has gone.

Wednesday morning. Well, my dear people, my paper went down like a glass of the best champagne. I had the group laughing whenever I wanted them to laugh. This morning someone told me that my paper was by far the brightest he had ever heard at the society. So it appears that I still retain some of the old fire. In this paper, by the way, I give a dressing down to most people. Defoe: I say people praise him because he is so true. That is hardly a decent criterion any more. Defoe, I said, remains a classic, because *Robinson Crusoe* was forced down the throats of children who were unable to offer any resistance. The children grow up, and their days of reading are mercifully over. Everyone sees *Robinson Crusoe*. Everyone has heard of it, no one reads it. It is bound to remain a classic. I parodied Henry James. I quoted a bit of Cecil Hunte, about the telegraphic style. 'A shot rang out. A man fell dead. Two more shots rang out. Two more men fell dead.'

All in all, I am quite satisfied. And I was surprised to find, in the discussion that followed, that my acquaintance with novels is really pretty wide.

It is a bright morning this day, the first bright morning for about six weeks. It is so warm that I don't need a pullover.

Tell Satti that I am very grateful for her letter and will try to give her a reply as soon as time permits. But judge for yourself: I have to write two essays by tomorrow morning about some poets who wrote in a Scottish dialect, four hundred years ago. Then, on the following day, I must have my essay ready on Anglo-Saxon verse.

Give everyone at home my love!

I am glad that you and Kamla have made it up.

Love,
Vido

University College, Oxford
February 24, 1952

Dear Everybody,

Sunday. It is warmer than yesterday, and one feels that spring is here at last. Five weeks of the term have past. Three more remain. This term has not been a very unsuccessful term. I have done some positive things. I have helped to publicise—and very well too—the college play. I have helped to edit the *Oxford Tory*. I have met a number of new people. I have written a good paper for the college society, the Martlets.

I saw some copies of the *Guardian* and *Gazette* at the British Council in Black Hall the other day. I saw an article by Pa. Something about textiles, I remember. I have done little writing this term, none at all, as a matter of fact. And yesterday I took a story I wrote in July last year to the girls in the college office. They are going to type it out for me.

I find that I really have little to tell you. I am living such a quiet life, doing the same things day after day. What shall I write about?

All I can do is to tell you, to bring it as close as possible to you, what I shall be doing today, a Sunday. In two hours, at a quarter past one, I shall be going in to hall, for lunch. The hall is a long, high room, with an enormous fireplace that is never used. The roof is timbered, and some of the windows have stained glass. Pictures of past great men of the college hang the walls. Attlee, by the way, is an old Univ. man. At the further end of the room is high table, where the Fellows sit. But they won't be sitting there for lunch. Lunch will be a cold salad—a terrifying experience on any day, particularly one that is itself cold. There will be some pressed meat, ham and other things which I don't eat. I shall tell the servant to take it away. He will. If I am lucky I will get a bit of cold chicken. Otherwise, a bit of cold lamb. After lunch, I move up to the Junior Common Room. There I shall have coffee and a doughnut. I shall drink coffee and read the newspapers. At two I shall come up to my room and work until three. At three I dress more decently than I am at present. For I am going to have tea with someone in North Oxford. I shall be out until 7. When, at seven, I get back into college, I go down into the beer cellar for a drink, usually half a pint of stout, costing fourteen cents. At 7.15 I have dinner—chicken every Sunday—and at eight I have finished coffee. At eight I hurry once more out of college, because I belong to the Oxford

Film Society and tonight they are showing a French film. I get back to my rooms at eleven, and work until about two. Tomorrow the round begins again.

Love,
Vido

University College, Oxford
February 26, 1952

My dear Kamla,

Thanks for your letter. I am indeed sorry to be a bad correspondent. I promised myself and you to write more often, but I still find myself unable to do so as often as I would wish.

Of course there is one big reason why I don't write more. There seems to be so little to write about. I had a rather hectic [experience] on the typewriter which is typing this letter. I wrote [letter after letter] after they had kept my [platen without] doing anything to it. I wondered what they would have done [had I] not made enquiries. The director replied and asked me to withdraw the implication I had made that they were going to keep the [typewriter] without making enquiries. I did withdraw the statement. They have paid for the repair, but the machine is so ancient that it cannot really be properly repaired.

I read my paper to the college society, the Martlets, 'Some Uses of the First Person Singular in English Narrative Fiction'. It was quite successful, and the little [gap] success has pleased me (ignore that big gap: that is only one of the tricks this machine has learned to play).

I am perhaps slightly disappointed that I shan't be seeing you this year, but time is flying so quickly that I am afraid we will both be old before we know it. And I don't mind really. I may surprise you, but I find that I want desperately to settle down and have all those things I despised a few years ago: job, wife, family, etc. Happiness is a very elusive thing. It exists and you don't know that it does. Only when something cataclysmic has occurred, something that destroys the placidity of your boring routine, do you realise what you had, and what you lost.

It seems hard to believe that Satti is no longer a girl, nor Mira.

I hope that you can work without any sort of emotional distraction and I hope that you work well. I shall be writing you in a few days.

Love,
Vido

Feb. 28th, 52

Dear Vido,

Congratulations on the fine way in which you came through with your paper before the college literary society. It should go some way towards restoring your old self-confidence. That rejection gave you, as it would have given me, a nasty jolt. But people such as you do not remain submerged for long. People like us are like corks thrown on water: we may go down momentarily; but we simply must pop up again. My advice to you is: take another shot, if you can spare the time for it just now; but leave satires alone for some time; go in for a bit of realism. I am dead sure you would come through with flying colours.

There are two signs by which you may know I am degenerating:

I am getting to like flower-growing more and more exclusively, and my handwriting is improving into the legible, well-formed calligraphy of the typical CM* School graduate. There is a third sign: I just cannot resist going into sweet sleep from about 1 to 3 p.m. every day. When I wake up, it is just time to take some milk or cocoa or what have you: smoke, look at the orchids, etc.; and maybe, water the plants. Smoke and eat once more; and, best of all, go to bed. To the pictures I seldom go nowadays. One can't see pictures and sleep at the same time.

Carnival is over. It was neither better nor worse than last year's. Savi wanted to go to town in jeans and shirt, but I didn't let her. For this I will be looked upon as being rather old-fashioned of course. I haven't seen Capo S. for about two weeks. I guess he is picking up the old threads gradually.

I have two stories (short); but one of them appears to be so stupidly humorous that I don't know whether the thing is any good. I have called it,

---

* Canadian Mission

'By St Peter, by Saint Paul'—a really fine sketch of the man you may have heard of as Laloo. However you look at Laloo, you see him only as one big joke. If you knew this man as I knew him you would know what I mean. I planned the thing as a straightforward sketch; finished it to the end; then found the stuff didn't have the liveliness of a short story. So I took a shot to make it a short story and found the thing began to live—so far as dialogue was concerned—only at two-thirds the length of the tale. No balance. So I am altering it again. By the time I am through, it may be no good! So you see I *am* degenerating. What to do?

Your Ma is not feeling up to mark this week or two. She has some stomach trouble. This afternoon she went to Dr Rampersad (Mavis) to get a check-up, but arrived late. She will be going back tomorrow morning. Don't let this get you down. It isn't anything very serious . . . Convent—and I understand Bishop's, too—is making it very hard for dull pupils. If you don't get through SC exam with a first grade the first time, no more chances! I wonder what Mira would do?

Love from everybody, Pa

University College, Oxford
March 2, 1952

Dear Everybody,

I had a letter from Kamla this week. Apparently she is very busy preparing for her examinations, which take place next week.

I also heard from Satti and was quite—oh exceedingly—happy to hear that she got a second grade. It is really much better than I thought her capable of. She must have been very childish when I left, or perhaps I was too wrapt up in myself to notice her. But her English has at last become the English of a reasonably educated woman. She should be proud of herself.

I promised Capo S. to write him sometimes, but so far I have not found time to write many letters, as you know. If you do see him, or anyone of his family, will you give him my regards and best wishes. I may write him one of these days.

I am rather interested to know whether you people at home have got used to being without Kamla and myself. I remember that when Kamla left, I was hopelessly unhappy for about a month, and could only slowly adapt myself to the thought of home without her. But then I got used to it. Thinking back, I find that I left home when I was not yet eighteen. That was truly adventurous. But the gigantic adventures of millions of unfortunate refugees and other victims of wars really dwarf my adventure and my problems. But I would not like to see Shivan leave home before he was rather mature. Intelligent Hindus are too easily prey to introspection. Introspection leads to very real unhappiness.

By the way, don't get too surprised if I come home for a short trip this summer. You see, I can use my allowance for four months (the length of the summer vacation) and easily buy a return fare. I shall make arrangements when I am in London in a fortnight. What do you think of the idea? I really would like to pop home for a while, and feel that I don't have to pay 12/6 for every night that I sleep in a bed here.

Today is Sunday and I have just had an excellent dinner—mushroom soup, chicken, cauliflower and roasted potatoes, followed by ice-cream and coffee. That should dispel any doubts about the quality and quantity of food here.

Today, for the first time in three months, I really am in fine spirits. I shall take advantage of this, and do some hard work tonight.

You really must forgive me when I don't write. I know what it means to you, but to write about the same things will probably tire you and, lord, they do tire me.

Once more, congratulations to Satti, and my love to her and all the rest.

Vido

University College, Oxford
March 7, 1952

Dear Pa,

Your letter amused me. Your handwriting amused me. Nobody's handwriting <u>degenerates</u> into CM style. It is usually the other way around. Besides, one has little cause for pride because one's handwriting is powerful and illegible. It is interesting, too, that there is in this country a movement towards the old-fashioned styles of writing, neat copperplate, etc., so what you have degenerated into is not something terribly appalling after all.

You complain, too, of an irresistible desire to sleep every afternoon. One should sleep every afternoon in the tropics. You cannot appreciate how difficult it is for me to do any work at all when the sun shines brightly over here. The day seems to be created for idling and lazing.

The college office typed out my story for me last Saturday. I sent it to Swanzy on Monday. Today, three days afterwards, he has replied. He thinks that my sketch was 'extremely well done'. It is being broadcast on April 27, and I shall probably read it myself. It means more money that way. Actually it is the first time that Swanzy has given me unstinted praise. The last page of my first story was too literary. My second was too involved and too drawn-out. This is extremely well done. I mean, there is definite progress, what?

I feel nostalgic for home. Do you know what I long for? I long for the nights that fall blackly, suddenly, without warning. I long for a violent shower of rain at night. I long to hear the tinny tattoo of heavy raindrops on a roof, or the drops of rain on the broad leaves of that wonderful plant, the wild tannia. But in short I long for home, or perhaps, the homely atmosphere. And I miss my bicycle rides, and the sea, and the pit at Rialto, and the sort of cigarettes I used to smoke, to everyone's scandal.

I shall certainly try to come home this summer. My only worry is about getting a passage back to England. I shall see the travel agents in London in about a fortnight.

I think my letters have become a bit more regular. I must stop now, for I have an essay to write for tomorrow morning.

> Yours affectionately,
> Vido

March 8th, 1952

My dear Vido,

I have been thinking a good deal about you this last week or two. In the first place, your last two letters had a pathetic tone about them. You seem to be lonely, even sad. Your food appears to be skimpy and chancy, much as was the case with me in Jamaica, because of my revulsion to beef and pork and ham and things like that. I wish we could be eating everything like everybody else. After all, we would at least have been more consistent—

and, in virtue of it, perhaps more physically fit. Many Hindus abroad eat beef nowadays.

I know I haven't been of much use to you; so painful is this thing that I rather not dwell on it . . . Today marks the end of the first week of my two-week vacation. I have been working harder than when I had no vacation. But I have been working with a great deal of pleasure, so that I hardly feel it. I have done a long short story—a thing I had worked on spasmodically a long time ago. I think I begin to see how the great writers go to work—when there is nothing else to do but to write; and when they know that editors are actually anxiously waiting for their stories, novels or articles. You feel lazy only until you approach the task. Then you get absorbed. Literary work is a matter of single devotion. You type or write till noon. Then you eat and relax, or mooch around the microscopic flower patch; or sleep. When you get up you are ready to have another go. That's how it has been with me. I feel so darned cocksure that I <u>can</u> produce a novel within six months—if only I had nothing else to do. This is impossible. <u>But I want to give you just this chance.</u> When your university studies are over, if you do get a good job, all well and good; if you do not, <u>you have not got to worry one little bit.</u> You will come home—and do what I am longing to do now: just write; and read and do the things you like to do. This is where I want to be of use to you. I want you to have that chance which I have never had: somebody to support me and mine while I write. Two or three years of this should be enough. If by then you have not arrived, then it will be time enough for you to see about getting a job. Think over this thing. I mean every word of it. I doubt you will ever be satisfied with a mere job. I know nothing else will make you happy . . . I mean nothing but literary success will make you happy.

I have only now looked to see what I have typed . . . So you see what I have in mind for you. You are no doubt having it hard just now. It is part of the travails of the upward-going. But this is only for a time. You must know exactly what you want to be; but there is one piece of advice that I should like to give you, though I know you will hardly need it. Do not get married too soon. It will handicap you. After you have arrived somewhere you can marry. And marry whoever you choose to marry. Who you should marry is entirely a matter for you; though for my part I should be more happy to see you marry an Indian, in the end it must be as you yourself choose. But give yourself plenty of time for this.

If you are thinking of getting a post at QRC, you should keep in touch with Hamer. He may be helpful to you in more ways than one. You could do with a post in the Education Dept. You could be an Inspector. But you must have a Dip. Ed. Oxon. Is not this how Rameshwar used to put it? But, as I say, you needn't have a job at all. You want to be a writer. I am dead sure you could be a brilliant one. I know you better than anyone else knows you. You'll have a free, unfettered go at writing for two or three years. By then you will have done something.

I have, of course, Mr Sookhdeo to pay off. I expect Kamla and Sati will help. The Naipauls just must make some extraordinary effort to get up. You people must plan and try to work according to that plan . . .

Kesso Ramcharan has got the Indian school for Medicine; QRC got all but the Science school. Bishop's got the Girls' school for the third time in succession.

You just try and make yourself cheerful. Remember, you haven't got to worry after you are through with Oxford. Your work is cut out. I stand back of you.

> Love from all at home,
> Pa

March 12, 1952

My dear Vido,

It is surprisingly good news that you could come home for the mid-summer vacation. Are you sure they will give you a return passage? Try your best to get the thing if it is at all possible . . . Thanks for the letter and copies of the *Tory*. It's very pretty and I'm sure you are doing a good job. Your pages are attractive without being overdone. I suppose Colonist is a columnist. What about using a by-line in signature? Or signed name at the bottom? At the first it struck me I should put the copies in the hands of Hitchens, with the remark, 'I think we have a future sub in the making.' And it occurred to me too that I should let Mr Hamer see them; but I wish you had sent these to him yourself. I am sure he would be very pleased and make a point of mentioning you and your doings in the Annual Report on Speech Day. We cannot afford to be shy of publicity, so long as it is decently done. I myself have been rather slack in this respect.

I have been trying to hurry through with a story, so I could send it to you right away. But this typewriter went dead on me yesterday when I had about four or five more pages to type. I'm doing it on letter-head-size newsprint. I'll be sending you it by tomorrow or day after without fail. I have two versions of it—one long and the other short: about 2,500 words; suitable for the BBC. I'd like you to read it carefully, and if you find it good enough, send it to Mr Swanzy, with a note that it's from me; and that it is part of a chapter of a novel I'm doing. Indeed, this is what I aim to do with it. As soon as you can, get working on a novel. Write of things as they are happening now, be realistic, humour where this comes in pat, but don't make it deliberately so. If you are at a loss for a theme, take me for it. Begin: 'He sat before the little table writing down the animal counterpart of all his wife's family. He was very analytical about it. He wanted to be correct; went to work like a scientist. He wrote, "The She-Fox", then "The Scorpion"; at the end of five minutes he produced a list which read as follows: . . .'

All this is just a jest, but you can really do it.

You know that Selvon is giving me some jitters. Can two persons be writing on the same themes and each be equally successful? Good Lord! How that man has mulched me of my ideas! He had all my stories with him at the *Guardian* for months; then he goes and writes on the same themes. Of course I have not seen the book, leave alone to read it. And I definitely will not read it. Doing so will do me a lot of harm. You read it and tell me what you think of it . . . You were right about R. K. Narayan. I like his short stories, but his novel, *The English Teacher,* is obviously immature. His English is often un-English, betraying the foreigner. Nevertheless, he seems gifted and has made a go of his talent, which in my own case, I haven't even spotted.

What more? Sati is mighty pleased with your compliments; so she is definitely going in for HC. That will mean two years. I have hopes of seeing Mira and Savi coming up too, though it seems Savi will be the more intelligent; no wonder she is the more rude or cheeky.

The too frequent harpings of your Mamee on the same old topic—how nice is England, and how hard is Trinidad—is sickening. I am sure both husband and wife are overdoing it . . . Have you met Mrs Jean Peremanand—Owad's wife? She's gone to join her husband of course, and oh could Miss Dhan be more cut up?

Be wary of Owad. Any secret he knows of you will be broadcast here in good time. I'm not saying not to be with him for a spell; only be careful.

Today, for the first time I bought a new tyre. I had no spare. Paid eighteen dollars down for it, and owe twenty-three dollars and a few cents. Bought a tube too . . . Last Sunday the whole Naipaul clique went down to Manzanilla Bay. Just as we reached Curepe on the outward trip one rear tyre went flat with a bang. Fault of the man who put pressure in town; put far too much air.

We had a spare and went to the Bay as though nothing had happened. The tyres held; and now I have a new spare. By the way, we had pilau and bananas and sweet drinks. Small wonder after we had eaten, your Ma and I just went kind of drunk with sleepiness. But we didn't sleep. The day was fine; sunny, with a fine breeze blowing all the day.

Johnson has given me my painting. It's a beach scene at Carenage, called 'Idle Boats' . . . Were you too 'wrapt up' or were you 'wrapped' up? I see Narayan using the latter word . . .

Your loving, Pa

University College, Oxford
March 24, 1952

Darling Kamla,

This is a desperate plea for help. I am broke, broke, broke.

Can you send me £5–£10. There is no hurry, but try to get it to me by the end of May.

I am doing my best. I am writing like mad. If I can collect an extra £30, I shall be all right.

If you can't send me any money, don't bother.

Sorry about this,

Vido

3/28/52

My dear Vido,

This morning I paid down one-fourth (25%) on your ship's passage to England.

All you have to do now is to book your passage to home. I don't know what boat you will be coming by, but if you left by the Colombie on the 19/6, which will arrive here on the 3/7, you'll have 62 days in Trinidad.

Your passage back is booked par the Colombie, which leaves Trinidad on the 4th October and reaches Southampton on the 17th Oct.

Since this will be carrying you back 6 days too late for the re-opening of your college, I have arranged a provisional passage for you on the Colombie leaving Trinidad on the 23/8 and arriving in Southampton on the 5/9.

But try and let your College Dean or Tutor know that you might be 6 days late for the re-opening, and then you needn't leave home on the 23/8, but on the 4/10; so you'll be spending 62 days with us instead of only 49 days.

Moreover, you may get a passage on board a tanker ($288) and then you may cancel the Colombie passage, but it must be done 2 months before sailing date of the Colombie. You'll have enough time to attend to anything when you are home.

Don't let the $360 passage worry you; you may get to go by the $65 berth instead of the $75 one.

Everything will be all right when you reach here. Don't worry but bring as much money with you as you can; it'll help paying on the balance we have to pay for the return trip. We all await you.

Your affectionate,

Pa

Malaga, Spain
April 6, 1952

Dear Everybody,

I should have written before I left England, but I found no time. Since March 30 I have been travelling constantly. Take out a map of Europe and follow me. On March 29 I left Oxford by the 2.15 coach for London. It was snowing and it had been snowing steadily for the past 36 hours. Which is rather unusual for the end of March—the month, they say, which comes in like a lion and goes out like a lamb. London was buried under snow. I spent the night at Mamoo's where Owad and Mamoo and Ruth and myself played whist. Ruth was quite friendly and she seems to be much better than when I saw her last Christmas at Brighton. On Sunday morning Jean, O's wife, made me breakfast and Owad and I hurried to Victoria to get the boat train. We hurried, but the underground trains were delayed by snow. We got to Victoria, then, just in time to see the boat train for Newhaven pull away. There was another train, though, at 9.30. This I took. To Dover I went and, forgetting the sandwiches Ruth had so charmingly provided for the journey, I boarded the steamer for Calais. A nice, cold crossing. Calais–Paris. A 5-hour journey, the first two hours through absolutely white country, white with snow. But it got milder as we approached Paris. It was too late to take the Barcelona express. So I had to spend the night in Paris—in a hotel (rather disreputable) in the Montmartre region.

Paris the following day. Austerlitz Railway Station. Romantic name—romantic journeys. Huge locomotives pulling expresses bound for all over Europe. Left Paris promptly at 8 p.m.. Did not sleep that night. Next morning, at N[?], decided to be luxurious and have breakfast in the dining car, just as the sun was rising. Beautiful. Paris–Châteauroux–Toulouse–Carcassonne–Narbonne–Perpignan–Po . . . Look at your map. The colours were exquisite. Blue, limpid sea . . . red, terraced mountainsides and the houses with corrugated slate roofs—red, with walls of yellow ochre and shutters of blue or sea-green. Seven long tunnels to Cerbère—crossing the Pyrenees. At C the frontier formalities leaving France. Passports checked and stamped. Then—Spain. Soldiers everywhere. Innumerable and irritating papers to fill. Change trains—leave the French for the Spanish ones that seemed like toy engines beside the masters of the

SNCF (Société Nationale des Chemins [de Fers] Français). Wouldn't deprive the French of their joy in impressive titles.

Four armed police go past the railway coach corridor in Port Bou. Later, passport inspected—3rd time in Spain. My temper rises and I swear loudly in English: the girl in seat opposite is American. She has been speaking flawless Castilian and now speaks flawless American and I am deeply impressed.

(All paper gone. Will continue later)

Hotel Granada, Malaga
Sunday Morning

Up at 10.30 this morning and went to the Railway Station to see about trains to Madrid. This hotel is too expensive. But I found one where—for 6 shillings—I can eat and sleep. This is very cheap and I am writing this in the writing room of the Hotel before moving on to the more disreputable one.

Well, back to the train at Port Bou. Presently all the carriage is chattering away. A Spaniard announces that he is a painter and that he has spent six months in Spain. A girl gets in at a station; and he promptly makes a pass at her. He takes out a picture of his wife and passes them around and swears that, despite the attractions of Paris, he has remained faithful. I look at his wife and agree with him that his fight against temptation must have been truly strong.

We get to Barcelona at 3—travelling constantly, then, for 19 hours. Ordinary station, nasty and blackened with smoke. At the exit hordes of scouts trying to sell you their taxis and their hotel. I ignore them and, following the advice of a woman on the train, take the Underground train, and then go to a hotel. The hotel turns out to be monstrously expensive. But—for 20 hours I have had no sleep and have eaten almost next to nothing. My eyes are blinking constantly and they burn. So I stay, have a bath, and then a rich full meal served with soothing decorum. Have coffee in a room that overlooks one of the beautiful avenues of Barcelona; speak to my hostess and her daughter—a slim, pretty little thing of 22 who had been playing the piano while I was eating. Presently I find that I am flirting with both mother and daughter. But the rules of Spain are strict. Respectable daughters are never seen anywhere except with their mothers. I rest until dinner time. After dinner I go for a walk—looking for Barcelona night life. There is light everywhere. But suddenly the broad, clean streets give way to tiny, dirty lanes overshadowed by houses five or six storeys high. A boy runs after me and offers to sell me a Swiss watch—black market. I refuse. Barcelona night life is tawdry and disgusting. It isn't even amusing. Barcelona cannot be gay as Paris.

Rain the next day. I browse away in the bookshops and have my boots cleaned by a bootblack. I also have laces put on for one boot had no lace at all! That costs me 4 pesetas—about nine pence.

The next day the sun is shining and I decide on some sightseeing. Interesting, but photographs can do better justice to Barcelona's views than my descriptions. I meet a Scottish girl, who is going to Malaga on a tiny cargo steamer. I decide to accompany her. I take the boat from Barcelona, then, and find myself in Malaga. I have last sight of my Scottish guide and don't care.

Holy week is now gripping Andalusia. Prices are high everywhere. Tomorrow I leave for Cordoba or for Madrid. I must stop now.

Love,
Vido

Aboard the Catalonian Express
Madrid–Barcelona
April 8, 1952

My dear Kamla,

I am sitting in a first-class compartment in a Spanish train. The compartment is animated, although it is midnight. Spanish trains are not like English trains. Everyone speaks to everyone else the moment the train pulls out of the station, and leaves people's separate and individual lives.

We left Madrid at 7.15 p.m. and we arrive at Barcelona tomorrow at 9.30 am (i.e. today).

I am sorry to spring this foreign-stamped letter on you without any preparation, but I want you to know that whenever I am upset it is to you that I usually pour out the suffering of my tortured heart. When I don't write it means that I am all right. (Nasty play of words but don't hold it against me.)

We are five men and one woman in this de luxe compartment (the train is exclusively first class). The woman sits on my right. She is extremely beautiful and we have just had coffee in the dining-car. Now she is telling the future of the gentleman opposite—a plump, oily man, middle-aged and with hair scattered sparsely around a shining, almost bald pate. The gentleman opposite me is without his coat. It is on paper supplied by him that I am writing this letter. Both pen and pencil have been lent to me by the man who sits on his right. A well-dressed ordinary-looking man sits on my left.

The man opposite me tells funny stories. To my surprise I still understand Spanish and am beginning to speak it better.

And now I must apologise for this letter. I find it difficult to write with my usual precise and legible vigour in a rocking train.

And yet it is hardly more than eight days that I have been in Spain.

Now, does that sound English? No, no—the construction is definitely French/Spanish.

The day after winter returned to Britain with a 2-day blizzard that spread snow all over the country, I left England, by the boat train for Paris. A fairly uneventful Channel crossing. Then a five-hour journey across a snow-buried North France. It was too late for me to get the Barcelona express that leaves Austerlitz Station in Paris at 8 every night. I passed the night in a pleasantly shabby hotel in Montmartre and the following day revisited some of the places I knew when I was last in Paris in September last year.

Austerlitz Station! Magnificent. Clean, with huge notice-boards announcing the departures of trains on *'grandes lignes'*—for all over Europe. What magnificent locomotives they have! And how fast they go. Take out a map and follow the train. From Paris to Châteauroux to Limoges to Toulouse (at 3 in the morning. The old peasant woman and the silent priest get off and some other peasants, smelling of garlic, get on) to Carcassone to Narbonne to Perpignan. I had breakfast while the left was speeding away from M [. . .]. The sun was just rising. Oh, how beautiful.

2 days in Barcelona. A large town—1¼ million pop.—and made up of 2 distinct areas, the old city, with its narrow streets and old buildings, and the new, straight-avenued town.

Just stopped to pass my cigarettes round. Only one non-smoker in the compartment!

At B. met a Scottish girl (26, it turned out) who beguiled me into travelling by cargo steamer to Malaga. So, a 2-day Mediterranean cruise travelling deck and being treated like a pig, while she, being a friend of the management and a flirt, travels like a queen.

Malaga, then, where I did my best to lose her, and did. Then train to Madrid. A beautiful city. We must visit Madrid when you come to England next year. I prefer Madrid to Paris.

Well, I must stop now. I want to take part in the life of the compartment. I am on my way to England and will get there in about 40 hours—most of it in trains—3rd class! Fun ahead!

Love, Vidia *[deleted]*

Everybody calls me Vidia—disgusting name—and even I have got into the habit of calling myself that way.

VII

April 21, 1952 – September 28, 1952

SUMMER TERM, LONG VACATION

University College, Oxford
April 21

Dear Pa,

The promptness and energy with which you have undertaken preparations for my return home this summer must, I fear, be wasted.

My financial situation is one that absolutely forbids returning home, and I am most unhappy to bring such a great disappointment to you.

The fact is: I spent too much money in Spain. And, during the nervous breakdown (yes, it was that) I had, I grew rash and reckless and threw money about with a don't-care-a-damn in consequence. My only opportunity of recuperating from my present chaos is to remain in England this summer and live very cheaply. This is what I propose to do.

Further, this is my last big vacation before my exams and I must work hard.

I shall be sending your story to Swanzy in a few days and I must say that you still remain a delightful writer.

When I am settled properly I shall write again.

Love,
Vido

University College, Oxford
April 21, 1952

Dear Kamla,

Thanks very much for your £7. It has helped me a great deal.

I am sorry to have burdened you this way, but I have done some very silly things, and I hope to do no more.

I had a lovely time in Spain. I shouldn't have gone, of course. But after the great nervous breakdown I had—travel was the only soothing thing I could think of.

I will write in a few days. Please don't think badly of me.

Love,
Vido

5/2/51

Dear Vido,

I am very disappointed indeed that you can no longer come home. A couple of days ago I got back my $90 from the shipping Co. I am sending you $25 out of it, and the remainder returns to my creditor, who happens to be away from the island, on a business trip abroad.

Why do you worry so much? Nothing at all is bad at this end; and this thought should go some way in keeping you cheerful. I'm sending you by sea mail the book *You and Your Nerves*. I think it will help you resolve a good many of your worries. Most of the things over which we worry are really no true causes of worry at all.

I was proud of your last short story. It was very well done. We all listened in, and the reception was quite good. I think we all easily made out all the people in the story. Why didn't you call Mrs Fred Mrs Fred?

Keep on writing as many short stories as you can. Lose yourself in the throes and thrills of your creative work; and write on WI or WI-Negro themes. We must not let Selvon alone get away with it.

What does Mr Swanzy say about my own stuff? I know it is long-drawn, but you should tell him that is so because it is a piece of novel, as indeed it is. Besides, it easily lends itself to cutting.

I am too tired to attempt any sustained work on my own; there is always some story or the other for the *Wkly Gdn*. In this struggle for existence I feel just hemmed in by hard, unescapable facts and forces.

We got some 2 letters from Kamla. She seems to have done not too badly in her exams. I think the last of her papers she'll get tomorrow. It's English, I think.

Write her a charming letter. And do, for our own sake, stop being downcast.

Your affectionate Pa

University College, Oxford
May 10, 1952

Dear Everybody,

I have no excuse at all for not writing before. I always promise to write more frequently, but never do so. If I may, I shall offer an excuse I made some time ago. In August last year, I think, my typewriter was fatally dislocated. You have perhaps already noted that it is only since then that my letters have grown scarce. I find it difficult to write with pen or pencil.

I have little news to offer. Only that spring is indeed here. The sun shines quite often, and the sun in the morning is a beautiful thing. The flowers are out, and in England they seem to come in true neat colours—chrome yellow, Venetian red, red, blue, mauve. The grass is green; and the wind is not too sharp. It is agreeable to go for bicycle rides into the country around Oxford or for walks. The countryside in Oxfordshire is not varied. It tends to be flat and monotonous. But I find it soothing. Even the rain has not become something which one tries to escape. It falls soft and it does not sting the skin. A week ago, we had a wonderful thunderstorm, after a particularly hot day. Lightning flashed, and thunder cracked and rolled—not as violently as in Trinidad naturally—and rain fell. The whole thing cannot be compared to a Trinidad thunderstorm. The T'dad rains are violent and seem anxious to remind you that nature is a horrid creature at times. The English spring showers are soft and sweet. I went for a walk in the thunderstorm, then, and got agreeably drenched. Much like old times.

About my activities: I am playing cricket this term, and I have taken up oil-painting once more. My technique has improved. I mean, I can get forms down all right. That is because I have done so much pen and ink sketching. But colour still baffles me. At some, if I remember rightly, I got wonderful colours, but then I couldn't draw.

Of course my cricket isn't hot stuff.

As you might have guessed, I wept and fasted, wept and prayed that my story might not be heard at home. But there! You realised, of course, how much I let my imagination roam. Most of the stuff was imagination. The idea alone was drawn from—well, you know. By the way, they paid me eleven guineas for it. I spoke to Swanzy about three weeks ago. Again he told me that I ought to get your stories published. He thought that you were throwing away your opportunities. He says you are a maturer and more delightful writer than Selvon. So will you kindly send me your stories? We need about twelve. I have not sent your story to Swanzy yet. I am still trying to patch it up for radio. It is deliciously written. I read it out to some of my friends in the college—and such delightful sentences as 'Mud and they were kin', 'Outsiders looked upon the Chandernagorean as a kind of amphibian' had them laughing.

I have written ten stories so far. You know that I can't write well. Not half as well as you. You manage a type of humour I cannot manage. Your view of life is surprisingly good-humoured. Well, don't write a novel then. Just let me have your short stories. And here: MAKE NO EFFORT TO THINK ABOUT DRAMATIC PLOTS. You can't manage them. Neither can I. Observe episodes. I can't express myself well, knowing that space is limited.

I asked Satti to tell me what French books and Spanish books she was studying. She has maintained an impregnable silence. I can help her now, but in two months' time I shall be too busy.

My love to all at home. Remember me to Capo S., if you run into him.

Vido

5.19.52

Dear Vido,

Three things in your letter please me greatly. The first, that you are playing cricket; the second, that you have done as many as ten stories; and the third, that you—and Swanzy—think I write even better than Selvon. I am sure I shall not allow this to puff me up, but it is good for me to hear this from people who <u>know</u> what they are talking about.

Why do I detest this Selvon so much? I know it isn't nice of me; but to see the fellow wearing what I might call quite a messiah beard gets me annoyed. But let him . . . All but one story in the *Gurudeva* booklet I have already typed. Your letter yesterday gave me a fresh impetus—the words, 'Swanzy thinks you are simply throwing away your opportunity.' So that what remain are those that were used by the BBC—including those that Swanzy rejected. These latter I still think are not bad stories, though perhaps unsuitable for radio. Let's see, then, what we have got so far—

1. *Gurudeva* (regard it as a novelette)   Typed
2. 'Panchayat'   Typed
3. 'Sonya's Luck' (BBC)   Typed
4. 'Obeah'   Typed
5. 'Copi'   Untyped
6. 'The Wedding'   Typed
7. 'Dookhani and Mungal'   Typed
8. 'Gratuity' (BBC)   Untyped
9. 'Canaan' (it's not a bad story)   Typed
10. 'The Engagement' (S. praised this)   Typed
11. 'They named him Mohun' (S. Rejit)   Typed
12. 'The Diver' (new—unpublished)   To be retyped
13. 'Uncle Dalloo'   Untyped (for book)
14. 'Escape'   Untyped (for book)

There are one or two other stories which I don't like and so have not included them in the list.

PTO

So you see I have about half of the typing still to do. Between today and tomorrow I hope to finish one more . . . But Francis X (Convent) wants me to write her a description of a Hindu marriage ritual, and D. Mahabir an article for his mag. on the Hindu Ecclesiastical Grant. I don't think I shall do it, though. If I didn't have to do this typing I might have had one or two more stories . . . The idea did occur to me whether we could include a few of your best stories—when the by-line would be by V. and S. Naipaul, or vice versa. What do you say? . . . I just asked Sati to check up on the vice versa, because when I ask her to spell the words, she did so, promptly adding, 'with a hyphen'. She was wrong, of course. It's so with Sati—and the other two graces (at Tunapuna since day before yesterday).

I saw Capo S. at Bhagwat recitation (a 7-day affair) at St James' last night, but forgot to tell him hello from you.

Nothing cheers us better than to know that you are cheerful; do make yourself happy—and *do* be practical in everything . . . Now I am going to eat. It's curried carite* and rice and ripe bananas. That's all, but I'm very tempted to get a pint or two of beer, which I prefer much more to rum. Rum is harsh.

We are all well, and you keep well too. Yours as ever, Pa

I have written a story in which the principal characters have been largely members of my own family. Sanyasi is Sadhu,† Gurudeva 75% Dinanath.‡ Gopi is myself and so on.

June 2, 1952

Dear Everybody,

About three weeks ago, two of my friends and myself threw a bottle party in my room at college here. A bottle party is a cheap affair. You merely provide the emollient opening drinks. Everyone who is invited brings his own bottle. There were about forty people—men and women. The party started at 7.00. The Dean came at about 8.30 and left at 10, the time when all women had to leave the college. But he saw me as he was leaving and gave me permission to keep the women on until 10.30. He had drunk so much or had such a fine time that he even forgot his pipe in my room. The party was a definite success. After taking the girls home, we discovered the Dean's pipe. Four of us went to the other quadrangle of the college and began to sing outside the Dean's window, *'Le pauvre Gilles a oublié sa pipe!'* 'Poor Giles has forgotten his pipe.' He did not appear. So we took the pipe up to him. He was preparing a lecture, but did not mind the interruption at all.

The weather has been quite good this term. I have done some painting, and some work. In a cricket match last week I bowled 11-3-25-3 and made 13 not out.§ In a minute or so, I shall be dressing for another match. I have been chosen for the 1st eleven. I hope I do well.

---

* A Caribbean fish
† Paternal uncle by marriage, Vidia's father's elder sister's (Phoowa's) second husband
‡ Maternal uncle by marriage, Vidia's mother's elder sister's husband
§ No attempt will be made to explain the mysteries of cricket

June 3

Well, there was some rain yesterday and the match was a pathetic little affair. I did nothing at all, did not bat, did not bowl, and fielded two balls.

There are three more weeks before the term ends. Then comes the long vacation of four months. I have been working pretty well once more and I hope to get a lot of work done in the vac.

Next term, in October, I move to lodgings. I have been living in college for two years. Peace of mind is the most valuable thing one can have in this world. Even if ambitions have to be abandoned, it is desirable. I cannot tell you what my three-month illness brought me. I have to take things easily. It is like a jar of muddy water that must be left still so that the mud sinks to the bottom, leaving the water clean on top. When, at the beginning of April, I slowly pulled myself out, I had to pause and look at the debris around me. I have been clearing it away this term.

Of course I know the reason for my breakdown: loneliness, and lack of affection. You see, a man isn't a block of wood that is sent abroad and receives two notches as a sign of education. He is much more. He feels and he thinks. Some people, alas, feel more and think more than others, and they suffer. It is no good thinking that the sensitive man is happier or greater. No one cares for your tragedy until you can sing about it, and you require peace of mind to do this.

About three weeks ago I saw the Indian team beat Oxford. When I got to the Parks the Indians were 38 for 3, and Hazare and Umrigar were in. Umrigar is a tall ugly man, very powerful. I saw him reach 95 just before lunch—4 4's in a row—and saw him hit 2 successive sixes when he was 205.

It may probably break you to know that I am shaving every other day now. I have to, and I find it a frightful bore.

Thank Satti for her letter. I have got the list of books she wants, but my money is short and I may only send them at the end of the month. I have pounds of books to buy myself.

I have nearly completed *Anna Karenina*, by Tolstoy. It completely breaks down in the sixth book. Its unity is destroyed. Tolstoy brings in everything he can lay his hands on, and the reading becomes tedious. I have come to the conclusion that undisciplined reading is no good. I want to start reading in an organized way—some history particularly, I know really very little of European history. Thanks to my study, I am now familiar with

Chaucer, Shakespeare, Spenser, Milton, Donne, Marlowe etc. One has to study these writers' complete works.

An article of mine on Spain was published in the *Oxford Tory* last month. I want to do something about Spain for the BBC.

My love to all, and don't forget me,

Vido

[From Kamla]

June 7, 1952

My dear Vido,

Only today, I was thinking whether I should send you a telegram to see if you are still alive. And really, I think that if you were before me I would have exploded like a Volcano. But you are a good brother after all and so I'll send nothing.

Before going any further I just want to tell you that in me you have a very faithful sister. Let nothing worry or depress you. Tell me everything and, believe me, I'll understand. At least you may trust that I understand you completely. Don't be afraid to say a thing to me. I can understand what it must have been like at Ruth's. You should never forget that strain of jealousy that runs in the Capildeo family. And since we know it, it now lies for us to show that the Naipauls too can rise to fame in their own lives.

You needn't be disappointed, I can manage to leave for England by the end of April next or maybe at the end of March. The music exams are usually held in July but they have already promised me that with special permission I may do it in March or February.

As you know, I have grown to hate this idea of marriage. I think it's the end of life. And besides I have begun thinking that marriage is concerned with all that's sexual and I don't like it. Now my only ambition is to get a good job somewhere and see to the education of Sati and the others. I would like to see them get out of Trinidad and make good. I don't know whether you have been told but soon there's to be another in the family. Of course, I don't think it is too heartening. And believe me I have only now got over it. Of course, I can't write a hard letter to Pa because he might cry. I have decided to ignore the thing and I think it would be wise if you would do the same. All these things, I see before me, however, and so the thought of marriage merely drifts farther away. The end of my life would be to see to the children's education and happiness and also to Ma's and Pa's.

You haven't much time left for your final examination. This year you should devote all your time to studies and don't disappoint me. Think that we are still poor and that comfort and money can come only after our period of studies is over. If that period is wasted away it means also that all our future happiness is also wasted away. So for my sake and for your own future make good with your college career. It is now my secret ambition to drag on entirely away from all our relatives—Capildeos or Sookhdeos. I detest every one of my family.

I don't think it's possible for me to get any kind of scholarship to England. Besides even if I get it, I won't accept. I have been away from home long enough. I think it's time I gave the others a chance.

Don't you think it would be better for me to come to England after your finals. Make your mind up and I will come whenever you think best.

I have just received a letter from Pa. (He sent me a cable congratulating me.) He complains of your not writing to him. He thinks you are ill. So do drop a line home.

As ever loving Sis,
Kam

If you'd write to me and to those at home regularly you'd never be homesick.

6/16/52

Dear Vidia,

Yesterday I typed out the last story, and I think altogether there are some 14 stories. The last two I do not quite like, but have included them because I had nothing else. I have the collection properly filed in a special folder, so that the whole reads like a book. However, I want you to read every story very carefully, line by line, for typing errors, mistakes in syntax, and whether certain words should carry a hyphen or not.

Now, I haven't posted you the thing because I am not sure just where you would be during the long vacation. So write right away and tell me whether it would be still Oxford. Do not make any too drastic changes in any story, but of course wherever you can add do so. I am sure you will find omissions and what not. By the way, what about trying Eyre and Spottis-woode, R. K. Narayans's publishers? Or perhaps the Penguin people. If one firm turns you down go to another. I suppose you would be having time enough during the holidays?

And what about adding a couple or so of your own stories? Ask the publisher whether this could be done, then we could have a good-sized book. And if you succeed in getting a publisher, mention that I intend—and in fact have already done so to some extent—extending *The Adventures of Gurudeva* to book length. I have planned out all the chapters, and have typed out two chapters already—'The Return of Gurudeva' and 'Guru-deva Becomes a Pundit'.

And I have in mind doing a book—my Trinidad Diary—something along the line of *Hindu Holiday*, by Ackerley, which you probably have already read. In this I could give short or long descriptions of things Indian or things Negro in a popular style: all about Mahabir Swami pujahs and Suraj Puran recitations,* and Tilaks† and marriages and this, that and the other.

You see, we have to work to plan: either you support me after you are through with Oxford, and let me devote myself wholly to writing the things I want to write; or I support you so you devote yourself to the same thing . . .

You must have been in some sort of money difficulties. I hope the five pounds I cabled you was of some help. <u>You</u> <u>really</u> <u>must</u> <u>be</u> <u>careful</u> <u>about</u> <u>money</u>, you know; your Ma and Sati and the rest keep telling me that you are ruining yourself by overspending; I believe somebody or the other has even been telling Sati that you have a lot of girls.

Do keep away from anything that is likely to become shackles to your progress. Your Ma thinks you are being influenced by Owad, and she wor-ries a lot about his. She doesn't trust Owad, neither do I; but of course all this may not be true.

Write promptly so that I may send the stories . . . Kamla wrote from Kashmir today. She seems to be all right.

> Your affectionate,
> Pa

---

* Mahabir Swami pujahs and Suraj Puran rectitations—Hindu scriptural readings
† Hindu engagement ceremony

University College, Oxford
June 23, 1952

Darling Satti,

I have just got two letters from home, including yours. Yours was written in a sloping, decisive hand, the style was incisive and to the point. In short, I think you have grown up. It has been a rather slow and tiring process, particularly tiring to the people who surround you. But I like your last letter. It has amused me; it has got my back up and so I sat down 30 seconds after reading it to write this letter.

I regret my development in your eyes, to the height of a character in a college novel. I have spent foolishly. This I admit. I also say that if I did not spend foolishly during the first 3 months of this year, there would have been no one to write this letter today—I shall give you the facts straight. I couldn't bear to see anyone. I couldn't bear to read, because it made me think about people; I couldn't go to the cinema; I couldn't listen to the radio. So please try to realise that for me it has been a near-miracle that I can walk in the streets without being afraid that I talk to someone and not feel to run away.

This desire to run away found full expression in my train journey to Spain. I kept on moving. My worries were about finding lodgings and about catching trains. It was a great help to me. I have not become an ungrateful son or anything romantic. I have at last become my old self. I have been doing some solid reading and feeling my old self.

Dear Sati, I shall get your books in exactly one week. Can you wait that long?

Now for some news about myself. As I write this, a man is pattering about my room. There is a bottle of champagne about one foot from my hand. It is not my champagne. It belongs to the man. From the window at my right there come the sounds of young men making noises that are in pleasurable anticipation of tonight. Tonight the college is having a Commemoration Ball; and a huge marquee has been erected in the main quadrangle. My room has been allotted to the gentleman with the champagne. He is a tall, silly-looking man with a broad, irritating grin anticipatory of tonight's pleasure. May I take you to the ball? It shall cost merely ten pounds. Shall I take you? Permit me a little extravagance. College balls come once a year. But have no fear. I am not going.

My name appeared in the *Oxford Mail* last Monday. For cricket, of all things. I was playing for the college first XI. I bowled 150 3m 33r 4w. Not bad! The best bowling in the match for the college. The side I bowled against made 142. We made 17 (VSN bowled for 0) in all! In my last match I top-scored with 25 (3 fours) and bowled 3 wickets for 33 runs. So I have developed my cricket, if anything.

Last Thursday the Martlets (the College Intellectuals) had a wonderful dinner with the Dean. I have been elected sec't'y of the Martlets. Not an honour to shout about, anyway.

About Owad. I have a mind of my own; and it is not an altogether pliant mind.

My love to Meera, Savi and, of course, Shivan.

Yours,
Vido

June 23, 1952

Dear Pa,

Thanks for the prompt manner in which you answered my plea for help. You may imagine how I felt about the whole thing. I did get both £5. Thanks.

My address for all the vacation is University College, Oxford; same as always. So there is nothing to worry about.

If I had known that Kamla's letters were as rare as my own I would have bent backwards to write more often. I hate you to think that your two eldest children are ungrateful.

Here term ended two days ago; we are now in the summer vacation. That runs till the end of September. This is the vacation for work and I have already begun.

My report for this term was most encouraging. 'Unusual ability . . . original . . . good style . . . well read.'

Please send me the stories. I shall send them around.

I have received two invitations this vacation. One is to spend a week at the end of July, in Kent; the other is for a fortnight in Harrogate, Yorkshire.

I have formed a very wide circle of friends. And it is with difficulty that I can avoid, during term, seeing people I know. One man has made a point of coming up to my room about midnight to tell me of his success or failure in love.

I intend to write no more stories until the end of next academic year—i.e. June. My exams shall have been over then.

I may go with the college 1st XI that is touring the west of England for a week in July.

My love to Ma.

Love,
Vido

University College, Oxford
June 30, 1952

My darling sister,

I was so happy to get your news about the examinations. Tell me, isn't it at all possible for you to get some sort of grant that will enable you to come to Oxford? Or is it possible for you to get into the Indian diplomatic service? Let me know.

I am disappointed to hear that you will be coming to England only next July. I was looking forward to seeing you next April, and to having your company for the last two months before my finals in June. But things have turned out differently. You see, my dear, I am very homesick. I am scared to be alive. For the past six months an air of unreality has hung about the things I have done.

Well, it has happened. I suppose you knew that it would. I had a row with Ruth. She and her husband started a campaign of humiliation against me; they hoped that I would be as jelly-like as the rest. For instance, if I say I played cricket, they wonder what sort of team I could possibly play for; if I say I am writing a story, they wonder who will ever read it; if it is broadcast, they announce their pity for the people who listen to it. They put me up in a room that forms part of the bathroom—no chair, no table—and charge me £1 a week. They also charge me for food. But I must wash up. I receive noisy admonitions about dropping ash on floors. (Compare, for instance, the charm of my present landlady, 'Just a minute, Mr Naipaul, I'll get you an ash-tray' with Ruth's 'Don't go dropping your ash on my floor.') Well, I have had enough. Thank God I have friends in this country. So I returned to Oxford (now the 2nd week of the vacation) the day after I went to London. Today I saw my Dean and he relieved me of worry by saying that one should never put up with anything one is not obliged to.

Oh, I do so hope that my depression doesn't come over me again. I want to work. I want to work very much, but I must feel free in my mind.

But tell me: when are you going to think about getting married. To judge by your letters, your life has been an unemotional blank. But this I find a little difficulty in believing. Don't take this in a silly way. You have a problem. I am perhaps too critical of people and you are probably scared to let me know.

Two of my friends have invited me to their houses this summer: one to Harrogate in Yorkshire, the other to Kent. So my vacation may be rather agreeable.

They have elected me secretary of the Martlets. It is not an honour to shout about, but the duties are light.

My two years in college have finished. Next term I move out into lodgings. I have found one in Wellington Square, Oxford—for £3 a week! Shocking, the cost of living in this country.

Having exhausted the 'true' Oxford, I find that yet it can be fun in work. It is a great thing, if one can lose oneself in it, so much the better. But my solitude weighs on me. Things never seem to turn out right.

I am sorry to be wailing all this time. But better a wail than no letter at all. I have turned over the new leaf in letter-writing—I hope and fervently trust, health, physical, mental and emotional, providing.

Write me soon, dear Kamla,

> Love,
> Vido

University College, Oxford
July 10, 1952

Dear Everybody,

I am writing this from Harrogate, where I am staying with the family of an Oxford friend. Harrogate is a very respectable town in the north of England; and, in the old days, was used by the rich as a place of recuperation after they had a spent a lifetime of indulgence.

On the 30th June I posted to Satti a parcel of books—all but one that she asked for. And, notwithstanding her protestations, I know that they were books that could be had in any Trinidad bookshop.

I may as well spend the rest of this letter relating the quarrel I had with the Capildeos. I have very little money at the moment (a position, thank God, that will disappear when I leave college and start living in lodgings). So I wrote to my uncle's wife and asked to be put up. I realised, of course, that I would have to pay. I got to London at 10.45 p.m. on the night of June 27. They gave me a meal. Shortly after the meal, I was ordered to wash up and help wash up. There were 2 women—Jean and Ruth—and Owad washing up. I ignored the request for a short time and finished reading a small column in the paper. Then I went to the sink. Jean told me to go away: it was all right, she would wash up. Then Ruth, 'Don't pamper him at all. He must learn to do these things.' All this may sound innocent, but it has formed part of a Capildeo campaign to humiliate me. (They were, for instance, besides themselves with joy when they heard that I had missed the train for the Spanish jaunt. Poor fools, they didn't know that I merely had to wait ½ hour for another. They thought I had lost all the money I spent on the fare!) But, at this sink, there was nothing for me to do. So I stood around idly.

I asked for a chair for the bedroom in which they had so kindly put me up for £1 a week. This bedroom was thus [little diagram showing bedroom half of a room measuring 8' × 10']. No furniture, not a table, not a chair—and $20 a month. Uncle is generous.

From this plan, you see that anyone wishing to get to the bathroom has to go through my room. So there is not even privacy. It was in such a room that they expected me to work for my exams!

Well, I asked for a chair. Ruth said that I was to take one and bring it down every morning. I said nothing. Then she suddenly shouted: 'Well, you can't expect chairs to walk up the stairs, do you?' I did not reply and, not wishing to lose my temper, decided to go up to my room. I was not at all moved. I was just realising that I couldn't stay there and work. I took my coat and made to go up. Then Ruth said: 'And don't drop your ash on the floor.' That was the last straw. I told her I had lived in rooms before, and perhaps in better rooms, that I wasn't going to stand her airs and I wasn't going to let anybody break me or my spirit once more; that I wasn't going to let myself be humiliated; and that, furthermore, I was going to leave the house tomorrow.

She was angry. I didn't know the fight that she had to allow uncle to take me, pictured as the poor destitute orphan—that she was on my side.

(This is amusing. Capo R. tried to imply that Ruth didn't want me. You see the plan: humiliate him.)

Well, next morning I left early. I returned later and said that I had come to collect my suitcase. Capo R. told me that my coming there had put him to expenses. That the room cost him £1 a week to keep: there was the gas and everything (a manifest lie; in summer, you don't need fires, nor gas). And, besides, the £1 for food was reasonable. If he were running a boarding house it would have been all right. But the shame-faced lie of the man: at the home in which I am staying at the moment—a big respectable home, where I have as big and as pleasant a room as I could have, with a window overlooking a garden—I pay not £2 a week for everything, but <u>30/-</u>, and from people who are upper class, not poor.

There is nothing here to upset you. Those people were never of any help to me. I thought that they were being kind to me in the Xmas; they weren't. My mental sufferings were objects of their mirth. Capo S. is perhaps a bit better but I wonder—no, they are just as bad. Expect nothing good from any of them.

Love,
Vido

Still writing from Harrogate, Yorkshire
July 1st, 1952

Dear Satti,

I have just finished Book II of the *Faerie Queene*, by Spenser (1552–99), and have decided to write you. It is 7 p.m. now, but the sun is still shining quite brightly and will keep on shining for the next two and a half hours. My window looks out to the garden of the house in which I am staying. I have been here one week already, and will be here for another.

Tomorrow we are all going to a play, or rather, a masque: *Comus* by Milton. It is being done by the girls of a famous public school for girls in Harrogate, Queen Ethelberga's. I am looking forward to it.

I am really quite happy now that you decided to do your HC. There should have been no doubt in your mind at all. A mere school certificate is practically worthless. But you seem to have chosen a difficult subject. English lit. demands more than a mere knowledge of the texts, and a familiarity with the criticism of your text editor. <u>You</u> <u>must</u> <u>do</u> <u>your</u> <u>own</u> <u>thinking about the books you read.</u> Learned criticism is what you need. In other words, if you are studying Milton, get to know something of his life, the temper of the times he lived in, the literary conventions. Take Milton: you read his life, and a short history of the period (this takes up less than 60 minutes and is invaluable). You realise that Milton was a fairly priggish man—austere, convinced that he was a genius, and always anxious to write a great and enduring epic. You learn that, because he toyed with several subjects for this epic, he really didn't care what he wrote about; but this is not to say that he wrote without conviction. Now, you ask yourself what Milton set out to do—justify the ways of God to man, and justify them particularly in the fall of Adam and Eve. What problems did he face?, you think, and you see (a) an epic must have lots of action like the *Aeneid*, lots of supernatural machinery—acceptable to the Romans because of their religion (i.e. Jupiter could send messages to mortals, etc.), (b) Milton tried to fix this epic machinery to his work, but runs into trouble. The Christian god is an incorporeal spirit; his angels are likewise incorporeal spirits. How can Milton bring one into almost fleshly life without ruining his thought?

In other words, thought is indispensable. You must realise in the first place <u>what</u> <u>the</u> <u>writer</u> <u>set</u> <u>out</u> <u>to</u> <u>do.</u> It is no use criticising a cricket reporter because he mishandles the report of Stollmeyer's* wedding. Having found out the aim of the writer, ponder on the difficulties of the achievement, and then see where he has failed. For heaven's sake, don't behave like one of my colleagues here and assume that every eminent writer is a literary god, unapproachable and infallible.

It is essential, if you are to understand the literature of the 17th century, to read a short book on the Renaissance in Europe. Make full use of the libraries. Read widely, and thoughtfully. Stop reading rubbish, and you shortly find that rubbish becomes boring.

I am sorry to be so pontifical, but I know how bad teaching is in QRC, and I shudder at what it must be at St Joseph's. By the way, you naughty girl, you made me buy you a *Mansfield Park* and it appears that you already have one!

Pa probably remembers Mr Earlforward in *Riceyman Steps*. Tell him

---

* Well-known West Indian (Trinidad) test cricketer

that I have come across a man in Harrogate who, I think, is Earlforward come to life. He doesn't care whether you buy or don't. His shop is shabby and books are piled anyhow. But he knows the value of books; makes no effort at conversation, and seems genuinely unwilling to sell. Like Mr E. he is nattily dressed always. He looks underfed. Extremely fascinating.

Love,
Vido

7.16.52

My dear Vido,

I have kept back a whole week or longer from writing you. The fact is I wrote a full letter almost as soon as I got yours (of June 23); but I didn't like it and never mailed it. Until I got your letter I was worried about you. News of your recovery was like a tonic and I went to work refreshed.

I am very glad you went to Spain. It was the best thing for you . . . I should very much like to send you two or three pounds on your having done so well in your term exams; but I can't very conveniently do so just yet, though I have some money with me. Last week I lost my glasses in the bush at Forest Reserve oilfield, and replacing them has meant $34. There are other things. <u>Still, if you very much need some money let me know at once.</u>

This will pain you: but your Ma will be having a baby—in September or October . . . I know it's a mess, but there we are. About your troubles . . . I should know a good deal about it, for I was the victim of a neurosis myself many years ago. You will perhaps remember our sojourn in Chase Village; and before Chase Village my hard days at your Nanie's, then at Wilderness, with Aiknath . . . But I got over it, and have done more work after that than I had bargained for. So do not be afraid. In my own case some religious literature helped, but only in a superficial way. They were a palliative, not the cure. The cure I got from the books *Outwitting Our Nerves* and *Psychology of the Adolescent*. The first mentioned book I shall be dropping in the mail box the same time with this letter. I am sure you will find it very helpful. You will get over all fear of the bogey, for that is what the whole neurosis amounts to. You see, my dear Vido, we are not just a mass of flesh and bone. We are also what our ideas have made us. There is no such thing as 'sick' or 'depleted' nerves. It is not a matter of tissue, but of thought. What gets us sick is our wrong ideas. The whole illness is often the outcome of a conflict between the demands of man, the animal in Nature, and the demands of Man, the creature of civilisation.

The best of us—from the Pope to the peasant—are three-fourths still very primitive creatures, and this primitive part of us sometimes gets over the 'censor' and invades our consciousness. Sometimes it doesn't come into our consciousness at all, but subconsciously expresses itself in all sorts of queer disguises . . . Adolescence is a stage that does not occur in the calendar of Nature. Biologically, most of us are mature in about mid-adolescence. But society at this stage has us very much in school. The instincts, be it that of hunger or of reproduction or any other, are just as insistent today (in spite of civilisation) as they were when we still stood at the ape or Neanderthal stage of our evolution. In this Nature recognises no sin, but society does. Hence the conflict. Consciously or unconsciously we think we have done wrong; we want to run and hide. We cannot face reality. . . . But there is no sin but society makes it so. Cure lies in re-education.

The book I am sending you will help. Read it diligently, and try and see exactly where your trouble lies . . . You say your illness was due to lack of affection. It can be. But it shouldn't. If it was so, it was because of what the psychologists call a mother or father fixation: the individual tarrying too long in the stage of mother or father love; a kind of retarded weaning, psychologically. You must get over it. All homesickness may be more or less a fixation; when it is acute it becomes an affliction. Tell yourself you are no longer a two- or three-year-old toddler . . . learn to choose your emotions. Well, I think I have preached a lot but you will find plenty more in the book.

Hitchens is at the Caura Sanatorium. When I told him yesterday (I went to see him) that you are Assistant Editor, Sub-editor and layout man on the *Oxford Tory*, he laughed . . . Shekhar is getting married next year to Dharry's daughter. Notice the term, 'married *to*'.

Kamla sent in some books for Sati yesterday . . . Geography and English Literature, or histories of English Literature. And some pictures. Nice prints. Since her cable passing her B.A. finals, she has not written us. Wonder why? Queer girl; like yourself! . . . I don't know what to say about those short stories. There are 12 all right, but they don't seem to come up to anything like a fair-size book! Should have three or four more stories.

Write us a long, nice letter.

Till then I am as ever,
Pa

University College, Oxford
July 19, 1952

My dear Kamla,

I was a fool. I wrote you in anger and irritation. But, although I think the whole thing is just damned silly, I am no longer angry. I shall ignore the whole affair in my letters, as you suggest.

I am not writing from Oxford, but from Harrogate, a town in the middle of Yorkshire. I am staying as a paying guest with the family of a friend. As you probably expect, I never hit it off with other people's parents. In this country, where the mother–son relationships are tighter and more sloppy than at home, mothers invariably look upon their 24-year-old sons as their own poor little babies, and treat them as such. So it is not surprising that an outsider and an intruder like myself is looked upon with suspicion. Heaven knows what they think of me. Perhaps they see me as a hard-drinking atheist, or worse, as a Communist.

As I told you, I have my finals next year, July. I think I shall do 2 more years at Oxford after that, doing a B.Litt., or something equally worthless. The prospects of a job are really quite dim. If I return to Trinidad it merely means QRC or the Civil Service. It also means the end of any ambition. It is really quite a problem. I find myself with a family to support as soon as I leave Oxford. So *'Que faire?'*

Satti has been writing me fairly regularly and I am replying as soon as I get her letter. I get so many letters that I find it quite a task keeping up with my correspondence. But I have decided to reply to every letter as soon as I have received it. That may waste time, but it keeps the conscience clear.

Love,
Vido

University College, Oxford
July 27, 1952

My darling Ma,

I had heard the news from Kamla about ten days ago, and I was rather surprised. But I have now got over my surprise and I am writing to tell you that I think it makes little difference, except perhaps for you. I hope the girls are helping you. Please write me if they are not and I shall write them—if my advice counts for anything.

I spent a rather pleasant fortnight in Harrogate. My friend's father had served in the submarine division of the Admiralty during the war, and has to tell a tale of corruption and cheating and sneaking that can rival anything Pa can tell about the Civil Service or the *Guardian*. Today, an old man of 60, he is retired and unemployed, living on a negligible pension. All he got for his services in the war was an OBE and a breakdown that involved a limp in one of his legs. So things appear to be the same all over the world.

I don't think that you should be too worried about Kamla. I think she is a fine girl, full of strength and determination. She wants to come home to help you out and I think that she will. Believe me when I say that not writing is no sign of dying affection.

For myself, you can rely upon me as long as my health lasts. Not that I am an invalid or anything at the moment; but I find, as I grow older, that I have grown infinitely complex, and not without a fair share of inherited nervousness. I have inherited several other things, too. I find that I button my coat in exactly the same way Pa buttons his, according to photographs. I sit in the same way, and have the same superficial light-heartedness. Perhaps you know Pa's habit of getting up at 5 or so in the morning, making a row to get everybody else up, and then going back to sleep. Well, I have no one to make a row with, but I get up sometimes at 5, and then go back to sleep too.

I suppose that the books I sent Satti will have arrived when you read this letter. I merely hope that the parcel is properly secured and that none of the books are missing. I posted some books to myself from Harrogate (to prevent my suitcase from being uncomfortably heavy). When the books did arrive, I found that 3 were missing and my original wrapper had been replaced. So I still remain careless. I still remain as forgetful as ever. The boy's mother at Harrogate had prepared some sandwiches for my 7-hour journey to Oxford. Of course I forgot them.

There is one thing I hope never happens in our family. I visited the Gockings yesterday and found the home in a state of revolting untidiness. I found daughters and mothers grovelling and talking at the same time and I was really oppressed. This, I hope, will never happen to us.

I shall write Pa in a day or so. But in the meantime tell him that I received his money. Tell him not to send me anymore just yet. The college is helping me out. They won't let me starve, and I have heard rumours of increased allowances. And, above all, take my love; and take care of yourself—Love, your son, Vido

August 21, 1952

Dear Satti,

Sorry to have delayed so long to reply to your letter. I am happy that the books please you. I also apologise for slandering you in the *Mansfield Park* affair.

I think that everyone at home is rather worried about Kamla or perhaps angry with her. I have just had a letter from her in which she tells me that she will be writing as soon as possible. So, cease from wrath, and stop worrying.

I have just spent a fortnight with a friend in Kent and I felt truly at home. The point that now worries me is if I will ever get used to living in a small house again. All the homes I have stayed at have always been elaborate St Clair*-style affairs. And I am beginning to look upon that sort of thing as my right. That, I think, is one of the dangers of Oxford.

My money problems are settled. The college gave me £40, but the following day the Colonial Office sent me £45, so I returned the £40 back to the college. Our allowances have been increased.

I think Kamla will be returning home in about ten months and I shall be coming for four months or so in 1953 or 54. So the odysseys that began in 1949 (only 3 years ago) are nearing their end.

Let me know how your work is going. And, remember, I shall reply to all letters that are sent me, the very day they reach me. I wrote many letters

---

* Upper-class district of Port of Spain

home about three weeks ago and only got yours in return. I am not annoyed. I suppose that people are busy. My love to Ma & Pa, and take the rest for yourself and the others—Meera, Savi and Shivan.

Love,
Vido

8.28.52

My dear Vido,

We haven't got a letter from you during the whole of August. Your letter to Sati arrived yesterday; and it seems that those you sent to 'Everybody' have gone astray in the mails. I had in fact been wondering why you were not writing. As to Kamla . . . I just can't understand her. She writes once in a blue moon, and always evades, if not ignores, questions asked. How long does it take to scribble down a letter? It is always good to write a letter immediately you get one. It becomes easier to write.

I am greatly relieved to know that your money difficulties are over and that you fellows have got an increase in allowance. How are your nerves? And have you got the book I sent you? Please read it; it will help you.

I hear the *Guardian* staff are getting some kind of increase in pay, beginning from September. This may either be a month's bonus or an increase generally. I don't quite know. I am hoping I come in for some.

The whole Naipaul menage—except of course your Ma and myself—have gone to Mayaro with the Sookhdeos. They left home on Thursday and will be back Saturday or Friday. Shivan is eager to go to the sea every time, but hardly touches water. Two Sundays ago we went to Balandra in the old 1192, which behaved commendably.

A lot of break-ups seem to be happening with the Capildeo clan. Mostly it is on account of the high-flying of the girls. Boy, are they going it? Some time ago Miss Sattin Ramnarine brought in a boarder—a Presby. chap attending the Government Training College here. Now she is going to marry him; he already a married man, with a child and another one on the way. Capo S. and his batch have stopped going to Robert Street because of this. As to the other girls—the Sookhdeos—you just can't time them. So far only the Naipaul lot seem to be still relatively unsophisticated. Good Lord! How humans change!

I suppose you have already heard that Shekhar is going to be married . . . By the way, some girl-friend of yours named Pat* sent you a letter from—I forget the place—and the closely-written dispatch somehow found itself home. Everybody read it; and Sati said to me, as she brought me the letter in bed, here, look, this is what your son is doing in England. And we all tried hard to find out just how the letter reached us at all. I suppose the registrar or somebody like that received it in your absence and sent it here, thinking perhaps you were vacationing in Trinidad. Take it easy. A boy must have a friend or two; or what sort of a boy is he? Only don't get netted . . . DO WRITE EVERY WEEK TILL IT BECOMES A HABIT. Write whether we write you or not.

Yours as ever,
Pa

University College, Oxford
September 6, 1952

Dear Everybody,

This week I got two letters. And, as I promised, I am replying straight away. The long vacation is nearing its end. It is, as a matter of fact, a mere month before it is over and my last year before the exams begins.

Last year this time I was in Paris. Now I am at Oxford and therefore am witnessing my first St Giles' Fair. St Giles is a broad avenue that runs from the north of Oxford's city centre to Banbury (yes, of the fine lady upon a white horse) and Woodstock. For two days this street is closed to traffic and becomes a fairground. Today (Sunday 7) the tents and amusement booths had been all up. The weather is going to be rather bad. It is cold and raining.

Now I must express my displeasure at something. A letter, addressed to me, was sent home because the college porter thought that I was wealthy enough to go home myself. There could have been no reason why this letter should have been opened, or, once opened, why it should have been read to its bitter (or passionate) end.

---

* Patricia Hale, Vidia's wife-to-be

But I shall satisfy in everything your curiosity. Patricia Ann Hale is a girl of 20. She is a member of the university, not unintelligent, nor altogether unattractive. I met her in February and have been thankful ever since. She befriended me at the height of my illness, put up with all my moods—my coarseness, and my fits of anguish. The relationship between us, while not a platonic one, is so far virtuous. The talk about being 'netted' is rather cynical and I do trust that you will not make things doubly difficult for us. Her father is making a terrible fuss about it, and I hope that the same narrowness will not be found in you.

About her character: she is good, and simple. Perhaps a bit too idealistic, and this I find on occasion rather irritating. She insists on looking at the good, and chooses to shut her eyes to the bad. She shares my literary tastes, and I have found my friendship with her most stimulating.

I would have written before, but I had no idea things would develop as they have. I have had girl-friends before who have rejected me. In none I found the qualities I found in Pat—her simplicity, her goodness, her charm. I should be grateful if Pa were to write her a sympathetic letter, or, better, write me an understanding letter. Such a letter will, I think, cheer her up quite a lot. She has seen pictures of all of you, and is, naturally, quite attached to Shivan.

I have not, I hope, given the impression that we are going to be married soon. We have to wait to see how things work out.

Love,
Vidia

September 8, 1952

Dearest Ma,

Thank you very much indeed for your letter and for your birthday card. I got three birthday cards in all—two from home, and one from Pat (whose letter was common property). Pat (dear girl) gave me a pair of socks because I complained some time ago that the last pair of socks I had were those that I was wearing!

A recovery from a mental breakdown is a protracted affair, and I can really write now and say confidently that the worst is over. I am thinking of going to a psychologist, but my recovery in the past two or three days has been accelerated so greatly that I don't think this will be necessary after all. But perhaps a check-up will do no harm. It is difficult to exaggerate the dangers of a place like Oxford—the retarding influence it has on people: the sexually unbalanced and the plain neurotics.

One has to be extremely careful in the making of friends, and the result is a fear—a terrible fear of nearly everything. It would take a really strong-minded man to go through unscathed, and I flatter myself that my fairly puritanical upbringing has stood me in wonderful stead.

I didn't think that mothers could understand the ways of their sons. The urge in a young man for a woman is a pressing thing that, if repressed, leads to terrible unhappiness. The life of a man in a boarding house that includes meals in restaurants and a fairly constant loneliness can do anything. So if I try to lose my loneliness in a woman's friendship, there is little that is reprehensible! I have been quite fortunate in finding an agreeable woman.

But I must stop talking of myself and reassure you of my love. I hope you are in good health, and that everything goes well. I am sure that it will.

There is a saying that, in England, the visitor from the tropics finds his first winter comfortable, but his second less so. There is much truth in that. I am feeling the autumn chilliness very keenly, but it is an invigorating and healthy cold, and not uncomfortable.

I haven't had a letter from Kamla for a long time; the last time she wrote me, she expressed disgust at marriage, saying that it all seemed grossly sexual. But I do think a girl of 23 ought to be married. I am sorry to hear about the goings-on of my cousins and I can trust my younger sisters not to make fools of themselves.

Please, darling, take care of yourself, and remember that I love all of you.

Vido

Wed.
Sept. 17/52

My dear Vidia,

Your letter was most interesting, but very perturbing too. On the one hand, I want to do or say nothing that will make you unhappy; on the other, I would hate myself for encouraging you into a situation which later may prove to be regrettable. (If only you had been older, say twenty-three or twenty-five, I might have had more confidence in your decision.) The girl, I have no doubt, is everything you say of her, and we are deeply grateful to any whose understanding and solicitude helped you so much when you most stood in need for such understanding and sympathy. But as you say, her father disapproves of the relationship between you.

I know in the end you will do only what pleases you, and I want you to know that whatever you do, the only thing that matters to me—and to all of us at home—is your happiness. I am glad that you do not intend to marry soon. I suggest that you go on knowing each other for another two years or so at least. By then you will both have been older and will have discovered not only your respective virtues but your shortcomings and incompatibilities as well.

Talk the matter over with her again and again, and see if she understands Trinidad's reactions to mixed marriages. Almost without variation, these marriages have never been successful—not because of the temperaments of the two people concerned, but because of the attitude that is shown them by friends on both sides; you will not be accepted by her people; she will not be accepted by anyone except those in our own home here.

This is an extremely serious matter, and we all want you to give it your most earnest consideration. Why not complete your studies at the university before embarking on a course which you may later regret? If at the end of this time you are still sure you are suited to each other, I shall give you my most affectionate good wishes.

Please convey our most heartfelt thanks to Miss Hale for her great kindness to you.

Your affectionate
Pa

PS Please let me know how you stand with winter clothing; and if you need money, how much?

Pa

University College, Oxford
Sep. 28, 1952

Dear Pa,

I received your letter about six days ago, and I must thank you for it. I don't want to break your heart, but I hope I never come back to Trinidad, not to live, that is, though I certainly want to see you and everybody else as often as I can. But Trinidad, as you know, has nothing to offer me.

The very fact that I can write about future plans ought to hearten you. You see, I have really been suffering from an abnormal mental condition. I was depressive. I have seen the psychologist twice and there is now no further need to see him. The first talk was inconclusive. At the end of the second, he discovered what was wrong with me. Put simply, it was this. Disappointed in Oxford, and myself, I had looked upon myself as a failure; yet was never willing to admit this fear. Accordingly this fear of failure became fear of something so absurd and horrifying that I shall not tell what it was for a number of years. When I discovered this, I suddenly felt that a weight had been lifted off me. And now, looking at myself, I see a young man, healthy mentally and physically, at a good university, with a year of preparation for his exams, and once more full of ambition. I no longer drag myself stupidly from meal to meal. This state of mind, the most normal thing in the world, now seems to me to be so extraordinarily wonderful.

Of course, I don't intend getting married for at least two years.

Love to Ma,
Vido

VIII

October 3, 1952 — August 8, 1953

FINAL YEAR

University College, Oxford
October 3, 1952

My darling Ma,

This letter is to ask you to remember at least one thing: that nothing will ever make me stop having all the respect and love in the world for you. So please don't make yourself unhappy because of anything. It would make me unhappy to know you do so. Please take good care of yourself. I feel sure that my sisters at home will be kind and reasonable enough to do all they can to make everything pass as smoothly as possible.

Do you know, about 2 hours ago, I got new glasses—the first pair since you got those from Dr Metivier in April 1948. The father of a friend of mine—at whose home I stayed in Kent for a fortnight—is an oculist; and he tested my eyes. Short-sightedness, thank God, is one illness that does not grow worse as one grows older. But I was shocked when I put on my new glasses. The world seemed such a glorious place. I could see people much clearer; and streets became more beautiful. The colours are sharper for me. And I feel rather sorry to have missed all those wonderful colours all this time.

Please take good care of yourself and write me as soon as you are well. I am indeed in the best of health. I am energetic; and my asthma protects me from most of the illnesses that come with winter. So there!

All my love, from your son,
Vido

University College, Oxford
October 3, 1952

My dear Miss 18 years,*

You feel like hitting me on the head, I know, for completely ignoring your birthday. I think you will admit that I have quite a number to carry round in my heard. Your birthday is Sep. 21, isn't it? Well, if I don't remember, it is up to you to kick up a row to remind me. Write me a month before and say, 'Oh, yes, you can send me a gold tiara for my birthday that falls, accidentally, in a month. Silver tiaras are the fashion, but I have no objection to gold.' That is the way to do it. Being tactful. The surest way of winning friends and influencing people.

Your silence on the subject of academic work forces me to believe that you are devoting some time to the house, as Ma is not well. Please don't let me down. It is difficult to make someone 18 years old understand the virtues of generosity and compassion. But, believe me, they are good things. So try and help. Help given with a smile repays itself ten times. Help given with a scowl is an insult and a humiliation.

Another thing you can do is to write Kamla. I haven't written her for a long time. I was awaiting an answer from her. But I will soon.

Remember that being 18 carries not only privileges but also responsibilities. Try to grow up. Treat yourself with respect and others will do the same.

Another time I shall write about LOVE to you. All I can say in the mean time is don't do anything that Ma will be ashamed of. Remember that most men are just rascals all their lives; all are rascals most of their lives.

Love,
Vido

---

* Sati

[From Kamla]

October 10th, 1952

My dear Vido,

You might be very surprised when you hear that a few days ago I became engaged to an Indian chap. He is Christian, though, and with the most awful name of Vincent Richmond, yet I don't think I can get the ideal person. It does not mean, however, that I am going to become a Christian. I am remaining a Hindu all my life and all my children will be Hindus. It will be three years before he will be finished with his studies and until that time, I won't marry. So it does not interfere with my programme of leaving for home soon. Of all the boys I met, I thought that despite the fact that he is Christian, Ma and Pa would like him best. Besides, I think it best to marry the person who is mad after you—almost worships you—than marry one you love. However, it will be years before I can get married, so please do not worry about anything.

Some recent events that have happened in this place have made me so disgusted with Benares and its staff that I want to go home immediately. I have written Pa that he should write a letter to the authorities and that he should send for me immediately. I really hope he does it. But as I told you, everyone at home now hates me like poison and I feel as though I would be out of place in the family. Well, such is the mental strain that one lives in Benares that I feel that I cannot trust even my own family. That is why I want to get out of Benares immediately.

Here is the result of the letter I wrote home to Ma—'if you had restrained those highly strung emotions of yours whether they were right or wrong (Sati)'. Well, that's it.

Will you kindly write Pa and tell him that he should send money for me immediately so that I could leave this place by December.

By the way, if there is anything special that I may bring for you please say so. I know about cigarettes. What else?

So many students from Trinidad have been coming to India lately that I wonder what's happening over there. Boy, I wouldn't let one of my sisters come here. One is sufficient. There is one Seta Muharaj who is here now and she has been only talking of going back. She's in for a pretty rough time, I know. The bigger cities may be tolerable but Benares is hopeless in every sense of the word.

Well, at the moment there is nothing that I am longing for as much as to leave for home. When I meet you, there'll be endless days of talking and I'm sure you would be very interested in India and everything about it. I don't mean politics.

Well, that's all for now. Hoping to see you real soon.

Yours,
Kamla

10/11/52

Dear Vidia,

This has been a week of letters. Some three from you; more than half a dozen from Kamla; another from Kamla's boyfriend—Vincent David Richmond (I wish the name rhymed—something like Rada Krishnan Dial). But it seems this is not to be.

Your letters were most cheering—and the one to Sati, charming. She showed me it. That is the sort we like. They lightened my own gloom—until one came in from Kamla demanding $300 'immediately', saying she is quite disgusted with Banares and wants to flee it right away.

That girl is unpredictable: the letter dated two days earlier was asking me my consent to her engagement. Richmond himself wrote a decent letter—requesting the same and saying they will be marrying in two years. Her engagement and her coming away do not click. I have told her so.

It seems from what she says that there has been some dirty mudslinging on her at BHO and she is demanding an investigation. The rumour spread on her is so nasty that I shall not tell you. It might be that between Oct. 3 and Oct. 5 these rumours grew more, then she wrote to say she wanted to quit Banares for good right away.

I don't know where I'm going to put my hand on $300. I have just 300 cents in the bank and I hope she changes her mind. But she says if I do not send her the money she'd be leaving Banares in November (no date) anyway.

VDR, by the way, is doing a course in pharmacy on a Government of India scholarship. You will recollect I had given K. a 'pulling up' on this chap a long time ago. The result was she wasn't writing us for months. Well, even here in Trinidad inter-marriages—he is RC—are becoming more and more inevitable. So I have given them consent, wishing them the best of luck. What more can I do or not do? Let them marry and be happy, that's all. Same for you. I am sure Pat is a good girl. Your Ma is the hardest person to win over. The others are 'diplomatically neutral', they want the girl's photograph and yours side by side. Send same.

Love,
Pa

Benares
Oct. 28, 1952

My dear Vido,

I received your letter yesterday afternoon. Sure I'll write to Patricia. But you haven't told me anything about what she does or what she is like. Well, if you both think that you would be happy with each other then I would only be happier.

Of course you've got to get through with your studies and get yourself a good job. In the meantime, it might be good if you'd just take a bit of advice and take things easy. You know, always try and keep on the safe side.

By the way, I intend leaving for home as soon as possible—most probably December. I guess I'll have to remain with [. . .] and I haven't written him for quite some time. So I had better do so immediately. Will I be allowed to stay with you?

You know, at home they were thinking of asking me to become the principal of some school with a salary paying between $300 and $350 a month. It will be a state-aid Hindu girls' school. Mamoo is the secretary but now that I am going to be married to a Christian, I don't think I'll get the job unless my fiancé turns Hindu. Well, I know Mamoo, and I think if he wants he can jolly well get that job for me. But honestly I have no faith, absolutely none, in him. Besides I am not going to be married for quite some time so I don't see the reason for objection. But gosh, it really would be fine if I could get that.

Well, that's all for now, and I wish you'd be a bit more regular in writing. Expect a telegram any time telling of my arrival.

My regards to Patricia and my love to you.

Your sister,
Kamla

49 St John St, Oxford
University Coll., Oxford
November 7, 1952

My dear Kamla,

It gave me a very real thrill to hear that you are leaving India. I am looking forward to seeing you. You can stay with me. The problem, of course, is one of money. And it is rather unlikely that you may be able to get a job here. You know—one must be specifically handed to do specific jobs. All part of the new socialism and what you will. I suppose you will have to put up with Capo R., swallowing your pride. I am poison to those people. The problem is difficult; please, however, do not spend sleepless nights over it. Things do right themselves.

I hope I am not being presumptuous, but can you bring me:

1. Gandhi's autobiography (sold only in India): *The Story of My Experiments with Truth.*
2. Some Indian brassware; and, if possible, some works of art. Can you possibly get a statuette of Siva Natarajan—the dancing Shiva?
3. A good, readable, authoritative and exhaustive history of India (does any such exist?). And English translations of the Hindu epics and dramas.
4. Something for Patricia.

Use your discretion. Bring some of these things, if you can, if you can't, don't fret yourself overmuch.

I am looking forward to seeing you.

Love, from Vido

A damned curt letter, I know!

University College, Oxford
November 11, 1952

Dear Ma,

I am indeed very sorry about not having written earlier. If it can make up for that, I offer the news that everything is really going marvellously well with me. My health is good; I feel ambitious once again; and I am managing to work pretty hard. It is another seven months' bout of truly hard work that faces me. Everything really depended on my health, but as this is now all right, there seems little to worry about.

Enough of me, however. I do hope that you are well. I was most upset to hear that you are under great financial strain at the moment. I myself find it difficult to understand Kamla's behaviour; yet I know her, I think, and feel that she will make up for this to you soon—very soon.

I think you should bear in mind that, in about two years or so, most of your children will be able to look after themselves, and help you. Frankly, whenever I think about you and Pa, I think that you have been noble. That is the only word I can use, and I use it in all sincerity. You have really done extremely well; much better than you perhaps realise.

At the end of December I shall send a tiny bit of money to you— £5—and I hope it will at least brighten the celebration of New Year's Day for you.

I was rather entertained by Nanie's last request. (And here I want to drop a pedantic hint to Satti: if, in her letters, she uses the phrase 'real big', a grotesque Americanism, I shudder to think what she writes in her essays. Tell her that it is necessary to think before writing. Remind her what Maugham says about American slang in *Cakes and Ale:* the American slang is so perfect that Americans can carry on long conversations without ever thinking about what they say.) I had, as a matter of fact, heard about it about a fortnight ago. I went up to London one Saturday, in the company of an American, whose typewriter I am now using, and went to Clapham (the abode of Capo R.) to get my overcoat. I had left it there last March. Capo wasn't there, but Owad was. He greeted me warmly, announced the sad news, and asked whether I was carrying any tobacco on me.

I am no longer living in college. That means I have moved out to lodgings. They are rather expensive, but are in the centre of the town which is rather convenient.

About that picture of Patricia which seems to be anxiously desired; the girl is so scared that she keeps on putting off the appointment with the photographer's, and she awaits the arrival of Kamla with a certain amount of apprehension.

I am writing another paper for the Martlets, the college intellectuals. I am secretary, and there seems little hope of getting someone to do a fourth paper this term. So I decided to do one myself.

My deepest love to all,
Vidia

11.23.52

Dear Vidia,

It felt good to get a letter from you at last and to know that you are all right. I had gone back thinking you were ill again. That is the worst of your not writing once every two weeks, if not once a week.

I cabled Kamla $300 for India–England passage on the 4th. She was anxious that I should do so and kept on writing home twice or thrice a week, saying she was anxious to quit Banares. But since my cabling her the money I have not heard from her. I can't say what is happening.

On the other hand, the Indian Commissioner here has threatened me that if Kamla leaves BHO before completing the music course, I may be made to refund the Indian Government whatever funds they have so far spent on Kamla for the music course. But the Secretary (unofficially of course) tells me that the Indian Government cannot do anything of the sort: I have signed no agreement to that effect. So I am not worrying about this.

As requested by Kamla, I wrote the Vice Chancellor of BHO. He has replied in a long letter to say, among other things, that though 'she is supposed to be doing the music course, she herself has confessed that she is no longer interested in it. The plain and simple reason is that she is continuing to be here because Richmond is here.'

If this is true—and it does seem true to me—it is obviously a tactless attitude on her part. You cannot be drawing 200 rupees a month (a sum that exceeds the salary of the average professor at BHO) on the score of your doing a certain course and yet saying you are not interested in it. It is bound to bring about jealousy. I have yet to write K. to this effect. If you write, be sympathetic and tactful.

It was grand of you to say that you'd be sending us some money in December; but we are really not in so much of a 'jam'. We are carrying on as well as usual. Of course, I have a monthly commitment to keep up on a loan for this passage for K.; but it is all right; I'll make it. Instead, I should be pleased if you spent the same money on some winter clothing for yourself, or get yourself something for Christmas. If you must send something let it be Maugham's 'The Gentleman in the Parlour' or 'Mrs [Craddock]'.

I have finished typing the stories—*Gurudeva* is more than twice the original length. I'll be glad to send it to you if my doing so will not interfere too much with your studies. Exams are near. Can you manage taking it to two or three publishers during the Christmas vacation? Let me know early.

You ought to visit my cousin Basdai* when you are in London. She'll put up nicely, I am sure. She'll be returning to England on January 10. Her husband and children are there. The address: 131 King Henry Road, London, NW3.

All well—Pa

Dear Vido

Nalini† and I are quite well, glad to hear that you also are well. Ma

I will send cocoa by Basdai.

49 St John St, Oxford
University College, Oxford
January 9, 1953

Dear Everybody,

The holidays are over; but, for me, there were no holidays. I stayed in Oxford for all the vacation, except for three days in London, spent almost

---

* Female cousin of Vidia's father
† Nalini (or Nella), newly-born (fifth) daughter, the seventh and last child of the family

unwillingly in a London slum with Owad and a man from St James—Twalib. By the end of this term I shall have spent a year in Oxford, practically without a break. That is too much for any man; and, at the moment, I am yearning to leave Oxford for a change. To get away to some village for a walk and be free.

My work is going slowly, but well. I am working like a steam-roller, much more effective for being slow. At the moment I am not quite well. I have a nagging cough and cold that leaves me enervated. But that's nothing to worry about.

I understand that Rudranath is going to T'dad in July. He wishes to settle everything. Apparently he began settling things three days after the old lady died. He has also expressed the hope that the ravenous, grasping sisters are not disturbing the [. . .] of Capo S. I don't care how brilliant that man may be, but I sincerely hope I never see him again. He has nothing for anyone. He is a petty being.

There really is little news to give you at home; all I wish to say—rather belatedly I know—is happy birthday to Meera, thanks to Satti for her letter (but, by God, I wish her handwriting could become simpler), and a happy new year to the rest of you. Of course I would like to get letters from other people—Savi and Meera and Shivan; but then, one can't expect everything. The principle seems to be—don't write first. To my letter of the beginning of December, the reply came four days ago—Satti's letter. Kamla has replied with a postcard. I do not wish to blame anyone. I know how difficult it is to write letters; and I have been none too zealous a correspondent myself.

Ideally, I should be leaving Oxford in June. But, since I am doing a B.Litt., my departure has to be delayed for 2 years. I really don't know why I am doing a B.Litt.

So, when I am ready to leave Oxford, in 2½ years, most of us shall be adult. Satti will be 21, Meera 18, Savi 17, Shivan 10; Kamla an old woman. And here I want to make a promise. When I am working, I shall move heaven and earth to send home a lump sum of money every year, a sum which, I hope, shall grow larger.

While I am doing the B.Litt., I needn't be at Oxford all the time; so I will do my best to come home for about 4 months in 1954—perhaps from Jan–May. All this is provisional. I shan't write any more on this subject. If I am not coming, I shall say so. If I am, I shan't say—I will surprise you all.

About jobs: I haven't the vaguest idea. But we have at Oxford an Appointments Committee that is a sort of Labour Exchange. I think I can get a job with the Shell people. They pay enormously; but Pat doesn't like the idea. She has got ideals etc. Neither do I, as a matter of fact, but it seems I am suited for so few things.

Pat and I went to the photographer's at the end of last term. It was not at all surprising that we should have a petty argument about five minutes before and, under the forced smiles as they appear on the photograph, we carry the marks of recent argument. But Pat has a camera and we shall send ordinary snaps in about two or three weeks.

I wonder what Satti is doing this year? What are Savi and Meera doing? No one writes me, and I am completely at a loss. I don't even know what Shivan is doing, or whether Savi is enjoying the benefits of a secondary education. Will someone help me?

Love, from Vido

Can you tell me
   a. The boat Capo S. is taking and the approximate date of its
      arrival, and at what port.
   b. Basdai's London hide-out.

Benares
Feb. 2, 1953

Dear Vido,
   This might be a very sad letter for you.
   Pa is very ill at home and has been confined to the hospital. The reason—worrying about you and I. I shall quote Sati's letter, 'It was a heart attack and a pretty bad one at that since he cannot walk. He has to take his meals lying down. Dr Mani told Ma that Pa would not be able to work steadily again, and, of course, if he knows that he might pan out right away.' According to Ma and Sati, Pa's greatest worry is that he cannot get his stories published. Sati wrote saying that he sent you one but you have done nothing about it so far. Now something immediate regarding the publishing of his stories means life or death for him and consequently life or death for us, especially those poor little children at home. Now, will you, in

the name of Pa's life, see immediately to his short stories and write him a nice, cheering letter. Ma says that, 'He (Pa) has written altogether about 14 short stories which he would be very glad that Vido should see a publisher to get them published. That is very important towards Pa's health. Please do your best to tell Vido that he would feel well if arrangements are made.'

These are Ma's words. I need not try to tell what Pa's being alive means to us—you know. So do take some time off and see about it. Write something encouraging to Pa immediately.

Tonight I have written for my passage. I am trying to make it as quick as possible—maybe this month, maybe next.

Write now to Pa. See about his stories. Write me saying what you have done. Carelessness about these means Pa's death.

Love, Kamla

University College, Oxford
February 3

My dear Pa,

First of all, I want to ask you not to worry. If you are unable to work, then you needn't worry, because I shall leave Oxford after my examinations in June. Please let Meera or Sati keep me posted. If I suspected that anything of this sort would have occurred I would have gone to the Appointments Committee some time ago. You needn't worry, though, about my leaving Oxford. Three years is enough for any reasonable man—and most people stay, as a matter of fact, for only three years.

You should not have thought that I was uninterested in your writing. You ought to know that I am perhaps more keen on your work than anyone else is. And, furthermore, as I have often told you, you have the necessary talent. Mittelholzer* has no talent, neither has Selvon, who has just written what he calls a novel, but what I call a travelogue. These people are just two of the twenty or so novelists who publish books every week; and reviewers praise about twelve of these books extravagantly. For instance, that poorly

---

* Edgar Mittelholzer, prolific West Indian (Guyanan) novelist, author of *A Morning at the Office*

written, contrived novel, *A Morning at the Office,* was highly praised. I have seen it in none of the public libraries here. The bookshops in Oxford that stock nearly everything have neither Selvon nor Mittelholzer. I went up to London two days ago to go to the Colonial Office. I saw a *Morning* going at the reduced rate of 2/6. This reduced price is the fate of books that are failures and recognised as such by their publishers.

If I try to hawk your book around, I wouldn't be doing you a favour. I would be trying to sell stuff that deserves to be published.

Allow me to tell you another story. The most successful and perhaps the best novelist today in the UK is a man called Joyce Cary. Cary began writing when he had served in the World War, served in Nigeria and had retired. For years his wife was the object of pitying derision. 'What is your husband doing?' people asked her. 'He is my man, and he knows what he is doing,' she said. Cary published his first book in 1936 when he was nearing fifty. It was a hopeless failure. And so was nearly every book he published—until 1944. Then the bad books became bestsellers. Critics began to recognise the patience and the art Cary had expended. Today Cary is an old man; he has tasted success only in the last six or seven years. He lectures in Oxford sometimes.

Please have courage and try to trust me.

Love,
Vido

[From Kamla]

Feb. 8, 1953

My dear, dear Pa,

I heard from Sati and Ma that you were ill. I feel very sad about being so far away from home at a time that I think I am really needed.

Are you worried about me? I am now very happy at Benares. You really shouldn't worry so much. At times in our own lives, you know, we all have difficulties. I had mine and for a time I fought them alone but then I was foolish enough to disturb you with them. You really shouldn't worry over so little. I am sure you know what you mean to us all.

Believe me, whether I am near to you or far, you may always turn to me. Whether married or unmarried, I will always see to it that I render some assistance to you all. I don't think that I would be so ungrateful as to just abandon home absolutely. And you ought to have that amount of trust in me. Should God help me, I would soon be rendering some financial assistance home.

I was given a medal by the Women's College for coming first class, third, in the B.A. (1952) results. I have given a graduation photograph of myself to be developed and as soon as it is ready I will be sending it on to you.

Send me a list of the books you'll like to have. I think Benares and Calcutta will be the best place to get them. I am trying to get some good statuettes, too, but the south is the best place for that. You get very crude ones in the north.

My dear Ma,

I know that you must be very worried about home. Pa's illness has really upset me. Can you tell me exactly why Pa is worried about me? Does he want me to come home now? I hope that he is better by now. Sati got me frightened about that working part. Well, I needn't say what Pa's not working will mean to all of us. For the next months you might have a difficult time at home. I hope that by that time I will be settled to a good sound job and then you would not have money matters to worry about. And this is not a vain promise.

How are the children at home? Well, I am not afraid because I know that you and Sati are there to see that everything goes well.

9th.

Received Mira's letter from home. I have no plans. I am really between the devil and the deep blue sea. I am now going to say everything and you ought to tell me what I should do. Vince is pessimistic about my going to T'dad. He seems to think that a separation now means a separation for ever.

In Fiji I am securing a job for around forty pounds a month. This will be roughly $180 in Trinidad money. Out of that I can send $100 home. The rest I will make do with. Now I will only accept that job when I have received information from Fiji in black and white. What do you think? Can

I get a better-paid job at home? Should I go to Fiji with Vince, work there and send money home, or do you think I could do better in Trinidad? Answer immediately and I will try and do exactly what you tell me.

Reply soon,

Love,
Kamla

University College, Oxford
February 20, 1953

Dear Pa,

I got your letter this morning and I was greatly cheered to find that you seem to be taking things in your stride. In a way I am not surprised, for the only test of man's greatness is his behaviour in times of distress.

I have been speaking to the Dean about getting a job. I have no wish to stay in England, nor do I wish to live the rest of my life in Trinidad. I lay down one requisite for any country I wish to reside in—it must be a big country. This does not mean that I shall give up my obligations to you. Far from it. It is only in the big countries that one can make money in reasonable quantities. The Dean thinks the prospect of my getting a job in this country is a pretty bleak one, and I never thought otherwise. He thinks, however, that I can perhaps represent a firm in some country—or something like that. But whatever it is, I am not worried, and I want you not to worry either.

My final examinations are drawing closer and I must step up the work.

Savi has been writing me some excellent letters and I long to get letters from Mira. By the way, I received a very charming photograph of Satti and Mira. They both look terribly attractive. Mira is developing an aristocratic, haughty beauty which the gauntness of her face emphasises.

At the moment I am doing a bit of work on the development of the English language; and I have grown infinitely tolerant of people's pronunciation—'coat' for 'court', and 'jine' for 'join' have perfectly legitimate backgrounds. Those words were pronounced like that in the eighteenth century. 'Tea' was pronounced 'tay', dream 'draym' etc. It is a most fascinating study.

The other day I was reading some letters of Horace Walpole—the 18th century gossip—about the balloon fad in his time. He was full of contempt for people who went up in balloons. I later discovered that great progress was made in the early nineteenth century in ballooning. In 1836, a balloon left London and—in 18 hours!—had travelled 500 miles to Nassau, in Germany!

Please send your stories as soon as possible. We shall probably place them.

Do all you can to stay well. Don't worry. Your troubles are almost at an end. Believe me.

Your respectful and affectionate son, Vido

3/5/53

My Dear Vido,

Thank you for your sweet letter. It comforted me and I know I can depend on you. But I feel so recovered I would like you to continue your studies for the B.Litt. you spoke of some time ago. I feel I can keep the home going well enough. Besides, Sati will be getting a good Mahasabha* school-teaching job as soon as she gets though her exams in December. Moreover, you are much too young to assume family responsibility; by the same token I do feel you should keep away from marriage for some years. First, make your way in the world; or at any rate wait and see which way the wind is blowing.

Please take good care of yourself; for, should anything untoward happen to you, 'the last hope of England' will have vanished.

Again, I shall be very happy if you continued your further studies as planned.

I doubt you will be ever happy in a more commercial post.

Do send a good close-up photograph of yourself with your very next letter—and do not worry. When you have gone beyond a B.A. you'd be in a position to command better situations.

Love from Pa

---

* Hindu political organisation in Trinidad

University College, Oxford
March 5, 1953

My dear Ma,

I am sorry about not writing last week; but I really have mountains to do. Last Tuesday, the Martlets, of which I am President, had their bi-annual dinner in the Senior Common Room of the college. Being President, I had to be at the head of the table. The Dean was at the other end. We had five visitors from Cambridge. Altogether there were nineteen of us. By the way, the Senior Common Room is the room where the dons eat and generally spend their time.

My examinations are a mere thirteen weeks away and in those weeks I have to concentrate the work of pretty well three years. It is unlikely that I shall do superlatively well; but I think I will do a reasonable exam and get a fairly good degree. Of course last year my illness prevented me from working. A great pity.

I am sorry that I didn't send Sewan* anything for his eighth birthday. But I think that I did send him my regards. But that is worth very little. I will do my best to send some money for the girls at the end of March. Not much. About $15. What I do hope to do is to take a job in the summer vacation and send some money then—about $50 or so.

I am quite in the dark about Kamla. She hardly writes me and I haven't the vaguest idea of her plans or anything. But I have not been a good correspondent myself, and it is unfair for me to say anything.

What you tell me about some things at home have depressed and alarmed me. But I think you will try to see that people behave wickedly to themselves—not because they have a natural bent to wantonness and indecency, but because they are flesh. I suppose Sero realised as well as anyone else that her actions would bring shame on her. The natural thing for her to do was to say, 'Damn it all.' The next step for her is to become very angry and very loud-mouthed if anyone tries to 'save' her. It is all very human and very sad. The reason is this: the old Hindus married their daughters off at an early age. We have grown modern—we decide to let them choose, but at the same time our Hindu prudery is struck by the gross-

---

* Another form (likewise Sivan) of Shiva, Vidia's only, younger, brother

ness of a courtship in the Western way. We put our foot down. Result: clandestine intrigues. Marriage is always the solution. I hope my sisters will profit by what has happened and be perfectly frank with you about what they do.

As soon as Savi starts getting fresh, marry her!

Oh, she will never write me now!

Aren't you impressed by the speed with which Capo R. is hurrying home to see about the will?

I really don't see why people should insist on behaving like characters from a book.

From what you write, it appears that everyone at home is helping each other. That is really marvellous, and I hope they keep it up. I am really impressed; and greatly moved. I am not trying to offer facile comfort when I say that in two years everything will turn out fine.

And now, Pa, if you are reading this, please don't feel that I have not been thinking of you. You have been in my mind all the time. It seems rather fatuous to ask how are you, when I know I cannot get a reply even as I write. Please, please, don't worry. Please have some faith in me. I wish I could be the knight in armour, hastening to avenge you and bring you help. But we have to go about things in a much more prosaic way. Don't write if you don't feel up to it. I shan't mind.

But now I must turn to the infinitely more difficult task of excusing my meanness to Sewan.

[In larger script]:

My dear Sewan,

I like the way you get to the bottom of something very quickly. I mean the way you asked point blank what I was giving you for a birthday present. You are too young to know the value of kind thoughts, without anything real. I know that I ought to have sent you something. But, please, I don't know what an 8-year-old boy likes. Tell me what you want and I promise to send you it.

Love,
Vido

Benares
March 11, 1953

My dear Vido,

Well, I think you got me all wrong. Or did the people at home write you saying I was only making promises and doing nothing about them?

I am quite satisfied with my engagement. And I write home regularly—once or twice a week. Of course if I could have afforded so many letters I would have written every day.

I am trying to see if I can secure a job in Fiji for £40 a month. Teachers without degrees get £45. All this I have written home to Ma. She seems to think that if I get that job I ought to get married and go to Fiji. That's a lot more than I can get in T'dad. I would be able to give quite a bit of financial assistance. But I won't go to Fiji without first securing that job.

Now, I could blow my top off like you did but it's patience that I have learnt in India. Before complaining about my not writing you, you ought to soundly whack yourself for not caring to answer me. I wonder who's really wrapped up and with whom? But I'll keep on writing.

Love to Pat.

Lots of love, Kamla

Sending a grad. photograph of myself. Got the Shiva Natarajan (it's black brass and rather graceful). If I don't come to England I'll post it on.

3.27.53

My dear Vidia,

At last I have got hold of an air-letter form. I have been asking all three of them—Sati, Mira, Savi—to get me one since the last two days. They just couldn't get the time (so they say) to stop at the PO that they pass and re-pass on mornings, noons and afternoons to and from school.

Anyway, here is charming news for you and all of us: I am quite recovered. Today is Friday, and I resume work on Monday. I was in the Col. Hosp. for six weeks, most of the time flat on my back on a bed, as ordered by the doctors who have had to deal with me. I was rushed to hospital from the *TG* office on the 1/19 and was discharged on the 3/2. I was given four weeks additional sick-leave at home, so that I have been absent from work for some ten weeks. The *Gdn* has been paying me the full salary.

I feel quite rested, but tired and nervous.

The last surprise I got on return from hospital was to realise what a neat little home we have in 26. I had never seen it in this way before. The girls are to be commended for this, though they are rather apathetic in other ways.

I began looking into the tail-end of the last chapter of *The Adventures of Gurudeva*, re-wrote a page or two and then felt like putting the thing away until I get in a readier mood for it.

Nalini has a cold but everybody else is quite well. The girls appear to be studying hard for their first term test.

Shivan is still going to a private school, but I intend to get him into the Boys' Western School when Romily is head teacher.

Keep your chin up.

Pa

University College, Oxford
April 4, 1953

Dear Pa,

This is a glorious Saturday, I think. I am working, alone, in the college library, and the clock of some church is striking six. The sun has gone down, but the days are growing longer, and it is still quite light.

The library is officially closed, but I was granted permission to use it during the vacation. It is rather depressing, though, working alone in a dead college.

I have just stopped working for the moment. I am preparing my final notes on Spenser. He wrote an enormous unfinished poem in 1590–6 called the *Faerie Queene*. It takes 400 pages in double-columns, with 40 lines in a column, i.e. 1,000 pages of an ordinary-sized novel. You can imagine how difficult it is to get a grasp of the poem as a whole. I have only read it through twice; what I have done is to close the poem and work simply from my notes and impressions. And I find it rather surprising to discover that I have worked fairly hard.

My examinations are but ten weeks away; but I have everything in hand, I hope.

I don't wish to arouse any hopes at all—but I'm trying to get a job with the Oxford University Press. They have three branches in India. I wish to be recruited on the same terms as people in this country—i.e. frequent and lay leave, etc. The advantages of this sort of job are great. I preserve links with England and Oxford. I get a good salary. I travel; and I play about with books. It seems so good that I feel sure that I won't get it.

I am glad to hear you are well once more. If I get a good job, I shall certainly leave Oxford. Commercially a B.Litt. is useless. But we will wait and see. I do miss home a great deal. The funny thing is that I always seem to have left home only yesterday, and when the sun shines brightly, I remember distinctly the road home, the Oval and all the signs and the Oval Café and those Chinese shops and the Police Barracks and The Post Office. Every thing is absolutely clear in my mind.

About ten days ago, I went with a friend to have coffee one morning. An Indian came in. He was too elaborately dressed to be a member of the university. I gave him no more attention than anybody else. Yet I could feel his eyes on me. Then he came over and said, 'Excuse me, are you Naipaul?' I looked at him, and didn't recognise him at all. I said yes. 'Vido Naipaul?' And I laughed and said yes. Then we had a little guessing game. Could I guess who he was. I ransacked my brain. Could he have taught me? No.

He said, 'Tut, tut! Do you forget that ah took you once to watch cricket.'

And then I remembered. Noble Sankar! Smaller than me; darker than I remembered; uglier than I remembered; stupider than I thought. Can you imagine a man coming to Oxford for the first time and not looking at the buildings, not looking at the bookshops, but just talking about money—how much he wanted, how little he had? That is the WI intellectual, I am afraid. He straight away assumed that his personal affairs were of great interest to me. And, as I talked to Noble, I fancied I knew, despite his elegant dress and demeanour, what culture was. I am so glad I came to Oxford.

Keep well. Love,
Vido

Regards to Savi. Her birthday, I think, April 21?

Let's get this straight: Satti: Sep. 25

Meera: Dec. 30
Savi: April . . . ?
Shivan: Feb. 25

University College, Oxford

Dear Ma,

I have a small bit of goodish news for you. If you listen on April 26 to the *Caribbean Voices* programme you may hear me reading a story.

The story itself is bad. It is a pot-boiler, and I am quite ashamed of it. But I think it is what Swanzy wants. It is vaguely about Mary in Louis St. I have added a lot of pure lies; so the story may have some interest for you. But I am sure you will be delighted to hear me speaking for about twelve or fifteen minutes.

This means that I shall be able to send some money—more than I expected—home. It won't be less than $30, but I do hope I can make it $50. I prefer to wait until the BBC cheque arrives. But if you want the money right away, please let me know. Waiting means that you will get the cash in about a month's time—about the first week in May. Please don't hesitate to let me know if you want it now.

I also think I can send you $24 at the end of June. I hope to get a job then and may be able to send more at the end of July.

What you can do for me is let me know the prices of shirts and socks and clothes generally at home. You see, I am terribly scared of buying English clothes. I bought 6 pairs of socks at $1.80 a pair last August and already they are gone. I am not asking you to buy anything for me. I don't need anything desperately. I did a pretty good bargain the other day. I bought a shirt for 10/- from a friend.

Springer sent me a postcard. Blue Basin, with a note reminding me of the time when I dived in fully dressed and swam to the waterfall and back!

Because of this, and a number of things, I find myself in better spirits than for a long time.

I must close now, and will write again soon.

My love to all,
Vido

[From Kamla]

April 21, 1953

My dear Vido,

You seem too worried about me. Really am quite all right. Everybody at home is asking what about your future. Well, I will give you an advice—that person has got to plan for the future who has money to finance the plan. For he or she who has no money, a plan should not be made for it might all end in spider's web. The thing to do is to try your best, and whatever strikes, take that.

Well, that's exactly what I am doing. I have no plan and never will have any.

I think that if I marry Vince, I will be very happy because he is quite a devoting kind of chap (quite contrary to me, because I don't think I can love anybody too much). I can understand your plans and I think you are right but if I were to get stuck, I'll say it. So don't worry, will you?

I don't know whether you have heard or not but Sati's engaged to Krisii Bissoondath (remember him). She'll be getting married next March if all goes well. I am quite happy about it. Because the three girls at home were the biggest source of worry to me. She's getting married of her own free will. Krisii is quite well off and the family's a good one. At least one of our sisters will be settled down to life. You are not to write criticizing it, understand.

I wrote to Fiji for a job but I'm afraid I haven't been very lucky. If I'd got one I would have gone. Now I have written to T'dad.

What colour does Pat like best and how many yards of cloth make her a frock.

Write a few lines to that effect.

All my love,
Kamla

Answer regarding Pat rather than no letters. If at all I am leaving for Trinidad or Fiji, it will be somewhere at the end of May. Continue writing.

4.27.53

Dear Vido,

It was grand hearing your voice over the radio last evening. Our own box at home did not carry the programme, so we all dashed to Shamar— you know, the woman next door, on the main road. The reception wasn't good throughout, though; and but for the fact that we knew in advance that you would be reading the story on Mary, we may not have known your voice at all. You spoke well, and we didn't find any nervousness or anything of the kind on your part. It was a pretty long story, wasn't it? What a pity we could not get the whole of the discussion that followed the reading. Here and there, of course, we caught up with a sentence or two, but for the most part the whole thing was drowned in static interference.

Some two or three days ago I sent in a short story to the BBC office in Kingston. It is 3,400 words long, and heaven knows whether they would accept it at that length. But I had no time to cut it. I have called it 'Ramdas—and the Cow', the principal character being my brother Ramparsad*, otherwise Rapooche. I have added a note to Mrs Lindo to ask whether Mr Swanzy could get you to read the story if it is accepted.

Sati has had an offer of marriage, and since the girl seems to be all in for it, there was nothing for me to do but give my consent. The suitor is Crisen Bissoon Dath, of Sangre Grande, Seedai's son, the people who carry on a dry goods store in that town and have a son studying medicine in England. Because Sati's HC exam comes in December, we could not of course agree to the wedding taking place this year—a thing for which Crisen has been pressing. We have, so far, decided for March next. Sati will be allowed to teach in Mahasabha School as a married woman. So they say. Your uncle Capo S. has told her that she would get $90 a month to begin with, with an HS Cert. He is Chief Secretary and one of the pillars of the Mahasabha Schools establishment movement. The next big man is Bhadase Marajh.

This will mean my borrowing more money for the wedding; but Sati assures me that she'll pay up at the rate of $50 a month—just the sum that

---

* Vidia's paternal uncle Persad (or Ramparsad)—see Pa's musings on 'Rapooche' in his letter to Vido of 10/5/50

I am paying to the bank here on a $300 loan for Kamla. She was to come home, remember? Now it seems she has changed her mind—after putting me to this trouble. Really, I doubt whether Kamla is using her imagination; yet she should surely know what I have to go through on a meagre salary of $165 a month, plus half that in bonus at the end of a year. Surely, if she didn't have to return to Trinidad, she ought not to have put me to this heavy commitment of $50 a month. She had said she would get a job here and work and pay it back within a year; now she sends offensively patronising letters telling Sati to see that when she sends us money we spend it wisely. As though she would be sending money for me! Every cent that she sends is to be used to pay the bank for what I owe them on her account.

I don't want you to tell her all these things, and I don't know why I should be telling you all this, either . . . But I think that Kamla has as much chance of getting work in Trinidad as she may have of getting work in Fiji, which is where she wants to go. The fellow she wants to marry is as needy as herself. In Trinidad K. could have been working with the Mahasabha.

It was understood that she would have saved enough towards her passage back home. She hasn't done a thing about that; but has spent even $250 that Rudranath gave her. I have already spoiled this letter by all this complaining to Kamla.

Although things are not easy for us I wouldn't be happy over the fact of your going to work during your vacation. So don't do so, just for us. What about applying for a job with the Trinidad Ed. Dept., or with the Indian Diplomatic Service? I don't know, and this is just a blind suggestion.

Yours affectionately,

Pa

Benares
May 22, 1953

My dear Vido,

At the moment I am trying awfully hard to get a passage on the Moja, which leaves India on the 6th or so and arrives in England after 21 days or so. An awful long time I should say.

I think for you, it'll be a bad time. Because you'll be writing your exams then. But really I can't help it.

I am not sure about the passage yet but there's a lot of hope that I may get.

I wrote a letter to Pa this morning. Well, I don't think it was a pleasant one. You know they borrowed some money for me. And in every letter they harp about it. Sati's last letter ended like this (keep it to yourself and don't mention it to anyone at home. Promise?). I asked her if she couldn't lay her hand on a bit of money with which I could have bought her a few things for her marriage. 'I would certainly love to have all those beautiful things India has to offer,' she answered, 'but at the moment all our money goes in food and in paying the $300 we borrowed for you.' This was a real slap in the face and it hurt deep. I cried for days.

And this morning I told Pa how I really felt and that is that they don't want me back home for my own sake but just that I may work. I also asked him to write me a nice letter which would help dispel this thought. If he doesn't I'll surely go home in a bad state of mind.

These things you are not to mention to anyone at home lest they create hard feelings. And I don't want that. You understand.

Be seeing you real soon.

Love,
Kamla

6.1.53

My dear Vido,

I have just read the letter you wrote to Sati. It has saddened me to know that you have not been working well enough for some weeks. I do hope you are not ill. Please do not be discouraged.

There is not a day—hardly an hour—when we do not think of you—and of Kamla.

I know quite well how very dull and depressing it must be for you not to get letters from home more frequently. Really, I am very annoyed at Sati and her sisters for their not writing you oftener. Of course, I myself am guilty.

About the stories: I shall most certainly be posting them to you by tomorrow or day after. You will have to re-type a small portion of 'The Return of Gurudeva', of course. It seems I shall never give it the finish that

I should like to. So I am sending the stuff as it is, well aware you will be disappointed with the work in many places. Please read the whole thing sentence by sentence. So keep a copy of 'The Return of Gurudeva'. What I have are mere disjointed scraps. But of the short stories and the printed portions of *Gurudeva* I have copies. I think 'Uncle Dalloo' could be considerably improved by some careful cutting or pruning. You may try your hand at this, if you like, after the exams.

I wish I had put Gurudeva's 'Lekchur' into indirect reporting, with descriptive interpolations. Like Bennett's piece of a Revival meeting in *Anna of the Five Towns*. Really, many parts of the story are so incompetent that I am ashamed to send it to you or to anyone.

If my own matter is not enough to make a normal-size book, what about adding your own stories? The by-line would thus be—By Seepersad and Vidia Naipaul. I don't know. It's up to you.

Kamla says in the letter received together with ours that from now on we are to write her care of Capo R.; so she is coming home at last and she will soon be with you in London or Oxford. She has had a lot of disappointments, so you'll have to soothe her.

Those Benares professors of hers could be vengeful. The music college has postponed the exams from April to July—without making corresponding arrangements for the continuance of her allowance for the additional three months. Consequently, I think she is leaving Benares without taking the exam.

She is annoyed with me, too, because I made Sati ask her whether she had received the $300 that I sent her through Barclays Bank last November. I simply wanted to be sure that she had received the money, for she had never said so in plain words, and money orders or drafts can go astray. Please explain to her and say we love her and want her home for her own sake and not for any money she may have to give us.

Now, Vido, please do not worry. You probably have done more work towards your exams than you are aware of, and everything will be all right, I feel. We all love you very dearly, however slack we may be in writing—

Your affectionate,

Pa

Dear Vido, Best of luck in exam, keep well health is precious don't be discouraged will always pray for you. Ma

Aden
June 4, 1953

My dear Vido,

I feel sick. As a matter of fact I have been feeling sick since I came on board.

It's almost monsoon time and the sea is choppy.

I happen to have as my cabin companions an Indian family who are really on their way to Trinidad to join the Indian Commissioner's Office there.

Well, that's all for now.

Love,
Kamla

6/10/53

Dear Vido,

This morning I posted you the MS of *The Adventures of Gurudeva and Other Stories*. As surface mail, of course. As I have already explained to you, you will have to get a small portion of the stuff typed. Due to lack of time I was unable to do this myself. However, just don't do anything until your exams are over.

Please put 'The Panchayat'* somewhere other than where it happens to be, for *The Adventures of Gurudeva* ends with a Panchayat, and this short, short story, being in the same theme, will be better placed elsewhere.

If you happen to dislike any of the short stories you are at liberty to exclude them from the collection; but if you do this, I think it will be a good thing if you substitute them with your own stories.

You must be very near your exams. My advice is the old one: keep calm and collected. Do your best without anxiety. Be a philosopher.

If you can snatch five minutes drop me a few lines to say how you are doing—and in particular, how is your health? Your last letter left me very depressed. It was that piece which said that had Sati kept writing you last

---

* Village or community council

year the letters would have been worth more to you than 200 friends in Oxford or London; that and your saying that you had not been working for six weeks.

The fact may very well be that you have studied harder than you are aware of, and I feel it in my bones that you'll come through well enough. Only keep cool.

Don't let Kamla and Sati get you down. The end of girls is marriage. Didn't we know? We all wish you best luck in the exams—Pa

June 22, 53

My dear Vido,

You probably have not yet received the MSS that I mailed you on June 10. When you do get the stuff you will have some work, but not much, I hope. At any rate you are not to do anything until you have got through your exams. Perhaps you are now in the middle of them; please take things easy and you will get through nicely. I have been worrying about you these last few weeks; I cannot get over a feeling that you are ill, and this makes me very unhappy.

The BBC will be broadcasting my 'Ramdas and the Cow'—what a dull title—on July 19th. I had asked Mrs Lindo to suggest to Mr Swanzy to let you do the reading; Mrs Lindo wrote back saying she has made the suggestion, but that the distance you would have to travel might not make it possible for you to do the reading. However, I do hope you will be listening in. The story itself is a chapter or episode in *The Adventures of Gurudeva*, but you needn't tell anyone this. I have changed Gurudeva into Ramdas. I am thinking that in case my stories—those I have sent to you—are not accepted for book publication, I can still get out a good many short stories for *Caribbean Voices*. That is why I want you to be careful about keeping a copy of *The Adventures*. Try more than one publisher; or try to get the thing through an agent, if necessary. Some of those recommended by Kilham Roberts in an old copy (1940) of *The Authors' Handbook*, include—

A. P. Watt and Son, Hastings House, Norfolk Street, Strand, WC2— 'who have the distinction of being the oldest established agency in the country'. Other good agencies recommended are—Curtis Brown Ltd, 6 Henrietta Street, WC2; A. M. Heath and Co. Ltd, 188 Piccadilly, W1;

Raymond Savage Ltd, 39 Jermyn Street, SW1; A. D. Peters, 10 Buckingham St, Adelphi, WC2; Pearn, Pollinger and Higham Ltd, 39–40 Bedford St, Strand, WC2—for the rest see *The Authors' Handbook*. I am sorry to inflict this catalogue on you.

As to publishers—try Michael Joseph, or Eyre and Spottiswoode, or Allan Wingate, the people who published Selvon's book.

Kamla will have arrived in England today. I hope you two meet each other in good health; and I hope you have no row with Capo R. Why do I keep worrying so much about you? I am getting sick with worry and all sorts of ugly forebodings. I want a good letter from you—and another about you from Kamla.

Do not worry about sending us money. It is bad enough we do not send you anything. What a wretchedly poor lot we are! Maybe, you promise to send us money, and then the time comes for you to do so and you find you have to get so much money for yourself. Naturally, this kind of thing will cause you to worry. Please don't.

Exactly how long do you have to remain in England? Please let me know. You could get good jobs right here in Trinidad, with the Education Dept., but you must arrange for all this in advance. You might be a Schools Inspector. Or you might get in at QRC. There is a new Government Secondary School at Barataria, but its opening has been delayed because of lack of proper staff. QRC's Acting Principal, Farrell, is principal designate.

Kamla will get a job with the Mahasabha schools. Capo R. is a key personage, of course, with Bhadase as President General. They have some twenty-six elementary schools all over the island, Government assisted, and the Mahasabha has plans for a Secondary School and a Teachers' Training College. Kamla will fit in one of these.

The most important thing I am asking you is to try to keep your health. Do not smoke too much. I am suffering the consequences of too much smoking, so I know what I am telling you. If you must smoke, do so only after meals. This is very, very important. Three cigarettes a day.

We are all praying for your success at the exams. As I am typing this your Ma is near me, rocking Nalini to sleep. The girls have just left for school. Now I must stop. There is another letter to write to Kamla.

As ever

your affectionate Pa

Home: July 1, 1953

My dear Vido,

Well, you have probably done with your exams by now. Don't worry if you have not done very well. Just pass, and that is all we need. On the other hand, you may have done better than you think. You know, you have worked much too hard, from early boyhood to date. Well, you are young, and that is the time when one should work hard; but I hope you will not have to keep up a grind, as has been the case with me. It doesn't pay, Vido; you wear yourself out sooner than you should. And then at the end of it all, you find you are as much a pauper as when you began years and years ago. As soon as you are through with your exams, take it easy, relax, play don't-care-a-damn. And come home.

I suppose you have seen Kamla, and I suppose the exams came between you two. Of course I am guessing. I was wondering whether you would go up to Capo R. to be with Kamla, and I thought your doing so might be rather hard on you. I have sometimes also wondered whether it was not due to your illness that you reacted as you did to Ruth's attitude. I don't know. Anyway, it might be a good thing if you and Capo R. and his wife made it up. I won't be surprised if your Mamoo travels in the same boat with Kamla homeward-bound.

Now, I imagine it will be very hard for you to see Kamla leaving you once more; and I hope you will take it lightly. I would like to know just how long you have to be at Oxford, and just what are your plans, so far. I know you have hinted in earlier letters that you will not live in Trinidad; you had also mentioned some slight chance of your getting a job with the University Press—in India, I think. Seems a good job for you. Have you heard anything more on this? Never despise money. If I had some money I would be a far more happy person and less of a bother to you and my other children.

Vido, please try and place those stories. I know parts would sound rather immature and crude, but it seems that is the sort of thing publishers want these days. Just read the thing through, type what needs typing and send it or take it to a publisher. I think you know what a godsend it would mean to me, if it was accepted—not for the name, but for the money it might bring me.

Remember they will be reading my story on July 19; I suppose it would

be Selvon reading it. I wish it could be anybody else. I had suggested to
Swanzy that you should read it. I am finishing off here now. There is
another letter to write to the Naparima Girls' High School, who in reply to
an application by Kamla (from India) is offering her a position as assistant
teacher at their new Girls' High School at St Augustine. I have sent a copy
of the letter to Kamla, c/o Capo R. I hope she gets it. Kamla is also being
offered a job by the Mahasabha, but as a teacher in an elementary school, to
begin with. Later, it is said, they intend to build a teachers' training college,
in which they say they will give Kamla a post. 'They' of course is Capo S.

Well, I must stop here, Vido, for after writing that letter to Miss Scrimgeour of the Board of the Naparima Girls' High School, your Ma and
Nalini and I are going to spend the day with the Sookhdeos at Tunapuna.
Send me a letter, telling me all about your exams and about yourself and
about your meeting Kamla.

As ever,
Pa

Home: 7/1/53

My dear Kamla,

Below I am typing out a copy of a letter which I received from Miss
Margaret A. Scrimgeour, of the Board of the Naparima Girls' High
School. I am not sending you the original because I am not sure whether
you will receive this letter; I mean you may have left England by the time
this reaches. When you come home you will have the original.

Naparima Girls' High School,
San Fernando,
Trinidad, BWI
June 25, 1953

Dear Mr Naipaul,

I received a letter of application from your daughter Kamla in
India. I have misplaced it.

Under the Board of the Naparima Girls' High School are
two High Schools—the other being the (new) St Augustine Girls'
High School.

St Augustine is in need of a qualified assistant teacher. Your daughter's qualifications seem good. Could she write Miss Constance Wagar, Austin Street, St Augustine—giving full particulars about her degree.

I have good recommendations of her, which I shall be able to give at the Board meeting. I understand that she is of the Hindu Faith. This will mean one or two things to be discussed when we meet her personally. Under those circumstances we would not be willing for her to teach Scripture.

Could you let her know that there is this opening if she is still interested?

I have spoken of this, as St Augustine is nearer home for her than here in San Fernando. True there is also a vacancy here.

I am sorry to write you and not directly to your daughter. I hope she will forgive me.

Yours respectfully,
(Miss) Margaret A. Scrimgeour (signed)

We have told no one about this application of yours and this reply thereto. The Mahasabha is also offering you a teaching post, but in an elementary school, to begin with, their own Teachers' Training College or High School not having been built yet. I think you should write accepting the offer, although I hope the Mahasabha people, including your Mamoo, will not be displeased. Sati is to get a job with them.

We are anxious to get a letter from you. Have you met Vido yet? Is everything all right with both of you? Do come home as early as you can. Wish I could send you some money.

Eagerly awaiting you,

Yours as ever,
Pa

49 St John Street,
Oxford
July 14, 1953

My dear Kamla,

Sorry to have missed yesterday. Hope you were not put to any inconvenience. Received a letter from Capo S. today—about you. A very short letter, saying couldn't I arrange for you to take a Vacation Course Diploma? But I am afraid that would be worthless. I have told him so.

I also wrote Basdai thanking her. Pat thanks you very much for her presents. She wouldn't have minded if you had come yesterday.

Let me know when you wish to see me. Do you want to go to the theatre? At Stratford or London. Please let me know.

Vido

July 17, 1953

Dear Pa,

Looking among my papers today I discovered a letter—written and addressed—which I thought I had posted. This accounts for the unnatural delay in writing. Kamla has, I hope, written about her arrival here. She does letter-writing so much more efficiently than me.

Your MS arrived 14 days ago (I wrote that letter then) and I have read it through. It is pretty good stuff and I feel sure it will be placed eventually. But the job of typing is a big one.

My viva voce examination is on the 23rd and after that I have nothing to worry about. I get results at the end of July. After that (23rd) I go to stay about 4 to 5 days with Kamla, see her off; then I have a 6-week job at a hospital washing dishes. But the pay is good. I have invitations from 2 friends (or 3) to spend some time and I will probably do this in the last weeks of September. The first 2 weeks of October I think I will spend on the continent—if my money holds out.

Kamla and I spent a weekend at Basdai's; to me it was pleasant, but a bit of a bore; Kamla thoroughly enjoyed it. I feel so isolated when I find the gulf between people from home and myself widening every day. The boys who come here quickly find their level. Oxford is really a fine place. One isn't aware, for instance, of the high level of intelligent conversation until one has to talk to a boy like Ramesh for an hour or so. People leave Oxford polished, competent, humane—or so it seems to me. So the gulf yawns with every day. Of course there are many Trinidadians at Oxford, but their ignorance and stupidity remain as impregnable as ever.

My health is much better; and I think not before long I shall be absolutely well. There is nothing wrong with me physically, of course; but there are periods of black depression, these are disappearing rapidly now, however. Understanding oneself is the biggest problem. Do not think I am the only man here who is not quite mentally alert. Several students are in neurotic messes. Oxford brings out all one's idiosyncrasies. One has so much time on one's hands, so much loneliness.

Kamla probably thought me frightfully lazy. But her stay with me had a strange psychological effect: I felt utterly tired—more tired than I have ever been and I wanted to sleep pretty well all day. I suppose you can work out the meaning of that.

This letter is not written in a mood of depression, you know. The fact that I can write about these things ought to tell you that at the moment I really am quite fit.

My love to all at home, and my apologies, too

Vido

Home: 7/20/53

My dear Vido,

Two things have cheered me up since last evening and this morning. Last evening we—the entire household—heard you over the radio reading my story; and this morning I got a reassuring letter from Kamla . . . Your reading of the story was very good indeed. I doubt whether anyone else would have done better. Thanks. I hope you got enough for the reading to pay your fare to and from Oxford.

I have been having a terribly miserable time this month. Your not writing to tell us you are all right in health was the main cause. Then again Kamla seemed to have landed in England quite broke. Her letter tells me this morning that Capo R. has refused to help pay up her passage. Well, that's how things go with this Mr Genius. She can have my entire payment—I mean the story money—whatever that may be; and if it comes to an additional fifteen dollars or so, I can somehow make it up from my last pay from the *Guardian,* which will be at the end of this month. But it will be so much better for all of us here if Kamla could raise a loan from India House, or, as she says, get some money from you. Then you let me know your own financial state and if things are bad I'll send you the BBC money as soon as I get it . . . On the other hand, about ten weeks ago Capo S. said that he was called up by the Indian Commissioner here at his office and made to sign security for a 45 pounds loan to Kamla—passage money from England to Trinidad. It appears that Kamla had applied for this loan at the India Office in London and the latter communicated with the Indian Commissioner's Office here. Capo himself has not told me a word about this, but simply mentioned it to Sati, who goes to No. 17 every Saturday and Sunday to coach up Sita. I am surprised that Kamla does not mention this Capo S. security business in her letter, which I have just received.

You will forgive me, but I cannot help thinking of Rudranath as some kind of monster, or a satyr. Yet I have to keep in speaking terms with these brothers because Sati is to get a job with the Mahasabha, and Kamla also—in a secondary school that they will be opening up in September. I hear Kamla is to get the principalship and Sati an assistant post. But Kamla is also offered a job by the Naparima Girls' High School—a new school at St Augustine.

I am so relieved to hear from Kamla that you are all right, and that since she is in England you are looking even better . . . I don't want you to worry about us here. Kamla will soon be here and we'll get through. My health is quite bad, of course, but I am not any more laid up in bed. I can do a lot of work, such as writing at a desk, but cannot cope with anything that entails any considerable physical activity. Cannot hustle. Thank God, I can write; so I can fill my otherwise empty hours with some kind of writing. But since the beginning of the year I have been so bad, have had to spend so much time abed, that my employers have seen fit to dispense with my services. They pay my salary to the end of this month. But I don't want you to worry over these things. After Kamla there will be Mira and then Savi to help for a year or two; and by then you will have finished your studies; perhaps working too. So don't worry, just be practical. Mother Frances Xavier suggests you do the one-year Education Dip. Course at Oxford. This will entitle you for better pay in teaching.

I don't know whether Kamla will be in England in time for you to give her some of the news from this letter. For instance, I had sent her a copy of a letter sent me by the Naparima Girls' High School secretary in connection with an application by Kamla for a teaching post. They are willing to take her as an assistant teacher at the new High School at St Augustine. Kamla does not say whether she has got this letter—which was sent her care of Capo R.

I cannot afford to show any but a good face to Capo S. Pending Kamla or Sati getting a job he has planned to let Sati keep on going to school so she can do her HC exams; and he will be paying her fifty dollars a month—just to help us out. So he has said at any rate. But for this Sati would have been leaving off school in order to teach after the August vacation.

I want you to tell me just how you went though with your exams, one of your very detailed and interesting and cheerful letters. Kamla taking money from you must leave you blank. Over here Kamla's real enemy is not her uncle or uncles, but her very stupid and jealous aunts . . . Can you turn the last chapter of *Gurudeva* into a 3,000 word short story? Do so if you can. I haven't got a whole copy, or I might have done the thing myself. The BBC (through Mrs Lindo) is asking me for more stories.

> With plenty of love,
> Pa

(Sati has mailed you some pictures and letter by surface mail.)

University College, Oxford
July 30, 1953

My dearest Pa,

I got your letter tonight, after coming back from London, where I saw Kamla off.

Well, first of all, don't worry. I shall give reasons why you must not worry.

1. I have got an Oxford degree. I am now B.A. (Oxon).
2. I shall set about immediately getting a job—for the best money I can find. You seem to have the idea that I can only

teach. This is not correct. There is an Oxford University Appointments Committee, which see to people like me getting jobs, and the difficulty is usually not one of finding, but of choosing. I am certainly not going to teach.

3. As soon as I have got a job, you are to come and live with me and fulfil an ambition of mine to have you idle, content—and I shall certainly see that you have some whisky to hand. This will not be very long now. I am looking forward to having you with me within a year. Kamla has promised to look after the children and Ma.

4. You are not to think that I am missing anything by spending only 3 years at Oxford. 95% of students do just that and are, like me, just dying to get away and earn some money. A B.Litt. is not essential and is a definite waste of time. Getting a job becomes no easier or anything, I know.

Now, I want to be informed of everything that happens at home. I don't wish anything to be kept secret. Tomorrow morning I go to the Appointments Committee.

It was rather silly of Kamla to complain that Capo R. was not helping her. Why should he? I certainly wouldn't have liked that to happen—for him to give Kamla money. The trouble is that Capo R. is so completely unimportant in our lives that the bother and fuss seem unnecessary. Kamla ought not to have written you about that especially as I had promised her the money. Anyway, the India House gave her it—a mere £15. Heaven knows why Capo S. should have signed security for £45!

Kamla would be shocked to hear what I am going to say at the moment. She is certainly still very thoughtless and inconsiderate, though wearing well. For instance, like writing you about Capo R., although I had tried repeatedly to show her how unimportant this was.

I would have looked after Kamla; but then we thought Capo R. would be hurt, etc., if I did. In the last week or so Capo R. was becoming more and more unpleasant and Kamla eventually did the proper thing. She left, and we spent the last five days very pleasantly indeed at Basdai's, listening to the interminable political discussions Carl held with all and sundry.

I could not finish this letter last night; and I am not writing it from Oxford. I'm writing it in a little village called North Curry, which is near

Taunton, in Somerset. I am staying here with a friend, and tomorrow I return to Oxford.

I went to the Appointments Committee and I have filled out the necessary forms. The important thing, as you can see, is to avoid making snap decisions which, after taking us through the next two or three years of crisis, will land me in the soup.

Yesterday I was talking to a very good friend of mine at Oxford—a middle-aged man—and he is convinced that you, only on the right side of fifty, can still consider yourself in the prime of life. But please wait until I get a job or something and you can come to live with me, before you do anything silly, like falling ill again. I will ask you again not to worry. At the moment I am writing a story and, if it is accepted, I promise faithfully to send the money to you. I gave Kamla a fairly important sum, and the people at home will, I feel sure, be agreeably surprised when they see the gifts Kamla and I have managed to send them. Shivan has a particular present—but I shan't tell what it is, because we want it to be a surprise. You remember that when Kamla left home he asked her for a pair of green trousers. I suppose he has now passed out of the green trousers stage.

Kamla wishes to be taken straight away to No. 26; and, as she wishes to have as little as possible to do with Capo R. and those aunts who are playing the damned fool, she wants to be guided entirely by you—as to who she should go and meet, etc. For heaven's sake, don't get annoyed by your sisters-in-law. Once you are, you do place yourself on their level. I have tried to tell Kamla over and over how damned unimportant her aunts or her detracting relations are, and I hope you take it well enough. There is no need for you to get worked up over Capo R., because he refused to help. Helping Kamla was my duty, and I hope I did it well. It came as a shock to a number of people that I could help Kamla. I can take care of myself now.

On Tuesday, August the fourth, I begin working on a farm. I am looking forward to it very much for the exercise, and because the English fields are such beautiful things. The ripe wheat looks like gold, and the field seems to swell in the wind.

Incidentally, if you are writing, I suggest that you begin something really big. Your life story written in the third person will make extremely agreeable reading. You have asked me to be a philosopher. I shall ask you to be a philosopher, and make as much as you can out of your enforced idleness.

Well, I must go to Taunton (take out an atlas, and see where that is) to post this. My friend is driving out there now, and I must close.

My love to all—my deepest love,

Vido

(Sorry to type my name, but the pen is dry.)

August 1, 1953

My dear Vido,

I have just returned from town, where I had been to attend to some printing matter for Sahadeo Maharaj of Tunapuna. Your ma and I left home together, but she has not yet returned. She has to buy some turpentine and other things: we are washing the walls so as to make home bright for Kamla . . . I am feeling very well indeed, and looking, I am told, much better than I ever have looked. I no longer have indigestion pains. But I am not working. Hitchens could not have treated me more callously.

Kamla's leaving you must be hard for you; I have many times tried to imagine how lonely you must feel; but we would all be so much happy if we know you are all right. I have often felt badly, too, over your illness. You must deny that dark depression, for it is not real. You must say, 'This is not true. It will pass away,' and in a day or two it will pass away.

Sunday, August 9, is a great day for us, the day Kamla arrives. I wish Rudranath was not travelling by the same boat. I intend to meet her on board ship in order to give her a few tips. She is getting an assistant teachership at the new High School for Girls at St Augustine (an impressive building just completed by the Naparima Girls' High School people, on the Churchill–Roosevelt Highway). Then again the Mahasabha has bought a building at Sangre Grande, wherein they will start a secondary school (Gov't aided) next month. Simbhoo—Mahasabha Secretary—says Kamla will be given the principalship of the school and that he is trying to get a salary of two hundred and forty dollars a month for her; also an assistant teachership for Sati in the same school.

Now, through Mrs Nobby, secretary of the St Augustine Girls' High School, Capo S. has got wind of the job that the Naparima people are offering Kamla, and of course he does not like it. So I have to see her on board ship and tell her what is what so that she does not show a bad face to Simbhoo, and spoil or prejudice things for herself and Sati.

Now, about yourself. The happier you keep the better for me here, for the truth is the only person I am often worried about is yourself. When I get no letter for a long time, I get convinced that you are ill, and I begin worrying. So you must write as often as you can. Everything is all right with us, I assure you.

What is happening with *The Adventures of Gurudeva?* I realise your exams have just finished and so I expect to hear about it. You don't have to type plenty of the story. Just do the pencil-written part, and send it to a publisher. I don't want you to delay over this business. If you cannot manage it, try getting it published through a good agent; but see that you pick an honest one. I understand many of these fellows are crooks. At any rate, do get going with the stuff. Now that you have no exams, I am expecting frequent letters from you—Your loving, Pa

My dear son,

I hope that Kamla's departure didn't hurt you a lot. You must remember that going and coming is a daily affair. Never let your feelings get the better of you, just remember there is happy and sad moments in everybody's life, not yours alone.

Nalini was ten months old yesterday. She can creep up the steps, holding and trying to walk, trying to talk too, saying Pa, Ma . . .

Everybody home is having the 'flu. We are all anxious to see Kamla on the Colombie Sun August 9th. It will be four years and two days since she left home.

Well, I hope the best of good luck in exam result and a lot of happiness and good health for the 21 years.

Loving Ma

49, St John Street, Oxford
August 5, 1953

Dear Pa,

This letter will be short, because I am very tired at the moment. This is my second day of work. I am working on a farm—and I don't think I have ever worked as hard in my life. I could have got easy office jobs, but I preferred the hard farm work—for a month or two. Yesterday I helped in the hay-making and I think few things can smell as sweet as hay. The farm at which I have this temporary job is a pleasant one and the farmer allows us to have meals in his dining room and if we work after five in the evening he gives us tea. A car picks me up at Oxford in the morning, drives me to the farm, and brings me back in the evening. Altogether a pleasant, refreshing and profitable change.

Kamla will no doubt be home by the time this letter is read and I hope no one did anything silly. Family relationships of this sort, once they cease to be profitable, at once become unimportant. No effort should be made to begin afresh, unless, of course, there is genuine goodwill.

I am still waiting for news from home: it will guide my actions.

By the way, Kamla has probably warned you that Capo R. will start telling stories about my wicked debauch. I expect you know me, and Kamla knows me, well enough to treat these reports with a smiling dismissal. Again the things become important only if you let them do so—i.e. the thing becomes important.

Shivan has his gun and he will jolt your nerves considerably in the next few days firing off pistols. I am so inexpert in the development of children that I am not sure whether Shivan has reached the stage where gun-toting is legal!

Two days ago I hacked out the first draft of a story. It's about Rosie, but I fear my dialogue will have a hollow ring. The people at home are becoming more and more indistinct in my mind, and I wish I were more alive to their affairs and speech. I am afraid I will use the name 'Rosie', because I can think of few names that are as appropriate—one chosen by an Indian family, one that conveys a coarseness and a voluptuousness—perhaps due to the echo of Maugham's Rosie.

I am working on your stories; so don't complain about my indifference.

I am waiting for news from home. Don't write now. Let Kamla do so.
With deepest love and equally deep respect, from your loving son,

Vido

Aug. 8, 1953

My dear, dear Vido,

That was a really lovely letter—the one you finished at the village called Curry. It took loads off me and left me happy and carefree. Savi, Sati and the others have begun facetiously calling me 'Englishman', because you say I am to come and live with you . . . But, of course, I should first congratulate you on your having obtained your B.A. degree. I am sure it must be a good one, I mean a good pass . . . You deserve a double present, first on your degree, then on your twenty-first birthday. I really ought to be sending you something, but as yet can't say what or when.

You are perfectly right about not picking the first job offered you. Take your time and be sure you get a job that you think you will really like. The people home have all been blaming me—not very rowdily—for making you leave the university when you could do at least another year, say to get the Dip. Ed. I quite agree with them. We could spare you another year, or longer; but, of course, if you do feel very 'fed up' with Oxford after three years, that is another matter. It is true that I mostly think of you as a teacher, and Trinidad is having quite a few secondary colleges and teachers' training schools and I'm pretty sure you could get a good post in one of them. But your ma is entirely against me for luring you to come to work here, and I too hate the idea, for I do feel there will be far better scope for you outside this pond. What about trying to get on the Indian Foreign Service; or on the BBC. You have a fine voice and diction. The time is coming when I won't need very much money on which to live.

I feel you will be sickeningly tired with that farm work. Try it for a fortnight, and if you find it too hard, chuck it . . . Home is quite well. And, strangely enough, although I am not working and not quite well, seeing me you'd never guess I am not in the pink of health; and indeed, I have seldom been happier. I am afraid I am getting to become naturally lazy. Sookhdeo is offering me a job in a store he is opening in town—'just to sit and watch the goods for me'. Pay of course will not be as good—far from it—as what the *Guardian* used to give me. But I must say I owe a lot to this old man. He has been very helpful to me in many ways. He came home one night, and because he learnt that medical advice was against my walking up the steps to get 'upstairs', he told me I could sell the house and buy another and he would not be in the way; that is to say, he would write off whatever I owe him on the mortgage. And I owe him a lot. However, I find there is no need now for me to take another house, for my health has improved, to the extent that I am even getting a bit pot-bellied, and I go up and down the stairs many times every day . . . David Ramkeesoon is appointed a master at QRC . . . Kamla will have to choose which of two teaching jobs she would take: principalship of a Mahasabha secondary school to be opened this September in Sangre Grande (wherein Sati will also get a teaching post) or an assistant teachership at a Girls' High School at St Augustine. The St Augustine school is run by the Naparima Girls' High School board . . .

I hear Simbhoo is trying to get for Kamla a starting salary of $240. Even if he succeeds in getting her $200, it will be a lot. But I'm afraid this St Augustine offer must have him rather peeved. But he shouldn't be. He never replied to Kamla's application, whereas the Naparima people were more prompt and courteous. Besides, up to some weeks ago nobody knew the Mahasabha would be getting a secondary school (state-aided) at Sangre Grande in time for the Sept. opening. Bhadase bought a ready-made building . . . On the sixteenth instant Sati will be getting her ring ($169) from Crisen Bissoon Dath; and I am having the Daths to dinner when the engagement will be announced. We are not inviting many people; it is going to be a small affair . . . I won't show Kamla your last letter in which you say she is still thoughtless; I quite see your point and agree with you; very good indeed; shows you can take care of things now. And have a nice sense of discrimination, a sense of values . . . But we won't tell Kamla anything; she might be hurt. She thought you would be 'drained' if you gave her all the cash she needed for the passage home. She was considerate in an inconsiderate sort of way. I could do a lot of writing before a typewriter and would like to begin the autobiographical novel; have, in fact, asked Shekhar to bring me some copy paper from the *G* . . . But there is this shop-watching job that Sookhdeo is offering me . . .

Keep well. We are all well, without fooling. And thanks again for that letter.

Pa

IX

August 10, 1953 — December 8, 1953

FAMILY TRAGEDY

[postmarked August 10, 1953]

My dear Vido,

Kamla's coming has caused some bustle and that made us at home quite happy, especially as Kamla has so much to say and has not in the least lost her sense of humour. But her immediate relatives—her aunts and others—are not so satisfied. They would have been infinitely more pleased if she had come down the gangplank twiddling a mala* or singing a couplet of the Ramayana. But, in fact, as she came with a pronounced accent, she really did surprise many—Mrs Dinan saying, 'Ei giol, don' speak so much Amwrican.'

Rudranath travelling in the same boat (kept aloof and away from Kamla throughout the voyage); but though she travelled third, she had a very good time and had lots of eats and several times dined and teaed with the captain himself. Arriving at No. 17, Capo R. sat to a Suraj-Puran Puja, and a minute later I was surprised to see Kamla take a seat on the coverlet-spread beside him.

I had been long suspecting Capo S. to be a bluffer, and I saw two days ago how right I have been. You know, for about a month or so Capo S. (through Mrs Capo S.) has been saying that he is trying to get Kamla the principalship of a secondary school the Mahasabha is opening at Sangre Grande; that she will be getting a salary of $240.00 a month. Well, two days ago Kamla asked Capo S. for an interview, since it appeared she couldn't see him otherwise, he being very busy with other matters. Kamla wants to discuss with him the Mahasabha job. He didn't see her himself, but caused her (with me) to appear before the Mahasabha's management Comm. or board or whatever you call it, in Bhadase's long warehouse on the following day. After making us wait for a whole hour or longer all he had to tell Kamla was

---

* Prayer beads

that she could only be given a teaching job under Lalee (Rikhi) in their Tunapuna school, for eighty odd dollars a month. There was a take-it-or-leave-it attitude about the offer, and of course Kamla thanked the gentleman for it and we left the place, feeling very humiliated; for Capo had simply made a 'pappy-show'* of us. Surely, he could have told Kamla in advance what was the position.

I was a bit annoyed with Kamla, and still am. She has not been showing a sense of dispatch or business sense; she relied, against my advice, too much on Capo S. She has had an offer for an assistant teacher's post with Naparima High School, and she should have got in contact with Miss Wagar soon after her arrival, by phone or otherwise, as Miss Wagar had suggested to her to do. But she remained almost a whole week to send a telephone message to her, asking for an appointment. I do feel Kamla will be better off working with the Presby. people here than with Messrs Bhadase and Capildeo and their henchmen. They have nothing good for us; and I shan't go to 17 to see Rudranath because I don't care to see him . . . The fact is that Bhadase and Capo S. have asked (I should say begged) Rudranath to become principal of a college they want to build at St Augustine; and Rudranath has accepted, on the condition that he returns to London and gets permission from his boss at the university, and returns in October. I was present at 17 when this proposition was made to him. He is to bring a tutor with him. He is asking for a salary of $600.00 a month, because, he says, that is what Jamaica University College was offering him. So you see, Kamla is a wash-out so far as these Mahasabha people are concerned, and it is a very good thing for her that this is so. Fancy her working under people like Bhadase and his illiterate and semi-illiterate henchmen . . . I think Capo R.'s idea is to work her during the long vacations, then return to his lecturer's post at London University; and do so year after year until he has brought down a sufficient number of B.A.'s and B.Sc.'s. But he had made it plain that he must be absolute boss all the time; and he will be doing all the training—for they are to have a teachers' training college, too.

My dear Kamla has given me a lot of hope and courage, but, you know, Banares Hindu University is not recognised by the Trinidad Board of Edu-

---

* Puppet show

cation, and I'm afraid this may go against her as far as salary is concerned; still, I think she will be given a better pay by the Naparima Girls' High School than by the Mahasabha.

Excuse the scribble in ink at the top of this letter-form. Kamla had started to write to someone, and I asked her to let me have the form . . . I am feeling very well indeed, and you have no cause to worry. Swanzy has paid me £16/16/0 for the story—the best fee I have ever had.

Pa

[Handwritten notes]:

I wish I could make my letters as good as you make yours. Write soon.

Are you doing the farm work? You must be very short of money, but if so, let me know. So I could send you two or three pounds out of my story money. Sending you by Krishna and Sita Rajcoomar some shirts and socks and an Indian vase as birthday gift. Krishna and Sita leave on 8/18/53.

Kamla will be seeing the principal of the St Augustine Girls' High School day after tomorrow.

26 Nepaul Street,
St James,
Port-of-Spain
August 12, 1953

My dear Vido,

I am finally at home. The Colombie was supposed to have docked at the wharf at 12 but it was there at 10.30. Ma, Pa and all the girls were there. Sati, Mira and Savi are so grown up and quite pretty. I really couldn't recognise them. Nalini is a lovely baby but she looks Chinese. Shivan is very shy and quiet, but Ma has told me that he is behaving in that spoilt manner only since I came home. He doesn't know a thing, but is very willing to learn. And so, I am giving him a few days to get accustomed to me before I start teaching him. He is going to somebody's private school. God alone knows whose. Anyway, I have been to see Romily, and Shivan might be in his hands from September onwards.

Barkah Mamoo* has been very kind to Ma and the children and promised them $50 from the month of August as Pa was given his pay until July. Also Ajah† and his family have been ever so kind to them. Surprisingly they had come to greet me at the wharf and those who couldn't come were at home in the afternoon. Baby and Bhaqurat (Mamee's brother and sister) were even there to see me. And many others.

I walked down Frederick St this morning with Phoowa and Sita and Goch. It seemed ever so small.

Pa's famous 'shade tree' has really grown to be one. And the house at first sight impressed me. Everybody has told me that Pa, ever since he heard I was coming home, is a different man—he became happy and less worried.

About my job—nothing definitely decided by me yet. When I next write I ought to say definitely where I am working and my salary.

We are sending shirts and socks by Sita and Krishna for you.

All at home send their love,

                                                                    Kamla

August 17, 1953

Dear Pa and everybody,

You see what happens to the letters I write. I write them and forget to post them, or have no time to post them. I didn't realise till about twelve today that it was my birthday. Then I rushed down to tell my landlady. This afternoon she sent me up a cake.

Sati's letter and photograph arrived today. I must confess that I have no recollection at all of Crisen. Sati tells me, in that atrocious handwriting of hers, that she is going to live at Mamoo's. She seems rather pleased, but I am afraid I am not shouting for joy about the idea. I have no doubt that Mamoo's motives are worthy; but the time has come for us to try being as independent as possible. Considerations of salary apart, I shall be much happier if Kamla, for instance, were to take the Naparima job. I have been waiting for a letter from her, but so far none has arrived. You see, taking the

---

* Simbhoo, Vidia's mother's elder brother
† Sookhdeo, Vidia's rich great-uncle by marriage who funded the purchase of the Naipaul family house on Nepaul Street, Port of Spain (see page 34)

Naparima job would prevent that peevishness about which you complain. But I am really not qualified to speak on these matters, because I am not in possession of all the facts. But it seems ludicrous to me that Sati should have to live in a house not her own. Only a saint gives something for nothing; and you are placing yourself within range of people's insults when you do that sort of thing. Sookhdeo is an entirely different proposition; and I should have no hesitation in accepting his offer.

I am really rather disturbed by the effect that man Capo R. may be having on you. But it is all unimportant, as I have tried to tell you. Please don't misunderstand me. I bear no ill-will at all towards Capo S.; I am, if anything, beholding to Mamee and him. But my recollection of family relationships in Trinidad is that they were on a tight-rope seeming to lead nowhere. I merely wish you to keep out of the way of petty and undignified squabbling.

This is the beginning of my third week on the farm. The hours are rather long, from nine in the morning till half-past eight in the evening, but I am not over-strained, and am really enjoying the physical exertion.

I am waiting for a letter from home, and shall write again in about five days.

Goodbye,
Vido

August 19th, 53

My dear Vido,

By now we have grown quite accustomed to Kamla. Her coming has had a wonderful effect for the better so far as the home folk are concerned; but I know, too, that many of our relatives seem to be put out because Kamla has been able to take care of things for us; but far more annoyed that she came as well turned as from an English university. They would have liked to see her wearing a tika and talking classic Hindi and speaking English as a native of Banares. This not being so, they are quite disillusioned, so that Kamla has gone to 17 but twice since her arrival—once when she disembarked from on board ship, and once again to pay a courtesy call. Many people are pained that she has come back to help us, and can help us, and will help us.

Last Monday I accompanied Kamla to the St Augustine Girls' High

School. She was interviewed by Miss Constance Wagar, Canadian-born Principal of the school. It was a very successful interview: Kamla will be teaching geography and English Literature, starting on the job from the beginning of September. According to the Principal, she will be paid a salary of $180.00 a month with increasement of $15 a year till she reaches the maximum of $270. The Mahasabha offered her $80.00 as an assistant teacher in an elementary school, of which Lalee is head teacher. She will write today declining the post.

Suppose Kamla had learned Hindi; she could have spoken in Hindi but would have learned little, if anything, of Indian history and culture. Far too many Hindus already know Hindi in Trinidad, but I fail to see where this is taking them. Intrinsically they remain as ignorant and superstitious as ever. Take Dinanath, for instance.

Yesterday Mrs Jules Mahabir visited us. Her husband, Mr Mahabir, is chairman of the Management Committee of the St Augustine High School. When Kamla's application (written from Banares) came up for discussion it was he who recommended her for the post very highly. Some time next month Kamla would be giving a talk on her Indian experiences to a women's group in Port-of-Spain. Mrs Mahabir has asked her for this and is making the necessary arrangements; but Kamla is not keen—she dislikes doing anything of the sort. However, she has promised to give the talk, not wanting to displease.

Last Sunday we had a few people at home. It was the occasion of Sati's engagement to Crisen Bissoon Dath. We had Mrs Capo S. but nobody else from the Capildeo clan; on my side we had Mr and Mrs George Rajcoomar. Sati is bent on this wedding; but for this she and Kamla could have brought in quite a pile of money. As far as I am concerned, I might be watching shop for Mr Sookhdeo within the next two or three weeks. The pay might be just about half of what the *Guardian* was giving me. But it will be a quiet and easy job, a thing that I should be able to cope with.

This is most important: do not leave the university yet. Take full advantage of the opportunity you have, for you may never have it again. With Kamla's help we can get along well enough for a year or two.

A while ago I had been teaching Sivan his parts of speech. He is not as responsive as you used to be. He lacks that precociousness that marked you out from others. He doesn't or wouldn't think. At the moment Kamla is taking him in his Robin Hood, a prize-book of Savi's. The King Arthur and

Sir Lancelot books you sent him are too profound for him. Do not imagine him a dull, listless fellow. Far from it; but he is too playful and just won't concentrate on lessons, though he is very proud of his having come first in his last test exam in the private school he is attending. From September he goes to Romily's school—Eastern Boys' Government. Romily has kindly promised to take him to and from school in his car.

I haven't been able to get him into Tranquillity.

Please read 'The Diver' and let me know whether it is good enough for Swanzy. I am informed that they have just now 'a spate of long short stories', so my next ('which I hope you will soon be sending,') must be a short one, say 2,500 words at the most. The last chapter in *Gurudeva* should also make a good short story, and I would be glad if you could send me a copy.

Just now we are living on the proceeds of the last story, and it is time I sent in another. Do work on this—I mean send a copy of either 'The Diver' or the 'Panchayat' piece of *Gurudeva*.

We are sending you by Krishna and Sita some shirts and socks and a brass vase. Please accept them—especially the vase—as presents for your 21st birthday—with love from all—Pa

The BBC has especially asked me for more stories.

Pa just confessed that he really has not grown accustomed to Ma! Lots of gossip about Rosie etc. in next letter.

Kamla

August 21st, 53

My dear Vido,

On Tuesday, Sept. 1 Kamla takes up her appointment at the St Augustine High School for Girls. There have been a hitch or two, but these have been finally and successfully settled. First, there was the question as to whether BHU was recognised by the relevant authority in England. Yesterday a letter was received by the Indian Commissioner here from London, stating that BHU is recognised; and a list is given of all the Indian universities that are also recognised. But for this timely assurance Kamla's salary would have been cut by half. Mr Loinsworth, to interview whom I accompanied K. to the Education Department yesterday, says everything is now all right regarding the validity or worth of the degree; but that if Kamla had done an honours degree, or had not come through with a first-class pass, her salary would have been accordingly lower than the maximum, which is $180.00 to begin with, but goes up to $270.00 at the rate of $15.00 a year increasement. So now we are all relieved.

No difficulties here with us. I am feeling better and better; but if I must be truthful I must say all sustained work entailing physical exertion is not for me. I can do a good deal, but only sitting before a desk—such as this typing I am doing. I am not worrying. As soon as I have finished this letter I shall start typing 'Uncle Dalloo', which I have re-done for the BBC. (By the way, whatever became of this story that I sent you?) When and if this is taken by Swanzy, I shall be sending him 'The Diver'. And I am pretty sure I could get at least one story from the tail-end of *Gurudeva*. I mean that 'Panchayat' episode.

Sati has not gone to Capo S. It might have been a coincidence, but I too was, and still am, against this arrangement. He hasn't given us the $50.00 he had said he would be giving us; and, thank God, we don't want it—unless of course he gives it unasked. Hitchens has promised me half-pay ($82.50) to the end of this month. He may or may not give it. But we'll get through. We may have it just a little hard for one short month; but I shouldn't say this even, for I find things—you see I do believe in a divine Providence—do come pat right just at the right time. No superstition, my boy, but a peculiar truth—but perhaps only for those who trust.

You couldn't shift Sati from her projected wedding. How more nicely things would have gone for us if she could have postponed the business for a year. But she wouldn't; and if you insist, showing her reasons, she begins to cry! And that fellow Crisen, he wants the thing to come no later than February. I tried to get him to agree to May, but not he.

There is one thing that makes life rather grim for me: I must not smoke; yet every now and then I take a puff or two, and immediately after suffer terrible guilt, not unlike one who has done a criminal thing. And it is very bad for me, for it brings on pains, even though they last but a few minutes. Every time after a smoke I vow I wouldn't take another, but no sooner than I have taken a meal, or a cup of tea—I don't take much of this, for this too is banned me—I want a smoke and indeed break my resolve. Yet I have gone weeks without a smoke.

Capo R. hasn't told me a word about you; nor have I asked him a thing as to how you are doing. I know he has a tendency to exaggerate, so though he may tell me things uncomplimentary about you—I'll take them with a pinch of salt.

Please do not think we have forgotten you and your 21st. We haven't. I am sending you some shirts by Krishna and Sita. And a brass vase, I hope, for a memento. But Krishna and Sita won't be leaving till September 18. Time their arrival . . . Got your two letters—one telling us about your farm work, and the other about other things.

Please continue your university studies, for it is a fine opportunity; and I should hate myself to make you spoil it. There is no real need to.

Pa

August 25, 1953

Dear Kamla and Pa and Ma and everybody else,

I should be writing first of all to Sati, to congratulate her on her engagement; but as it is now a quarter-past eleven and I have had a long day at the farm, I think I shall leave that for tomorrow.

The letters I have had from home since Kamla arrived have been truly marvellous. They bring with them excitement and happiness, and this pleases me greatly. I am particularly pleased with Kamla's job. The whole thing, at this distance from home, seems too good to be true. In a way I am rather unhappy that I was not told about the plan to sell No. 26, etc. But it is of little importance.

I am having 'The Diver' typewritten. I am afraid that your letters were not really necessary for that. I had decided on the story some time ago. I shall make one change. The story slips into the present historic about half-way. I shall use the ordinary preterite. The story has a beautiful beginning—'There was this inconsistency about Jaimuni . . .'—I am quoting from memory. I would have typed it myself. But this typewriter is really an American's, and I should have taken it back two nights ago. He is collecting it in the morning.

I have an odd little anecdote to relate. I was looking for the lodgings of this American. The directions he gave led me to a very old house, dusty and unkempt, past narrow passages and up a shaky staircase. The first room I looked into was covered with litter. But there was the smell of paint about and I assumed that the house was being redecorated. Just then a voice from the adjoining room called out 'Hello there' and I said, 'Is this No. 80a?' The door opened and a man came out. He was old. He wore spectacles and a beret and he was carrying a pot of paint. I looked into the room. The ceiling sagged and the floor was not level. The panelling was old. The man gave me detailed instructions about getting to where I was going, to the house, showed me a fifteenth-century room and told me a lot about himself. He visited prisons to speak to lonely prisoners. The room in which he lived—the 15th-cent. one—was hung with paintings of the sort one finds in antique shops. Everything in the room looked as though it might have come from an antique shop. Before bidding me goodbye, he said, 'That room you found me in, the one I was painting, do you know about it?' I said no. 'Lewis Carroll lived there. In that room he wrote *Alice in Wonderland*.' I had no idea. I must have passed that house a hundred times since I have been in Oxford. But it is hard to imagine the charm of Lewis Carroll's Oxford. The streets around that area just begin to get shabby. The toughs move around it. In Carroll's time, Nuffield didn't build his Morris cars just outside Oxford and Oxford had little attraction for the spiv and the factory worker. All that has changed now.

I think I shall remain for one more week at the farm. Having stayed so long it seems a pity not to stay longer, especially if the weather is fine and we go out combining. The combine is a marvellous machine. As the name suggests, it combines in one operation all the jobs of harvesting. It cuts the wheat stalks, threshes the wheat and sends out the chaff and straw in one direction, while the grain comes into a bin. My job is to bag this wheat. It can be a fairly tricky job, for the bags are big, and I must prevent the bag folding up. A bag of wheat weighs 252 pounds. The fact is that at the end of my eleven-hour day I do not feel absolutely worn, as I did for the first two weeks, I merely feel pleasantly tired, and I have the satisfaction of having done a good day's work. Mere clerkship seems insipid now. Besides, working an eleven-hour day fills one's time completely, and the spare time one does have in the evening seems more precious. Physically I feel fine. My arms, though not developing, have become very hard and very wiry. The muscles on my shoulder have hardened too and I feel very light and comfortable.

I am having an interview with the Appointments Committee on

Sep. 14. I have looked through the jobs folder in college, and jobs in the United Nations seem to be just up my alley. Failing that there are jobs with firms in the East or overseas. I have to go on with Oxford, theoretically at any rate. I need the money while I am getting a job—which may come in four or six or eight months. The Colonial Office will not pay if I remain at Oxford not doing a course of some kind. The problem is, what course? I am tempted by a degree in modern languages—French and Spanish. It would be largely the work I did in 1948, though I fear much of that has grown rusty. I don't know. But I am not over-worried. These things normally work themselves out.

I hope that you are writing seriously. I do wish I could see Trinidad more clearly. And my, the stories that I seem to be writing. There is no lack of material. I feel sure a three-month stay in Trinidad would keep me writing for three years. I shall send you, as soon as I have the opportunity, James Joyce's *Dubliners*. James Joyce wrote that story 'Clay' in the Everyman selection. The one you liked so much that you read it to me—about the nurse going to call on a family, and discovering that she has forgotten a cake.

My regards and love to all. It is late, and I must close.

Vido

University College, Oxford
September 7

Dear Satti,

You ought to have received this a long time ago; but quite a number of things managed to delay it.

I am very happy about your engagement and I wish to offer you and Crisen my best wishes. You needn't feel at all guilty because you don't want to wait to get married. So don't get upset because Pa says to wait. I feel sure he will understand.

I have very little news to offer about myself. Kamla must have told you all that you really wished to know. But I think I shall definitely stay till June—i.e. for 9 more months. By then I hope I have a reasonable job.

There is one thing I do earnestly wish, though—and that is for you to change your atrocious handwriting. I don't think it is very hard to do. For it is easier to be plain than to be flashy. Your handwriting will really put people off. After all, A B C D E F G H I J K L are very easy to write and read.

I shall be very glad to hear from you from time to time and though I do not write a reply to every letter, it is not from want of wishing to do so.

My best wishes once more,
Vido

[From Kamla]

September 7, 1953

Dearest Vido,

Until last night Pa was literally going around in circles—you must be very ill. Well, the picture Pa has of you is amusing to me. I have never come across such a vivid imagination in all my life. No wonder he writes so well. He seems to think of you as a skeleton—a perfect specimen—walking along St John's Street. He is just dying to see you.

Look, Vido, do try and make the best of Oxford, now that you are there. Look at the whole thing sensibly and do what you think will be best for your future. Pa seems sad that you want to leave. So, do the best, will you?

We bought 2 white, 1 grey and 1 blue shirt—quite de luxe—for you. I am giving you the price, so that you may be able to compare. We paid $15.30 for all four. I personally thought the price was excellent. We also bought 3 pairs of pure wool socks and we paid $2.64 for each. When you wear them, you will be able to tell us whether they are good or not. If they are, write and tell us. I'll try to send one or two now and then by anyone going to England.

Home has really become happy since I returned. It is just as though Hope herself came to them. I am happy too, seeing that my return has made them so happy. I am enjoying teaching at St Augustine. 80% of the girls are Indians and some of them are real cute.

Pa and all at home are planning on your returning home for the summer vac. next year. It could be very easy. The Gov't can pay your passage to T'dad and we can do something regarding your return passage. You can help me by taking some of your stipend in advance and paying down on the return. Don't think this is selfish. You know I am just working for a little. But to make it possible next summer I will help all I can.

My driving lessons are the present source of amusement at home. In some way or the other, I am always the source of amusement and Pa loves that. This afternoon, I drove all the way on the Churchill–Roose Highway from school. I am improving. The first time, I turned the corner on two wheels. These days I am doing it on four. Pa said, I can perform in any circus.

The Rosie lowdown—she is still round and rosy, Richard is in England and Ma said, 'Man, that is a feather in she cap.' She still hasn't netted a husband. Rosie was engaged but she 'caught her fiancé doing something and, girl, you know me, I don make bones, Ah pelt 'im with de scissors and cut him.' She then hooked a man with a car and her Aunt Beti encouraged her because Beti wanted for herself a provision shop. But now everybody is disappointed. Rosie's man found her ugly. So that's home—the present position. Rosie is ugly. She is old. She is unmarried. She is frustrated. Beti has no provision shop so she has [. . .]. Rosie advised me, 'Gul, I glad I ne married. You think I will marry any fool?' I am sorry for Rosie.

Kamla

Univ.
September 7

Dear Kamla,

I should have written some time ago; but I was working on the farm. I am afraid I had to stop at the end of August, and I have been ill since—with the worst attack of asthma I have had since I left home. The doctor tells me that many people have it at the moment. I think it is the weather. Whenever it gets hot, I feel unwell. Of course my not being able to work puts me in a financial fix, and I shall have to ask you for enormous help. But not yet. This is just a warning. I am sending 'The Diver' to Swanzy tomorrow and the carbon copy to Pa. I haven't been able to do much more.

I am not unhappy or anything. I have had asthma for too long now and I have several medicines on my table—peculiar-looking inhalants and pills to take before meals and mixtures to take after meals. I have never taken so many drugs in my life.

I haven't heard what your job is like. But I feel you ought to play fair and devote some time to your work. Read all Shakespeare for instance and all Milton. You will get a much better perspective and you'll be able to teach more effectively.

The worst thing about asthma is that it is such a bore. I thought I had grown out of it, but there we are. Still, I suppose I'll be all right in a day or two.

Please try to be nice to as many people as possible, whatever their attitude may be.

Yours,
Vido

September 24th, 1953

Dear Vido,

Krishna and Sita Rajcoomar left for England in the Colombie on September 18. The boat should reach England in about ten or twelve days; so you can guess the time the two people will be home. We have sent you by them two things—four shirts, three pairs of socks and a vase and two half-tins of salmon. I bought for you a picture, a Chinese thing done in cork, a river scene; but the thing is so fragile that I was almost sure neither Sita nor Krishna could be trusted to hand it to you whole. In fact, Sita said she would not guarantee the thing reaching you in one piece. So I decided to keep it home until your arrival here in June or July next. Of course we have all discussed this arrival of yours. Kamla thinks you can do it with your quarterly allowance; then we can make up the passage money for your return. I will be very glad indeed if you can do this. Plan for coming home from now.

There is one thing that is a sorry topic here, and I have been trying to postpone mentioning it all this time; I have been pretending that everything will be all right, and I might have gone on pretending but for Kamla's insistence that I must tell you this thing that is becoming a worry. Well, I need not beat about the bush: it is felt by everybody at home (not excluding myself) that if you get married at all you will be lost to us. We cannot afford losing you; I am not good any longer for any hard work. And one or two must work to see the younger members of the household come through, so that they are able to do for themselves. I am asked to remind you that your own uncle Rudranath is the best example. He has made it blatantly plain that he has nothing to do with any of his sisters; as to the sisters' children—well, they are less than nothing to him. As though to prove this to them he has never visited a single one of his relatives; though every member of the clan did kow-tow by going to see him off on the boat taking him back to England.

Kamla is doing a lot, in fact she is doing everything; she is doing a man's job, and I do very much want to assure you that, grateful as I am, it is no pleasure to be a burden to her. Moreover, sooner or later—the sooner the better—she will marry. I have been trying to get a job, but for the same reason that the *Guardian* no longer wants me, nobody wants me. And my job has to be select; it must be an easy job. Nobody wants to give anybody an easy job—except Sookhdeo, who, by the way, is not yet ready and heaven knows when he will be ready.

Nor do I want to become a lifelong burden to you; but you should be in a position to help. I thought Kamla would help one or two years; then Sati would have taken her turn (but you see what kind of turn Sati is taking); and after Sati there would be Mira and then Savi, to help. But you can never tell with girls. So if you could put off marrying, say for three or four years, you would be in a better position to help. I am not ignoring the problem of loneliness.

If you get a well-paid job, some one of us will be able to join you in England or wherever you are, and, on the whole, we would try to make things as home-like for you as we possibly can.

This letter may make you very unhappy, and it is no pleasure for me to know that I am the cause of it; in the end you will do just as you please, but I had to say a thing or two and I have said it.

There are more teaching jobs in secondary schools here now than there are suitable candidates. The new (Government) St George's College at Barataria had to postpone the opening because of lack of teachers. Several denominational secondary schools are being built or are soon to be built.

A fellow named Abdullah, who has had a four-year course at Oxford, has been appointed languages master at QRC. That fellow Rowel Debisingh has left for Oxford for a three-year course in something or the other.

QRC is paying $400 a month to the teacher with the right qualification. All this is not to say that I want you to live in Trinidad, but it is just giving you some news. You probably will have better opportunities outside this hole; but I am sure you will enjoy a holiday here.

> With all my love,
> Pa

University College, Oxford
October 8, 1953

My dear Pa,

I am terribly sorry about not writing for so long; but you will no doubt be considerably amused when you learn how I have been spending my time. During the month of August I worked on a farm, as you know. Then I had an attack of asthma (the doctor told me that everybody in the area who was susceptible to it had it then). This made me spend my time in bed for a fortnight. Then one day a friend said that he was going to Bristol. Get out a map and look. He was going by car and I decided to go for the ride. He was going to see his branch manager. He was working as a salesman for a book company: *Home Encyclopaedias, Books of Knowledge,* etc. It turned out that I could get a job selling these books at 15% commission. The *Home Encyclopaedia* brought me 7/10 per copy sold. Up to now I have sold 23 copies of that. I have also sold one dictionary.

The business is, in fact, so profitable that I am thinking of selling these books when I come to Trinidad next summer. I think we can sell quite a lot there. Anyway, the money earned was enough to keep me going through September. The work involved is not much and one works when one wishes.

I am greatly handicapped by the lack of a typewriter with regard to your stories. But I have arranged to rent one at 7/6 a week.

Now, about my plans. You can count on seeing me within 10 months— in June/July. I can assure you that your desire to see me only equals my wish to be with you again. I have acquired such a revulsion for English food that two weeks ago—in a mood of severe homesickness—I went to bed solaced by the mere idea of roti and pumpkin and bhaji—those very foods which you dislike. English food is a calamity and a tragedy. The ignorance and crudity the people display in their handling of vegetables make the eating of vegetables a painful task.

I know and can understand your wish for me to settle in Trinidad. But let me explain why, if I did so, I shall die from intellectual starvation. Two days ago I met Solomon Lutchman.* I never realised the man was so utterly ugly, so utterly crass—low forehead, square, fat face, thick lips, wavy hair combed straight back. Now S.L. is an educated man. Yet to me he appears uncultured. The gulf that I felt between people and myself at home— people called me conceited, you remember—has grown wider. Take Lutchman. Narrow, insular, still looking upon Trinidad as the source of all effulgence. Bigoted, and adamantly refusing to consider that there may be another side to any question. Not interested in books for themselves; like most people, he reads only when forced to. He is not like you, who reads a book for its style, and for the man behind the style. He cannot talk. He is coarsely rhetorical: says 'preférable' instead of 'préferable' (i.e. he says 'prefer' [pree/fir] and then adds 'able' [ubble]: pree-fir-able. One ought to lay the stress on the first 'e' and say 'preff-er-able'). In Oxford he wears a sky-blue blazer with a badge of a club called Sunbridge League. I wished to draw his attention to it; because that blazer can be spotted a mile off. 'Tee, tee, but you don't know us? Cricket club in Caroni, man.' Wearing the blazer of a Caroni Cricket Club in Oxford. I ask you—can you conceive of anything narrower and stupider? I talked to him about politics. His lack of vision, his impregnably stupid preoccupation with the 500,000 inhabitants of T'dad as being the hub of the universe, annoyed me. He ignores the bigger things ('Why should I care about Dominica or the starving Jamaicans?'), he does not see the injustice done to the Africans in Kenya or South Africa; the fact that 12 years ago Indian troops were being killed in the desert by the Germans and today—Indian immigration to Kenya stopped, Germans invited. The bigger issues of global injustice and global wrongs do not appeal to his mind. Everything begins and ends with Trinidad.

And S. Lutchman is an educated Trinidadian.

Let us take the other side now: the Trinidad upper class. I take Sita and Krishna as good members of this class. Samples of Sita's conversation: 'Ah belong to [. . .], Palm Beach and a few other clubs. They have a club in Piarco with tea-time dances. There you begin to dance at three and you go on till midnight. Ah had a good time on the boat. It was de captain's las'

---

* 6th Form schoolfriend of Vidia

journey and we had dancin' every night.' I don't even believe she knows what education is. Education isn't a matter of getting a degree—where Capo R. fails; it is a lot more: it should create a mind that can adapt itself to the humanities, the leisurely interludes of life, the mind that thinks. If one can translate the social graces (read Chesterfield's letters to his son—they are delightful things) into 'mental' graces, the purpose of education will become a little clearer. Sita is merely literate; Capildeo is a technician, the worst type of the modern barbarian—the man who thinks he has the right to pronounce on all things because of a limited excellence. If you can get a book called *The Rebellion of the Masses* (it was in the Central Library when I was at home) read it. It is by a Spaniard called José Ortega y Gasset. What money is to Sita, degrees are to Capildeos. The English upper classes may spend their time in frivolous debauch just as much as Sita; but they find time to read *The Times* every day and take some interest in world affairs; they even subscribe to The Times Library ($20 a year). Even their society magazines have sections devoted to book reviews. Sita doesn't even read.

I feel at home neither with Lutchman nor with Sita. And it seems difficult for me to find a society to which I could belong, without effort. But Trinidad is out. A salary of £1,000 a year is tempting; but in Trinidad it is worthless.

R. Debysingh is not coming to Oxford. He is at some sordid engineering school in London's East End.

About the business of marriage, I myself am rather unsure; and I can understand your reasoning. I shall explain everything in another letter soon.

On Oct. 18 you can hear me in *Carib. Voices*. It is a funny sketch—very funny, I think. I wrote it more than two years ago. Willy Richardson* has asked me to do a six-minute talk about the British Farm—as much as I could gather from my month's experiences. Perhaps, after that, I can do something on being a salesman. Never before have I felt so urgently that I must write. But the frustration kills me. I have trained myself on the typewriter and I find that I can't do without one. I have no typewriter at the moment that belongs to me.

The best news of all that I have for you is that I am in glorious health.

---

* West India Producer on BBC Overseas Service; was a librarian in Trinidad when Vidia first met him

My horrifying nervous illness that made life this time last year a nightmare has slowly and surely disappeared. I get up every morning and feel glad to be alive. Every day has become an adventure. Kamla's stay in England, despite its shortness, really began the healing. But when she came I was still unwell. Her presence comforted me and has cured me. She has brought much joy to us. She, much more than I, is the heart of the family.

On Tuesday (13th) I am going to see the Oxford University Appointments Committee. I hope that by the time I am ready to leave England next June, I shall have been settled in a reasonable job.

What about British Guiana? Sita had some pictures of BG. I rang up the *Daily Sketch* and tried to sell the pictures; but they were not interested.

At the moment I am wearing the grey shirt and the socks. A splendid set; for which many heartfelt thanks.

Keep well and give my love to all.

Vido

CABLE AND WIRELESS (WEST INDIES) LIMITED

OCT 10 1953

= NAIPAUL 26 NEPAUL STREET PORT OF SPAIN TRINIDAD

= HE WAS THE BEST MAN I KNEW STOP EVERYTHING I OWE TO HIM BE BRAVE MY LOVES TRUST ME = VIDO

University College, Oxford
October 14, 1953

My dearest Ma,

I was more worried about you at home than about anything else. Please don't worry about me. Of course I had looked forward to seeing him; everything that I am is directly due to him. But, as Satti has said, one must now settle down and try living again. Tears and regrets, though they cannot be helped, are of no avail.

Things could have been worse, you know. And though nothing can replace him who was our guide, we must all hold together and stick together. So, first of all, I would like to know as soon as possible what our financial position is. How much we owe, etc. Please let me have details of this. Yesterday I went to the Appointments Committee, and have got a list of jobs. I am writing for an interview with the Western India Match Company. I don't think I will come home until I have definitely settled a job. And I can only look for a job here. The prospects are bright. If everything fails I can always get a job for £50 a month with an Oil Company. But I do want something a little better.

The person who worries me at the moment is Shivan. He will need me; because you know how boys need older men around. But we can discuss that more fully when I get home.

I don't think Satti should put off her marriage; unless, of course, she wants to. But I have my doubts about holding it at No. 17.

Kamla is doing a grand job; but I hope she does not think she will be bound for several years. I shall do my best to relieve her as soon as possible.

Ranee and Dravid shall remain in school. I don't know how well the Dravidian is doing at school but I expect Kamla will let me know soon.

The main thing now is not to exhaust yourself in regrets. He worked for all of us; what we are he has made us. And when you think from what he started, you ought to feel proud.

Above all, try to be of good cheer and remember

Your loving son,
Vido

[From Peter Bayley*]

University College, Oxford
October 17, 1953

Dear Kamla,

I was extremely sorry to hear the news of your bereavement, and I send you and your mother and the family my sincere condolences.

But I was touched and pleased by the fact that you felt you could write

---

* Vidia's English tutor at Oxford

to me, and also by the trust you place in me. I am extremely fond of and interested in Vidia, and you may be sure that I shall continue to be so. And shall continue to see as much of him as I can, despite the fact that now he is doing work for a research degree he does not come to me officially at all. However I think he knows that he is very welcome at our home at any time, and we both hope he will continue to look upon us as friends whom he can drop in to see whenever he feels like it.

I received your letter on Monday afternoon. It was waiting for me in the college lodge. I had not been in to college in the morning as my teaching programme had not properly begun. I immediately went to Vidia's lodgings, but failed to find him there, as indeed happened when I called again early in the evening on my way into college for dinner. But I left a note, asking if he could come and see me, and he came round at about ten that evening.

However, he had been called to London and had already heard the news of his father's death, and by the time I saw him had had time to get over the first shock. As you know, he was deeply attached to his father, and loved and admired him, and has often told me how much he owes to his family, his mother and sisters, but in particular ways to his father for all his interest: in languages, literature, writing, even printed type. But he had obviously stood the shock very well indeed, and was no doubt grateful to his sisters for their solicitude (though I have no doubt he will row you when he writes for having bothered me in the matter!). But you must not worry in the least, nor Sati (I'm so sorry, I'm not sure if it was Sati who wrote as well, as of course I passed her letter on to Vidia), for I did not at all mind, and was in fact, as I have already said, very touched and flattered to think that the Naipaul family felt that they could approach me. I am exceedingly glad that Fortune made it possible for you to come round and see us in the short time you were in Oxford, not only because it was a pleasant and memorable occasion which we all enjoyed very much, not only because you made an entrancing impression on us, but also because, having met me, you cannot, I hope, feel that Vidia is quite alone in a foreign land!

I assure you, and I hope you will tell your mother and sister, that I will do what I can to 'look after' Vidia.

My kindest regards,

Yours very sincerely,

Home: Oct 22nd, 1953

My dear Vido,

There are so many things I want to say but I don't know how to say them. That Pa is dead—well, I guess I have to reconcile myself to that, but I can't. There are few things which haunt me—he didn't see you, who he so much wanted to see; to see England, and most of all to have his book published. What really hurts me is that he worked so hard all his life, all for us.

He had a huge funeral and his cremation was so quick and effective that everyone who witnessed it thinks that cremation is best.

Financially, we are as you know home usually is. But I feel dull without Pa. You know how interesting teaching could be and whenever something funny occurred, I always kept it—'I must tell this to Pa when he comes for me this afternoon.' As for instance correcting a form IV paper, I came across, 'Bins was lived in Scotland and when he got big, he study and he study and wrote down his references.' I am sure you could imagine Pa laughing heartily at this. But now he is not there and there is none who could see so much the humour in that.

To change the subject. We want you to come home definitely next June—even though for a short while. If you come, Pa's dream, though he is dead, would come true. He died a proud man though—very proud of me and proud of having a son at Oxford. He always thought of you as being good and considerate. He trusted you and told everyone so.

Regarding finances at home, Pa died so suddenly that I can't say anything yet. Some time later I would. We heard you over the BBC and heard the tribute to Pa. As usual—why haven't you written yet? You have Ma very worried. Think of her.

Love,
Kamla

University College, Oxford
October 28, 1953

My dearest Ma,

You are right to complain about my not writing; but, however much I wished, I just could not bring myself to do so. Something inside me just jibbed at the idea. Pat, without prompting, wrote a longish letter which I have not read.

I think it was rather kind of Henry Swanzy to pay a tribute over the radio; especially when he was at that time at the other end of the life-scale; he was about to become a father for the first time.

It hardly seems necessary for me to tell you how lonely and unprotected I feel. Everything I did and did well, as I thought—always prompted the thought, 'Pa would like to hear of this.' He didn't know, for instance, that my translations in the examination were the best in the year. In a way I had always looked upon my life as a continuation of his—a continuation which, I hoped, would also be a fulfilment. It still is; but I have to abandon the idea of growing older in Pa's company; and I have to get the strength to stand alone. I only wish I have half Pa's bravery and fortitude.

I do not want to encourage any false hopes just now; but in about 3 weeks I will definitely know about what appears to be a splendid job. I am to go to India as an executive assistant in the Western India Match Company which controls ¼ of the match industry in India, Burma, Ceylon and Pakistan. The company is ½ owned by the Swedish match company. My contract can be renewed every three years. For the first 3 years I get Rs 1,000 ($360) a month. After that, regular increments every 3 years (Rs 300 a month) which means that in six years time I shall be earning $7,200 a year in Trinidad money. Every 3 years I get 6 months' leave (with passage to Europe and back 1st class paid). There is, besides, the usual 2 weeks' local leave every year. Usual amenities are provided: car, housing, etc.

Jobs like that are fairly easy to come by. Simply because one has an Oxford degree! If Pa could only have waited! I did my best to tell you that there was no difficulty about getting a job.

I have asked the match company to give me 3 months' notice—so that I can come home, if they are going to employ me right away.

The problems that face me are knowing what to do with Shivan; and whether Meera or Sati wishes to go to university somewhere. But it is silly looking for solutions just yet; and I hope to have made plans when I come home. I would hate being separated from Kamla while she is unmarried.

It appears that Pa had been dead for four days when I went to collect the shirts and the vase and the socks.

I have worn the socks. They are—well, just a little too gay—you know, bright red diamonds etc., the vase is on my table in front of the window and at the moment is full of chrysanthemums, but rather poor specimens. It is a lovely vase, but so expensive!

It is autumn now; the season when the leaves grow old and trees seem to flame. It gets dark about tea-time and the mist comes. In the countryside it can be romantic; but in town it is a little irritating.

Bayley was very nice about breaking the news to me; but unfortunately I had heard of it two days before. Owad was very sympathetic; the night I got the news, he came to Basdai's. I wished to say nothing about it, and he didn't press me. Capo R. wrote me a letter and came to Oxford; but we missed each other. That was as well, for I am in no mood to melt and kiss and make up.

I have been going through the Children's Bookshop in Oxford; but I really don't know what Shivan can read (Pa said the King Arthur books were above him) and I have forgotten what I liked at that age. It is a great pity for Shivan; my reading tastes were formed by Pa and Shivan hasn't this guide.

Please forgive me for the delay in writing, but don't worry.

My love to all,
Vido

University College, Oxford
November 25, 1953

Dear Kamla,

As soon as you read this letter I would like to see what you can do about sending me some money. I warned you a long time ago that I would be needing some money. And, I am afraid, the time is now. I have postponed writing from day to day, expecting this and that and the other to turn up. But nothing has, and I am really flat broke. I realise that the strain would be enormous, but the money I spent in the summer could not be replaced by my efforts. The sum I need is between 150–200 dollars. I have had to buy so many things that went to pieces since I left home. I have had to buy two pairs of shoes (43), I had to pay the college 75 and my landlady 60. Believe me, Kamla, I am deeply grieved to have to ask you to do this, but I can see no other way out. My big expense here is food. I have tried eating cheap food, but that was nothing but masses of boiled potatoes, and it made me ill and weak. I have now decided that I cannot risk losing my health, and so I have a good meal twice a day. This costs a little more than a dollar a meal. If you can get the money please cable it, so that I will get it before term ends. I really feel very badly about this, but please don't think that I am cruel or inconsiderate. I have postponed writing from day to day, but I am now forced to write.

The India job has fallen out. I have now to try another firm. But there is little need for you to worry.

I think it will cheer you up to know that I am really quite well again, and it is already beginning to seem strange that I should have had that nervous illness. What a pity, though, it prevented me from writing home, it prevented me from making friends, and it prevented me from working as I should have done. But, thank God, it is all over.

I think it would be excellent if you can get Sookhdeo to write off the debt. If he doesn't, well, there is nothing to worry. It is my debt, and I will be able to pay it off. Whatever happens, though, we must see that Shivan and anyone else who so wishes have a university education. These days I think of home nearly all the time.

I took my degree last Saturday. You get no paper or anything. The ceremony is a short one, and you dress in dark clothes and gowns, etc. So I am now a fully fledged B.A.

My story about Rosie was rejected, just one of a number of rejections. Still, this is my apprenticeship, and one expects rejections.

Please don't stop writing me because my letters are so few. Now more than ever, I need letters from home.

My regards to all at home, and give my love to Ma,

Vido

December 8, 1953

My dearest Ma,

I feel very ashamed to write now, after my last letter, asking for money. But please realise that I am not really a bad boy and I asked when everything else I could do failed.

I do not want you to be unhappy or to worry about me. I think every day about you and I wish you to feel that, just as I know that you think about me. Please remember this and remember that you and everyone else at home enter into whatever plans I make for the future. Of this you must be sure, and then perhaps you will fell better.

Seromany is here in England and—well, just the same, as far as I am concerned. She showed me the *Sunday Guardian* in which Pa's death was recorded, and I was pleased to see it on the front page. I suppose it was the best thing the *Guardian* ever did for him, and I must say I have no goodwill towards them for treating Pa while he lived as they did.

I think it was splendid of Pa's family—the Sookhdeos—to rally round as Seromany told me they did, and when I return home I shall express my thanks. But look, Ma—you must not feel lost. You have us and I hardly feel that any one of us will ever let you down. Please don't worry.

I am a little worried about Shivan, though. He seems to be running wild and I hope soon to see him and see what we can do with the little wretch. Does he like the cinema as much as I did? I used to go to the old London every Sunday, remember? Rialto is much closer for him.

Satti must think me unkind not to have sent her any greetings for her examinations, but she ought to know that I really wish her the best and feel sure that she will do well enough not to let the side down. And how is the Dravidian getting along?

The great thing I wish you to preserve at all costs is your independence and self-respect. Don't be dragooned by anyone into doing anything you don't wish.

I am quite well. I wish I could be with you for Christmas, but you will be seeing me soon now. So don't worry.

I realise now that I have not told you that I received the money yesterday. Thank you very much. I would like you to regard this as a loan which I shall repay as soon as I can.

I will write again in a few days and I hope to keep it up from now on. Please think of me with love, just as I do of you.

Your son,
Vidia

Postscript

May 3, 1954 – June 20, 1957

THE WRITER

My dearest Ma,

It is wrong for you to think that I do not wish to come home, and that I intend to forget everyone there. Nothing is going to give me greater pleasure than the return home. I fully intend to return home this summer, but I can give no definite date. It may be next week, or next month, or three months from now.

The fact is this: I don't see myself fitting into the Trinidad way of life. I think I shall die if I had to spend the rest of my life in Trinidad. The place is too small, the values are all wrong, and the people are petty. Besides, there is really very little for me to do there. Ideally, I would like first of all to arrange for some sort of job in India or elsewhere, and then come home for a vacation, which I do desperately need. You must try to understand that it is no use trying to get a job from Trinidad. It will be all very well to come home and spend six months. Nothing would give me sharper pleasure. But there remains the problem of getting a suitable job even at the end of that six months. Do you see? It is much better for me to spend two more months in this country getting a job than returning home to eat lotuses. But whatever happens, you can rest assured that I shall return to Trinidad to see you this year.

Do not imagine that I am enjoying staying in this country. This country is hot with racial prejudices, and I certainly don't wish to stay here. My antipathy to a prolonged stay in this country is as great as my fear of Trinidad. I hope you understand my position now, and I think you will stop believing that you have seen the last of me.

I spend much of my time thinking of home—not Trinidad in that sense, but you. Every now and then I dream about you, and I wish that I could return home immediately. Sometimes I even think it would be nice to go to sleep here and wake up miraculously in Nepaul Street. And it is because I have no exciting news to tell you that I find it painful to write home. If all the things I think about home could be transmitted to you mentally, I feel sure you would come to look upon me as the world's greatest bore.

Now that the time is drawing near for my day of departure from Oxford, I am discarding all my English friends and acquaintances. I shall spend the rest of my life trying to forget that I came to Oxford. But it may not take as long as that. Oxford is perhaps the best university in the world, from many points of view. At the same time it is a treacherous place that insulates you from the world around. You forget that people outside are perhaps even stupider than Oxford people, and incredibly coarser. You forget many important things, and you are heading for unpleasant surprises.

Fortunately for me, the nervous breakdown I had in 1952 and 1953 has prepared me for any number of things and I am reasonably happy, as happy in fact as a man in my position can be. When I was ill I used to say that I would give both arms to be able to regain my peace and serenity of mind, to make my mind healthy again. But I didn't have to give anything except two years of my Oxford career, and now I am really very well. Being well has its dangers, though. Do you know I now weigh 147 pounds, and that I put on something like fifteen pounds in the last three weeks? So you must not worry about me. If anything happens to me I will squeal soon enough, believe me.

Sati sent me a postcard from Barbados. She seems gay and happy, and I am greatly pleased. Can you give her some advice for me: don't have more than two or three children.

I think about everybody in turn. Kamla, of course, nearest to my heart. And Mira's funny face and funny mouth, and Savi with her robust and quavering songs. Shivan with that pleasant little Naipaul face, a proper Chinee. The last girl I don't know of course, but I will soon. I wonder if Shivan remembers me. And you, whom I love very much.

So you can expect me home, but I can't say when, and you must not worry about anything. The world is a pretty awful place, but our star will shine bright yet.

> Love to all, from your silly son,
> Vido

University College, Oxford
May 17, 1954

My own Kamla and all at home,

Isn't that little rascal Shiva just like me? Cricket, and the small lies to get away from school. In 1940, you know, when I was in 4a at Tranquillity, Ma and Pa decided it would be a good thing for me to take private lessons from the older Romily. I didn't think much of the idea, and got away rather neatly by telling Romily that they had decided after all that I was to have no lessons. So I went home, and then trouble broke. Romily called me 'a little scamp' when he found out, and I had to submit to the ordeal of private lessons five days a week.

I would seriously ask Ma to think again about that couch-cum-bed. These things work well for a few months. Then they become troublesome and awful. I have been looking at Basdai's couch (Owad now has it). It is not very good. It is a very uncomfortable thing to sleep on. It is all right to use once in a while. But if you contemplate using it every day, you had better find something else. There are other things.

Sati sent me a card from Barbados and a letter. I have not yet replied to the letter, but I hope to do so soon. She seems to be happy. I hope the Sangre Grande bush is not too much for her. Is she working? I thought she was going to do some teaching before settling into the glorious routine of keeping house for her husband. Oh dear, isn't it a bit odd having a brother-in-law? So very strange. I feel very old, and I shall soon be looking out for the grey hairs.

I shouldn't worry about Marian. She is a bitch. She treated me in a most offhand manner, and this hurt me. I went to bed in floods of tears, and had to mop the room up next morning; everything was salt with my tears. It just provides me with another reason for wishing to escape from Trinidad, and I think I owe it to you to do all I can to assist you to leave that place. Who has all the vices—the dancing, the drink—of the Western way of life or whatever it is? Certainly not me. I have been rather stupid to concentrate on the books and the paintings the West has to offer us, haven't I? People are going to be disappointed when they meet me. I have nothing about me that will say that I came to Oxford. If Marian thinks my accent is what, erroneously, is called Oxford, then she reveals her own ignorance.

I am deeply grieved that you are being troubled by those damned silly fools of the family. All I can say is that you must do your best to cut down intercourse with them, and ignore their lies and insults. They are such stupid people that it would be a pity to let them upset you. It is rather unfortunate that you were born into the family that contained them; but the ties are not very strong ones. They give neither pleasure nor profit, and little can be lost if you are just coldly courteous. Let them say what they wish. I hope they were not invited to Sati's wedding. We have to live to ourselves, remember that. We are surely strong enough to do that.

I am enclosing two photographs. They may interest you. Kamla will doubtless recognise the one against the Marlborough Column at Blenheim Palace. The man on the left is a Turkish friend of mine, very kind and hospitable. The girl in the centre is Seromany, who is desperately unhappy still. She spent a week-end at the Randolph some weeks ago, at my invitation. (As usual, I did little more than sleep during the mornings.) The other picture was taken on the bridge at Abingdon, about five miles south of Oxford. Four of us—the Turk, the German in the middle, and an Indian from Tanganyika who took the picture—went on Good Friday for a two hours' row on the river. The main stream is not the one shown, but a little to the left.

Will you keep well, treat each other nicely, and love me?

Vido

St Julian's Road,
London, NW6
April 6, 1955

My dear Kamla,

I have just got your letter, which has worried me greatly. One always hesitates before giving advice of such a personal nature. But one thing I do feel is that you must never by any means marry just for the sake of being married. I really don't know why you are so worried about getting married. If being single has become an intolerable burden to you, then by all means see about getting married. But if that is not so, then I think it wiser for you to wait and find someone you really like. I couldn't bear the thought of you being unhappily married to a man you couldn't like. You will almost certainly find yourself in a greater mess. So you see how hard it is for me to advise. But, my dear Kamla, you are only twenty-five, and I see no reason why you should start to get panicky. Of course, I understand everything, but I don't want you to make this thing an affair of night and day deliberation. It is not good for you.

And now, before I return or rather carry on with the subject, I want to answer the second part of your letter. I promised you that day when I saw you off at Waterloo that I would do everything in my power to bring you back near to me, to take you away from Trinidad. That promise still holds good. I am making slow, but definite progress in the radio business, and if things keep up this way, I PROMISE YOU THAT WITHIN TWO YEARS FOR THE MOST I shall relieve you of all family duties. Do not think I am saying so just to keep the burden off my own shoulders. But I strongly feel that I will be able to help all my family. Because, I promise you, if I don't start making good money soon, I shall take a well-paid job in Africa or somewhere else. My dearest Kamla, I know that we have both been given a raw deal in life, you a much rawer one than me; but I beg you, can we look upon ourselves as partners in this business of looking after the family. You won't have to hold out for much longer. And that is the reason why I don't want you to commit yourself to any rash action you may regret later. I want you to understand that. But if, say, you meet someone you feel you like, someone you can imagine yourself linked to for a long time, then please get married, and do so without even asking any questions. I know that you just despise me, always putting off the way I do the day when Vido will take up arms and rescue the family. But I am working on that. And I am not making promises just for the sake of making them. But I need a little time, to get going. I wonder if it will make you any happier if you look upon Trinidad, not as a hole, but a place of stop-over, if you see what I mean. Look, I am going to be a success as a writer. I know that. I have gambled all my future on that possibility. Do you want to throw your lot with me or don't you? So you see that I really don't want you to do anything that will really keep you unhappy. And I want you always, always, to feel me working for you. Because I am.

I don't know, from your letter, whether you want to leave Trinidad right away or not. Perhaps you can explain later on, in another letter. Please let me know, because I want to do all I can.

Another thing, I don't want you to worry about money. I am sending some more to you in a couple of weeks and WHENEVER THERE IS NEED OF

MONEY AT HOME please ask me at once. I shall move heaven and earth to send it to you. I am sorry I couldn't send more than the fifteen pounds that time, but if things remain as they are, I shall send some more. Will you always ask me, then?

The reason why one cannot send money regularly is with the BBC one is always dependent on cheques coming through, and there can be an awful amount of bother and rigmarole and delay.

Give my love to everybody at home,

Vido

14 St Julian's Road,
London, NW6
October 3, 1955

My dear Kamla,

I will be sending you the money in four days, and if I think it wise I will cable it.

I owe you and everybody at home a great big apology and I trust that you never lose your own faith in me. You see, nearly every plan I have made so far for me and for the rest of us has gone wrong, and I am bitterly ashamed.

So here now is the last—definitely last—plan. I do intend coming home next year, but I hope that it won't be for very long. Frankly, you see, I am expecting something fairly big to come from my writing. I want to establish myself in some manner so that I could get away from England into something worthwhile. I still have my eyes on India. So whenever you feel like cursing me, remember that I am cursing myself even more violently. So far this year I have written two books. The first, of which I have big hopes, is at the moment with the publishers, and I am expecting a reply any day now. As a matter of fact it was to have come because I was hoping to have some good news to send home. I have big hopes about this book because everybody who has so far read it in typescript thinks it is good, and that is a good sign. The second book has to be re-written. I finished writing it last week, and it is very rough. But you can see, then, that I am not idling, but working hard towards a definite goal, and that I am not having a life in London, as you call it. I have many more ideas for books, but an acceptance now will give me a lot of badly needed confidence.

There is another item of news which you have no doubt guessed by now. Pat and I are married, and I have thought it wise to keep it silent up to now because I feel it will upset you greatly since I have done nothing for you. But you must know that this makes no difference whatsoever to my plans for the family. As a matter of fact Pat keeps on urging me to return home to help, and she only reluctantly agreed that I should remain here and write. The plan is that, if my writing fails, we both return to Trinidad and work and take the weight off your shoulders as soon as possible. I know that this news will upset Ma and you a great deal, but I do hope for the best from you.

So you will see that the reason why I am remaining in England is really my writing: and I think this is something you will sympathise with, and encourage me. The short-term solution of returning to Trinidad and paying off the debt will cripple all of us in the long run; whereas if I can do something big—with effort—all of us will benefit. Bear with me, I beg you. I am not having it easy: I am not starving, but I worry about my responsibilities towards you a great deal, and I feel ashamed of myself.

I don't want to see anybody who is coming from Trinidad, and I will be glad if you ask them to keep away; because the time has now come where I am finding it increasingly difficult to be polite to people I don't like, and I can't bear hypocrisy.

Thank you all for everything: for the letters you write in spite of my silence, for the cocoa and the pyjamas which I have received and gratefully use, above all, for your continued love. This last means a lot to me.

Hope, with me, that soon you will be getting a letter saying that my book has been accepted. It will make the world of difference.

My love to everybody: to Sati, to whom I have been unforgivably rude; to Meera and Savi, whom I remember with pleasure; to Shivan, of course, of course! To Nalini, to Ma and to yourself.

My love to all, and please, no rude letters!

Vidia

CABLE AND WIRELESS (WEST INDIES) LIMITED

DEC 8 1955

= NAIPAUL 26 NEPAUL STREET PORT OF SPAIN TRINIDAD

= NOVEL ACCEPTED LOVE = VIDO

The British Broadcasting Corporation
Broadcasting House, London, W1
February 10, 1956

Dear Kamla,

This is the letter I have been longing to write home ever since I left Trinidad. It is about my book. Some time ago I sent you a telegram saying that it was accepted. This letter will explain why I have been silent since then. First of all, last year I wrote not one, but three books. The first I sent to a critic who criticised it so severely that I gave it up altogether and didn't even send it out to a publisher. I think it was the best thing. Because after that I decided to change my style of writing completely. In the beginning of June or thereabouts I began a series of connected stories about a street in Port of Spain. The stories please all who read them. I wrote seventeen of these stories in seven weeks. The girl who typed them for me took five weeks. I sent them to a publisher—in fact I had a friend take them together—and there it remained for eleven weeks. I rang up the publisher. She said she liked the stories and everyone else did. But that they didn't know whether they should publish because no one likes to buy a volume of short stories, even connected short stories. She herself liked them and wanted to publish but her partner said no. During these eleven weeks I had written—in under seven weeks—the draft of a new novel and had finally written the first three chapters. I told the publisher this and she was interested. She wanted to see the finished three chapters. If they like it they would publish the novel first and the stories afterwards. So, at the end of November, I took in four chapters of the novel and eleven days later I got a telephone message that they liked them and they were going to pay me £25 as an option on the finished novel and £75 more when they received the finished novel. So I worked hard until the end of January to finish the novel. They like the finished work as well. This evening I am going to the publisher's home to have a drink and to discuss some changes she wants to make in the end of the novel. I have not yet got the £75. The interesting thing about the whole thing is the fact that I had no rejections. The ten pounds I sent home for Christmas came from the advance of £25. I do not want to touch any more of this money for the time being and this is the reason. I want to leave that money in the bank. If the novel sells ten thousand copies—and the average novel sells about two thousand—I will have enough money to pay off the debts we have at home—I mean at 26. So everything depends on the novel and the book that comes out after the novel. The novel is called *The Mystic Masseur;* the publishers are ANDRE DEUTSCH; and I believe the book will come out in September or October, at the earliest. If this book is a success it will be followed by *Miguel Street: Sketches of a Street in Port of Spain.** I am working on another, a third, which I have just begun, to be called *Life in London.*† But this last is still very much a sketch as yet. I think I may make something big out of it. I know it is bad to predict, but I feel that I may make some money out of *The Mystic Masseur;* and that is all I can promise, Kamla, for the time being. I still intend to come home in the summer, if only for a short while. But there is something more concrete I can offer, Kamla. The novel stands a good chance of being published in America as well, and Kamla can have the money from the American sales. So it is really in all our interests for the book to do well.

I think from what I have said you will see that I have not been idle and I have not forgotten anybody at home. I have all of you in mind and everything I do I really do for you. I myself believe we are coming to the end of the hard road. And I cannot tell you how glad I am to know that I haven't been wasting my time writing. I believe I have a little talent, and in the past year I have learnt so much about writing that I am now writing about six times as well as I did at the beginning of last year.

On the other hand, the book might make no money at all. But I shouldn't let this thought oppress you too much. I will be writing soon.

Love,
Vido

---

* See Bibliography

† Abandoned attempt at writing, fully explored in *The Enigma of Arrival* (see Bibliography)

14 St Julian's Road,
London, NW6
June 20, 1957

Dear Ma,

The day after I wrote to Kamla about the critical reception of the book, the *Daily Telegraph* carried this splendid review: it is so good I am going to quote all of it:

> V. S. Naipaul is a young writer who contrives to blend Oxford wit with home-grown rumbustiousness and not do harm to either. He is a kind of West Indian Gwyn Thomas—piquant, charitable, Rabelaisian, who deals in the small change of human experience as though it were minted gold.
>
> His first novel, *The Mystic Masseur,* describes the career of Ganesh Ramsumair from his early struggles as a teacher to his final metamorphosis into G. Ramsay Muir, Esq., M.B.E. In between Ganesh writes books with titles like *What God Told Me,* and scores a tremendous success as a consultant mystic ('spiritual solace and comfort may be had here at any time on every day except Saturday and Sunday').
>
> Mr Naipaul has a Dickensian exuberance over his minor characters (they include a terrible pair of matriarchs known as King George and The Great Belcher) and a shrewd eye for political rackets. When he observes that 'the history of Ganesh is, in a way, the history of our times,' we can only speculate on the probable effects of TV's impact on Trinidad.

I suppose the publishers have sent this review to St Aubyn;* but if he wants to use it in his advertisements, the reviewer's name is Peter Green.

Now, about jobs. I went to that interview last week. It went off well enough although I was forty-five minutes late. (I got lost, going to the wrong address.) They were ready enough to give me a job right away, but at only £600 a year. I told them I couldn't accept that: I needed £1,000 as a

---

* Bookseller in Trinidad

starting salary. They told me that they didn't know whether I would be worth that to them. I agreed and suggested that I do a trial piece for them, so they could see how much I was worth. So I am going to do a trial piece for them. They sent me all the stuff this morning. It wouldn't be an exciting job: it is for the Cement and Concrete Association, and my job would be to describe concrete buildings all day long, but they are good people to work for: they raise your salary by at least £100 every year.

There are a few other things on the boil. To be perfectly honest, I fear now that I might be offered two or three jobs: choosing will be difficult.

I have a lot of work on hand now. I am writing about six new paragraphs for the novel (at the publishers' request): this is hell. I just can't add to a finished novel, just like that. I have got to do 2 more talks on Henry V (total value: 30 guineas). And I have to write that trial piece.

My love to all,
Vido

Bibliography
of Published Works

SEEPERSAD NAIPAUL (1906–1953)

Gurudeva and Other Indian Tales (privately published, Port of
Spain, 1943); published as *The Adventures of Gurudeva and Other
Stories* (London, 1976); reissued as *The Adventures of Gurudeva*
(London, 1995)

V. S. NAIPAUL (1932–)

The Mystic Masseur (1957)

The Suffrage of Elvira (1958)

Miguel Street (1959)

A House for Mr Biswas (1961)

The Middle Passage (1962)

Mr Stone and the Knights Companion (1963)

An Area of Darkness (1964)

A Flag on the Island (1967)

The Mimic Men (1967)

The Loss of El Dorado (1969)

In a Free State (1971)

The Overcrowded Barracoon (1972)

Guerrillas (1975)

India: A Wounded Civilization (1977)

A Bend in the River (1979)

The Return of Eva Perón (with The Killings in Trinidad) (1980)

Among the Believers (1981)

Finding the Centre (1984)
The Enigma of Arrival (1987)
A Turn in the South (1989)
India: A Million Mutinies Now (1990)
A Way in the World (1994)
*Beyond Belief: Islamic Excursions
Among the Converted Peoples* (1998)

SHIVA NAIPAUL (1945–1985)

Fireflies (1970)
The Chip-Chip Gatherers (1973)
North of South (1978)
Black and White (1980)
A Hot Country (1983)
Beyond the Dragon's Mouth: Stories and Pieces (1984)
An Unfinished Journey (1986)

INDEX

ALSO BY V. S. NAIPAUL

"For sheer abundance of talent, there can
hardly be a writer alive who surpasses V. S. Naipaul."
—*The New York Times Book Review*

AMONG THE BELIEVERS

On the basis of his seven-month journey across the Asian continent, V. S. Naipaul here explores the life, the culture and the
current ferment inside four nations of Islam: Iran, Pakistan,
Malaysia, and Indonesia. Naipaul depicts an Islamic world at
odds with the modern world, fueled only by an implacable
determination to believe.

Current Affairs/0-394-71195-5

BEYOND BELIEF

Fourteen years after the publication of his landmark travel
narrative *Among the Believers*, Naipaul returned to the four
non-Arab Islamic countries he reported on so vividly at the
time of Ayatollah Khomeini's triumph in Iran. *Beyond Belief*
is the result of his five-month journey through Indonesia, Iran,
Pakistan, and Malaysia. In extended conversations with a vast
number of people, including a rare survivor of the martyr
brigades of the Iran-Iraq war and a young intellectual training
as a Marxist guerrilla, Naipaul deliberately effaces himself to
let the voices of his subjects come through.

Current Affairs/0-375-70648-8

A TURN IN THE SOUTH

Continuing the Naipaul tradition of political and cultural rev-
elation, his first book about the United States is a revealing,
disturbing, elegiac book about the American South—from
Atlanta to Charleston, Tallahassee to Tuskegee, Nashville to
Chapel Hill.

Nonfiction/Literature/0-679-72488-5

VINTAGE BOOKS
Available at your local bookstore, or call toll-free to order:
1-800-793-2665 (credit cards only).

Some of the finest pieces of V.S. Naipaul's reportage,
collected in one volume for the first time.

Winner of the Nobel Prize in Literature

V.S. Naipaul
THE WRITER
AND THE WORLD
Essays

Available **August 2002**
from Knopf
Hardcover • **$25.95** • 0-375-40739-1

"For sheer abundance of talent, there can hardly be
a writer alive who surpasses V.S. Naipaul."
—*The New York Times Book Review*

Please visit www.aaknopf.com

Also available in paperback from Vintage:

Between Father and Son • 0-375-70726-3
Beyond Belief • 0-375-70648-8
A Way in the World • 0-679-76166-7
A Turn in the South • 0-679-72488-5
Among the Believers • 0-394-71195-5
The Enigma of Arrival • 0-394-75760-2
A Bend in the River • 0-679-72202-5
Guerrillas • 0-679-73174-1
In a Free State • 0-394-72205-1
The Mimic Men • 0-375-70717-4
A House for Mr. Biswas • 0-375-70716-6